THE COMPLETE IDIOT'S GUIDE® TO

Business Success in Your 20s & 30s

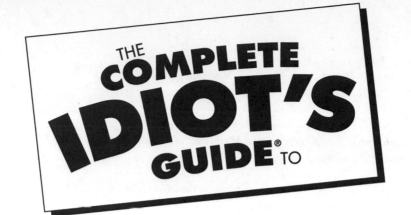

THE
COMPLETE
IDIOT'S
GUIDE® TO

Business Success in Your 20s & 30s

by Robert Sofia

ALPHA
A member of Penguin Group (USA) Inc.

ALPHA BOOKS

Published by the Penguin Group

Penguin Group (USA) Inc., 375 Hudson Street, New York, New York 10014, USA

Penguin Group (Canada), 90 Eglinton Avenue East, Suite 700, Toronto, Ontario M4P 2Y3, Canada (a division of Pearson Penguin Canada Inc.)

Penguin Books Ltd., 80 Strand, London WC2R 0RL, England

Penguin Ireland, 25 St. Stephen's Green, Dublin 2, Ireland (a division of Penguin Books Ltd.)

Penguin Group (Australia), 250 Camberwell Road, Camberwell, Victoria 3124, Australia (a division of Pearson Australia Group Pty. Ltd.)

Penguin Books India Pvt. Ltd., 11 Community Centre, Panchsheel Park, New Delhi—110 017, India

Penguin Group (NZ), 67 Apollo Drive, Rosedale, North Shore, Auckland 1311, New Zealand (a division of Pearson New Zealand Ltd.)

Penguin Books (South Africa) (Pty.) Ltd., 24 Sturdee Avenue, Rosebank, Johannesburg 2196, South Africa

Penguin Books Ltd., Registered Offices: 80 Strand, London WC2R 0RL, England

International Standard Book Number: 978-1-59257-936-5
Library of Congress Catalog Card Number: 2009926598

11 10 09   8 7 6 5 4 3 2 1

Interpretation of the printing code: The rightmost number of the first series of numbers is the year of the book's printing; the rightmost number of the second series of numbers is the number of the book's printing. For example, a printing code of 09-1 shows that the first printing occurred in 2009.

Printed in the United States of America

Note: This publication contains the opinions and ideas of its author. It is intended to provide helpful and informative material on the subject matter covered. It is sold with the understanding that the author and publisher are not engaged in rendering professional services in the book. If the reader requires personal assistance or advice, a competent professional should be consulted.

The author and publisher specifically disclaim any responsibility for any liability, loss, or risk, personal or otherwise, which is incurred as a consequence, directly or indirectly, of the use and application of any of the contents of this book.

Most Alpha books are available at special quantity discounts for bulk purchases for sales promotions, premiums, fundraising, or educational use. Special books, or book excerpts, can also be created to fit specific needs.

For details, write: Special Markets, Alpha Books, 375 Hudson Street, New York, NY 10014.

Publisher: *Marie Butler-Knight*
Editorial Director: *Mike Sanders*
Senior Managing Editor: *Billy Fields*
Executive Editor: *Randy Ladenheim-Gil*
Development Editor: *Jennifer Moore*
Production Editor: *Kayla Dugger*
Copy Editor: *Catherine Schwenk*

Cartoonist: *Steve Barr*
Cover Designer: *Kurt Owens*
Book Designer: *Trina Wurst*
Indexer: *Heather McNeill*
Layout: *Ayanna Lacey*
Proofreader: *Mary Hunt*

Contents at a Glance

Contents

Appendixes

Introduction

Everyone wants to be successful. Some might not admit it, but deep down, they do. Doubtless you do, too.

The funny thing about success is having the desire alone isn't enough. In fact, you could spend your entire life sitting around cultivating the desire to succeed and getting absolutely nowhere. To be successful requires certain attitudes, behaviors, and actions.

It's noteworthy that everyone measures success differently. To some, the idea of being successful may conjure up images of a small family in a suburb of Middle America and a picket fence; to others, life in an uncharted region of the globe immersed in humanitarian efforts; to still others, success is represented by the corner office of a high-rise building in a major metropolitan city.

So what is success really? This book is not designed to answer that question for you. What it is designed to do, is help you become successful in one key area of life—business. More than that, it's designed to help you do it while you are still young enough to enjoy your accomplishments.

So why not pick up any old book about business success and read it instead of this one? Because attaining success while you are still in your 20s or 30s requires special effort. It also requires you to overcome a unique set of obstacles.

Here's how things work for most people:

1. Their 20s and 30s are spent bouncing between different jobs while trying to eek out a living and find their "niche."

2. They finally find a job at a place they like, begin saving a little for retirement, and work there until they get laid-off, fired, or retire.

3. They turn 65 with a few hundred thousand in the bank, collect Social Security, and work through retirement to make ends meet.

Here's how things can work for you:

1. Decide what you want out of life, find your internal motivation, and establish your goals and priorities. Get to work on them.

2. Learn about the traits of other successful people and apply them in your life. Maximize every opportunity.

3. Refine your skills until you become the successful person you set out to become.

There are more barriers to success today than ever before. The job market is ultra competitive and oversaturated. The value of a college degree is declining. The economy is in a constant state of flux. Social Security is being depleted. The list goes on and on! How can this book help you overcome such challenges?

How This Book Is Organized

Each section delves into a different area that impacts your professional life. Here's a quick overview of what they contain:

We all have to start somewhere, and **Part 1, "It All Starts Here,"** shows you where. It explains the advantages and disadvantages that come with being young in the business world. It helps you set reasonable goals, decide on the career that is right for you, and take your first steps down the road to business success.

Once you decide what you want, you have to be able to go out and get it. **Part 2, "Getting on the Right Path,"** shows you how to land the job you want and then use it as a catalyst to jumpstart your career. It also teaches you how to make stellar first impressions that get you noticed and rapidly promoted.

When it comes to business, the relationships you form either rocket you upward or drag you downward. **Part 3, "It's All About Relationships,"** teaches you how to build strong, mutually beneficial relationships and how to network. It also furnishes you with the expertise to brand yourself so others notice you and want to contribute toward your success.

Not everyone is a natural born leader. You can, however, learn to be a good leader. **Part 4, "The Leader Inside You,"** helps you do just that! It equips you with valuable skills that cause others to acknowledge you, respect you, and follow you. It also discusses the power of teamwork and shows how to use the expertise of those around you as building blocks to your own success.

If there is one thing every successful business person possesses, it's an eye for opportunity. How do you recognize a good opportunity or distinguish a bad one? How do you know if it's time to start your own company? **Part 5, "Opportunity Knocks,"** answers these questions and more.

Part 6, "Life Lessons," examines common pitfalls to progress and teaches you how to avoid them. It addresses business ethics, appropriate work/life balance, and how to find satisfaction in your work.

How to Use This Book

All the knowledge in the world is useless if you don't apply it. If you desire to get the most out of this book, I challenge you to do the following:

1. Buy a small notebook and keep it with your copy of this book. Bring them both to work with you every day. If you don't have a job yet, keep them in your car. If you don't have a car, keep them on your bike. If you don't have a bike … Well you get the idea.

2. Each time you read out of this book, pick *one* thing you would like to apply. Write it in your notebook. Trust me—only *one* thing. I'm sure you'll want to apply everything at once, but it's not possible. Choose one thing at a time.

3. Every day, take out your notebook and read through the items you made plans to apply. Once you've applied an item, put a line through it.

4. On the first of every month, flip back through the notebook and review all the items you put a line through. Make sure you're still applying them. If you've started to slip in a certain area, add it to the end of your list again. Repeat. (This entire process takes less than five minutes a day. Is your career worth five minutes a day?)

5. Keep the book as a permanent reference tool. Refer back to it when challenging obstacles arise.

So are you ready to become successful in business? Good! Let's get started!

Extras

The following sidebars appear in each chapter and will assist you in understanding and applying the information contained in each chapter.

Best Practice _____

Tested and proven tips you can implement to accelerate your career growth.

FYI
A little extra something you might like to know. File these away for future use.

Heads Up! _____

These are common pitfalls to avoid. Evading these snares save you a considerable amount of time and aggravation.

Acknowledgments

I owe this book to what I've learned from the dynamic men and women it has been my privilege to know.

Dad, thank you for teaching me to work hard. Mom, thank you for teaching me to love literature. Bob Demarco, thank you for teaching me about responsibility. Steve Hollosi, thank you for helping me realize my true potential. Chad Noble, thank you for being such a good friend. Dale Cebert, thank you for giving me a wonderful opportunity. Rich Rollins, thank you for your savvy advice. Robert Fross and Thomas Fross, if I thanked you for everything you've done, it would fill volumes.

Thank you to my capable and reassuring literary agent, Ron Benrey. Thank you to Randy Ladenheim-Gil, Jennifer Moore, Kayla Dugger, and all the other talented people at Alpha Books.

Last, and most important, special thanks to my brilliant and supportive wife, LeAnne.

Trademarks

All terms mentioned in this book that are known to be or are suspected of being trademarks or service marks have been appropriately capitalized. Alpha Books and Penguin Group (USA) Inc. cannot attest to the accuracy of this information. Use of a term in this book should not be regarded as affecting the validity of any trademark or service mark.

Part 1

It All Starts Here

Achieving extraordinary business success is never easy—achieving it in your 20s or 30s is downright hard! If you hope to do more in 10 or 15 years than most people do in 30 or 40, you have to know yourself, know what you want, and know how to go about getting it!

In this part, you learn how to find your internal motivation, how to set achievable goals, and how to choose a career that is right for you. You also learn about some of the unique obstacles you face as a young person in business, and how to overcome them.

Every great journey starts somewhere, and the journey to business success in your 20s and 30s starts right here!

"I know, Bridget. I want to make it big by thirty, but you have to do it by four, huh?"

Chapter 1

Business Success for the Young—A Reality!

In This Chapter

- A brief history of the young and successful
- Embracing the advantages of your youth
- Understanding the challenges you'll face
- Getting started down the path to success

The road to business success isn't an obscure pathway reserved for discovery by the privileged and genius. Rather, it is a road well traveled by those who possess the desire and will to walk it.

This chapter is designed to help you get started on your journey. We explain the unique challenges you face as a young person in business and show you how to overcome them. Along the way, we help you determine your strengths and make the most of them. And once you're ready to embark on your journey, we walk you through the first five steps you need to take.

A Wasted Youth?

The famous playwright George Bernard Shaw wrote, "Youth is wasted on the young." Apparently this statement resonates with more than a few people because a quick online search for this quote returns anywhere between 95,000 and 225,000 hits. So what is this supposed to mean anyway? Is youth really *wasted* on the young?

Heads Up!

This book is about success in business—not success in life. Success in life depends on balancing your career with a number of other factors. A satisfying career alone won't bring you happiness. Too many people have learned this lesson the hard way.

Unfortunately, in many cases, it can certainly seem that way. Think about how many young people idle away valuable years on useless pursuits under the guise of "having fun." It's a sad proposition to roll out of bed one day in your 40s with a backache and a hangover only to realize you just spent the last 20 years accomplishing nothing meaningful with your life.

So what are you doing to put your vitality to good use? Committing to a meaningful career is a good place to start.

Those Who Came Before You

Accomplishing remarkable things while you are still in your 20s and 30s is well confirmed by history. Alexander the Great, for example, began ruling at age 20 and had conquered most of the known world by his death at 33. And while violently subduing world powers may not be your forte, the world of business has its own share of impressive warriors. Warren Buffett was a millionaire by 32, Donald Trump by 25. Bill Gates founded Microsoft at 21 and went on to become the world's richest man before 40. Jerry Yang and David Filo started Yahoo! in their 20s and are both billionaires today.

But these people were extraordinary, right? Totally different from you and me? Maybe, in some ways. And maybe you don't desire to be anything like them. The point is, being young doesn't have to hold you back from achieving business success.

To bring things a little closer to home, you might want to take a look at *INC Magazine*'s annual 30 Under 30 list of entrepreneurs. Among them are chefs, inventors, designers, computer programmers, humanitarians, and more. Some went to the best schools in the country, and others dropped out of them. As you read through their profiles, you will likely discover some of them are very similar to you.

What is one thing they all have in common? They believe in themselves and their ability to accomplish great things in business. Do you have the same kind of confidence in yourself? You should. Let's consider a few reasons why.

Youth Gives You an Edge in Business

Everybody has an edge of some kind. It may come from their culture, upbringing, schooling, personality, or from another source altogether. The edge you have as a young person, however, is different because it is limited by time. In view of the fact that you can't stay young forever, you need to make the most of these formative years. In other words, use the edge you have while you have it.

Fresh Perspective

There's nothing like a fresh set of eyes to breathe new life into a dying venture. And if you are a young person in business, you might be just the one to provide this precious commodity.

Many businesses perform well for decades, only to suddenly find themselves out of date. How does this happen? One of the major reasons is they don't infuse their organization with fresh talent. The result is aging leadership who loses touch with their market, their employees, or current industry trends.

Think of it this way. A seasoned team of basketball players is at the top of their game. They win every National Championship for 10 years in a row without ever having a single player join the team. They figure because they are playing so well, there's no reason to make any changes. How long do you think they are going to remain National Champions? The answer should be obvious. Eventually they are going to be overtaken by younger, stronger, faster players.

Just as any sports team needs to continually draft new players, businesses continually need to attract fresh talent.

Best Practice

Spend your first weeks on any job as a keen observer. Take note of how people do things and how smoothly their procedures operate. If you notice what appears to be a deficiency, make a brief note about it, research it, and see if you can come up with a better way. You can share your ideas with management down the road.

It's common for businesses to get so used to a certain way of doing something that no one recognizes it's being done the hard way, the expensive way, or the ineffective way. Often, everybody just keeps doing the same thing because it's the way they've always done it. This is one of the reasons businesses hire consultants—so a new face can come in and tell them all the things they are doing wrong. If you've ever done any consulting work, you know what I mean when I say, sometimes you sit back scratching your head and wondering how on Earth all these smart people missed something so obvious. Often, it's just because nobody ever questioned it.

Heads Up!

Be careful not to start pointing out deficiencies until you are comfortable with the fact that management is willing to listen. You also want to make sure you have a solution for the problem, or you risk looking like a complainer.

So how does this apply to you? If you are new to the business world, many of the standard practices you'll be introduced to won't make any sense to you. This is a good thing. It simply means you are looking at things with a fresh set of eyes—a fresh perspective. Just because you may not have developed a tremendous amount of *business* sense doesn't mean you don't have *common* sense. A healthy dose of common sense can go a long way toward helping a business improve, and toward making you look like a hero.

Less Baggage

That's right. I said it. The "B" word that nobody wants to hear, *baggage*. If you are still in your 20s or early 30s, you probably don't have too much of it yet. And good for you if you don't!

Truth be told, we all have some degree of baggage, but it's unlikely at this stage in your life that you have a giant house to maintain, two kids who have to go to ballet and baseball, two cars (one of which is a minivan), a second mortgage, $20,000 in credit card debt, and in-laws to take care of. The advantage of this is it allows you to devote more time to your career.

When in life are you better equipped to be a dedicated employee? What holds you back from going in early, staying late, and working on an occasional Sunday evening? Yes, you have the ability—far more than your older colleagues—to demonstrate the kind of commitment that gets you noticed and rapidly promoted.

The question is: Are you willing to?

Boundless Energy

The vitality of youth is truly something to be treasured. No matter how hard you try, you only get to hold on to it for a limited amount of time. So while you have it, use it wisely!

As I write this book, my own energy reserves are being significantly tapped by the pressures that go along with running one company, starting a second, volunteering several hours a week, working out in the mornings, and yes—writing a lot. Quite frankly, the only reason I am able to do all this is because I am still young. It's a fact I won't be able to continue at this pace forever. I am determined, however, to put the energy I have to good use. How about you?

Granted, everyone needs a little rest and relaxation, but when recreation becomes your sole pursuit, other more important things get crowded out. Now is the best time to put as much energy as possible into your career so you'll have something to fall back on when your energy level starts to wane.

Plugged In

In recent years, the advent of new technology and new ways to communicate has a number of organizations scrambling to catch up. For them, trying to understand and use social media and other technology has become a chief priority. Why? Because their customers are using these tools and they realize they risk losing touch.

While you may be an experienced blogger and be comfortable using sites like Facebook, Twitter, and so on, many companies aren't. In fact, there has been a huge push in the staffing industry to recruit Generation Y because of their expertise in this area.

The fact that you are technologically savvy can go a long way in helping you land the job you want. When given the choice between a seasoned businessperson with marginal computer skills and an energetic young person with outstanding computer skills, many forward-thinking companies opt for the latter. Use this edge to your advantage by featuring it on your resumé and mentioning it in interviews.

Heads Up!

When employers check your background, they are likely to search for you on commonly used social-networking sites like MySpace and Facebook. Be sure to remove any incriminating photos or language before you start applying for jobs. Better yet, keep everything clean from the start.

If You've Got It, Flaunt It

Yes, as a young person, you truly have an edge in business. The four areas we just discussed can help you distinguish yourself in a very positive way. The key is to be aware of the advantages you have and then showcase them.

Even if all these areas don't apply to you, you can still pick one or two that do and maximize them. The reason this works is because most people aren't willing to put forth the effort to stand out because it's so much easier to blend in.

Imagine, for example, you are driving down the interstate. How many cars actually turn your head? Percentage-wise, it's very few. Isn't it always the red one, the sleek one, the fast one, or the new one?

Wherever you are working, you can be like that car. In no time flat, you can have people turning their heads and saying, "That new guy has so many good ideas!" Or, "That new girl is always the first one here. She seems ultra committed!" Wouldn't you like to have your bosses saying things like that about you? You can! All you have to do is step out of your comfort zone with your best foot forward.

Of course, making your way as a young person in the workplace isn't easy. There are also significant challenges to be met.

The Disadvantages of Youth in the Business World

Trying to get ahead in business without knowing what you're up against is like running hurdles blindfolded. Let's consider four key areas where young people face noteworthy challenges. Doing so helps prepare you for the road ahead.

Preconceived Notions of Others

Conventional wisdom would have you believe people receive the treatment they deserve based primarily on their merit—that what they do and how they act determines the way people treat them. Unfortunately, in some cases, conventional wisdom is just plain wrong. Young professionals experience this fact firsthand. Regardless of how skilled you may be, you are likely to face prejudice simply because you are young.

If you're in management, for example, the preconceived notions and ideas of the people in your organization can make numerous conventional management ideas worthless for you.

Consider the conventional "management wisdom" about how to give instructions. Most management resources tell you to take plenty of time to outline exactly and completely what is required, ask the person lots of questions to make sure they understand, and finish them off with a deadline and a confidence-boosting pep talk. Some even suggest you draw a visual diagram to illustrate your instructions.

While this may be good advice for your average middle-management Joe, it isn't good advice if you're supervising people who have been in your industry longer than you've been alive. As a young manager, if you try this kind of strategy on a company veteran who is 5, 10, or 20 years your senior, all you're going to get is comments behind your back about what an arrogant, know-it-all, greenhorn you are. (We discuss a more fitting way to give instructions in Chapter 16.)

So why does this happen? It's because, fair or not, the people around you can't bring themselves to see past your baby face. It's not that you're young; it's that they associate certain attitudes and behaviors with "young people." The result is when they look at you, they connect you with things like inexperience and lack of work ethic.

Let's face it, the status quo says your generation wants it all, doesn't want to work for it, and thinks they're entitled to it. You probably have friends that fit into this category. If you were born anytime since the late 1970s, you are also considered part of the MTV generation. Think for a minute about the value system portrayed by this network, and you can see why people have preconceived notions about you.

But you're different, right? You're a real professional. You're responsible, friendly, and sharp, right? So, why don't you get the credit you deserve?

Basically, here's what happens: let's go back to the scenario we just mentioned about giving instructions. From the minute that seasoned industry veteran sits across the table from you, he is already sizing you up.

While you're trying hard to be a good manager and give clear, detailed instructions, he is thinking:

Why is he talking to me like I'm a child? I already know all this. My kids are older than this guy! … Ooh! I need to call the kids!

And just that fast, you've been tuned out.

Granted, this isn't true of *everyone*, but it proves true with enough people to make your professional growth a bona fide challenge.

What this really boils down to is winning people to your team long before you walk into a meeting or sit an employee down to counsel him. You have to make others view you as someone they *want* to support because they *like* you. You want to be viewed as someone they yearn to see succeed because you're such a nice example of how young people should be, of how they used to be, and of how they want their kids to be.

All of this can be accomplished with a good first impression (see Chapter 6), a strong network of allies (see Chapter 12), and a track record of results (see Chapter 13).

Lack of Experience

If you ever decide you'd like to take an excursion into one of the world's jungles, you would doubtless hire a jungle guide. Besides keeping you from getting lost, a good guide watches for dangerous animals and clears your path of hazardous debris, poisonous plants, and other entrapments. Why is a guide so well equipped to do these things? Because he has been into the jungle many, many times.

The world of business can often seem like a jungle. There are unscrupulous people who take advantage of you, hidden agendas that can trip you up, and pesky things that come back to bite you. What is one thing you lack on this journey? Experience. Because experience comes from undergoing and observing things as they occur over the course of time, your older colleagues have more of this than you, which clearly gives them an edge.

What can you do about this? Following are three things to try.

Find a Mentor

A mentor can be an invaluable resource in helping you develop your career. If you find the right person, they become your trusted counselor, teacher, and supporter. They can also help you widen your circle of influence.

The best place to look for a mentor is among those whom you admire and respect. Look for those who have considerably more experience than you and who seem to be somewhat interested in you as a person. It might be your boss, or even your boss's boss. What position they hold isn't necessarily the main thing. What really matters is if they are willing to mentor you.

After you identify the person you would like to ask, don't be afraid to approach them. What do you have to lose? Even if they decline—which they likely won't—they'll still be flattered that you asked.

Once you have a mentor, you can ask him to evaluate your work, help you handle complicated situations, and introduce you to others.

A healthy mentoring arrangement is beneficial for both parties. You get to benefit from someone else's experience, and your mentor gets to enjoy the satisfaction that comes from contributing to your success.

Best Practice

When you send an e-mail that makes a new suggestion, ask your mentor to review it first. If he agrees with its content, have him send a follow-up e-mail to all the recipients vocalizing his support for your idea. If your mentor is well respected, his input can enhance your credibility.

Read

The world is full of books that can make you wise beyond your years. Why not take advantage of them? Commit to your personal career development by reading other business books like this one. Try picking up some that deal with your specific field, provide motivation, equip you with better communication skills, or help you improve as a manager. If you don't have a lot of time to read, you can even purchase books on CD or download them as MP3s so you can listen to them during your commute.

Trade journals and industry publications are another great resource to tap into. If there are any available for your field, you should certainly subscribe to them.

A habit of regular reading increases your vocabulary, keeps you on top of business trends, provides you with fresh ideas, and broadens your mind.

Read more. Not sure what to read next? Check out the Top 100 list in Appendix B.

Observe Others and Ask Lots of Questions

One of the most effective learning techniques of all time is to observe others and then ask questions.

Think about it for a second. What is the primary way young children learn about life? Isn't it by incessantly asking questions? Yes, fundamentally, we all learn the same way—by watching what others do and asking questions.

Unfortunately, later in life some of us stop asking questions. This might be because we are afraid of how others view us, afraid of what the answer might be, or because we stop caring what the answers are.

If this is true of you, rekindle your inclination to ask questions. Here's why this is so important:

- ◆ It keeps you from making stupid mistakes.

- ◆ It helps you build relationships with others.

- ◆ It demonstrates you are a good listener.

- ◆ People gradually start asking you all the questions because, by asking questions yourself, you become the one with all the answers. Isn't that a nice role reversal?

In order to ask meaningful questions, you must first be a keen listener and observer. Take note of how top performers and managers do things. If something is new to you or doesn't make sense, ask them to explain it. If the timing isn't good, write down your question and ask it at a later time. You'll benefit from their experience, and they'll be pleased you sought their guidance.

By finding a mentor, reading regularly, observing others, and asking questions, you can considerably compensate for your lack of experience. In fact, in a relatively short period of time you'll likely surpass older individuals with more experience than yourself.

Connections

Business is all about connections. Business to business, business to customer, employee to manager, manager to shareholder—the influence of all these connections is what powers the free market. It can also power a successful career. The right connections can help you get jobs, promotions, raises, and recognition.

Herein lies the challenge: it takes time to make connections. If you are new to the business world, you likely won't have as many connections as your colleagues. Fortunately, this doesn't have to be a problem for you.

First, you can make connections rather quickly if you put your mind to it. Second, most people don't make good use of their connections anyway. The real power lies not in the *number* of connections you have, but in the *quality* of them.

So how can you make quality connections? The main key is to stay in touch with your contacts. You can do this through e-mail, phone, snail mail, or even a personal blog. Keep your network in the loop about what is happening in your life. Let them know about job changes, promotions, relocations, and so on. Send cards on special occasions, and invite them to social events when appropriate. All these things can make a person feel like they are invested in your life. Down the road, when they hear about a great job that opens up, they just might say, "I have a friend who does that! I'll get in touch with her for you." Networking isn't about shaking hands and walking away. It's about making and sustaining real connections.

So who's in your network? Probably more people than you realize. You're apt to have connections with former classmates, professors, employers, instructors, co-workers, and just about anybody else you've come in contact with. Now is a good time to start making use of all these connections. We'll analyze how this can be done in Chapter 12.

Best Practice

When you meet new people, make it a practice to get their business card or enter all their contact information directly into your personal digital assistant (PDA) or smart phone. Contacts aren't really contacts if you can't contact them.

Reputation

A good reputation is one thing you can't earn overnight. What you can do is work especially hard to make sure you don't do any damage to the reputation you have.

Think of your reputation like a blank canvas. With brush in hand, each call you make, each project you complete, and each interaction you have makes its own unique mark on your canvas. Over time, you can either paint a beautiful picture others will be drawn to, or a distasteful one that turns them away.

View outbursts, sloppy work, and unethical behavior like buckets of black paint ready to be splattered on your canvas. How long do you think it would take to remove such unsightly blotches? Do you want black marks on your reputation?

It's not only the reputation you have with your boss that matters. Co-workers, other department managers, former employers, and vendors you conduct business with all have an impact on your reputation.

Imagine what might happen if an employee you mistreated moves on to become manager of a department you frequently need assistance from. With one small example, I'm sure you can see the kind of complications you create for yourself when you damage your reputation.

Work hard. Be honest. Respect others. If you do these things, a good reputation comes to you, most likely sooner than later.

Best Practice _____

"Be more concerned with your character than with your reputation. Your character is what you really are, while your reputation is merely what others think you are."
—John Wooden, collegiate basketball coach, Hall of Fame member

Get Moving!

Success doesn't come to those who wait around for it. It comes to those who create it! Following are five steps to get you started.

1. Analyze your current situation.

Are you happy with what you are doing now? Do you like the field you are in? Can you see yourself working in your current field for the rest of your career? Are there any real opportunities for growth? Your honest answers to these questions can help you determine if it's time to move on.

2. Brainstorm for career alternatives.

This is a big one! Start daydreaming about what you would like to do for a living. Ask your friends and family what they think you'd be good at. Use the career advice section of job hunting websites and do extra research about fields you find interesting. Ask other people about what they do. As you gather information, try to narrow your options down to fewer than 10. We'll talk more about this in Chapter 3.

3. Do you have the right education?

While a college degree isn't necessarily a prerequisite for attaining business success, it is required if you aim to become a brain surgeon. A high school diploma, on the other hand, is required for almost everything. As you consider your career options, it's important to make sure you have the proper education. If you aren't sure what you need, do the research to find out—it will be time well spent.

4. Work to develop your skills.

Every experience in life can teach you something. Start looking around for opportunities to learn new things. Ask your boss or college professor if you can help them with a complicated project. Enroll in specialized training or shadowing programs when they are available. Even if they aren't available, ask if you can create one. If online training classes are offered, sign up for all of them. Offer to create a company newsletter. View every new challenge as an opportunity to grow.

Heads Up!

While it's good to broaden your abilities by taking on new things, be careful not to bite off more than you can chew. It's better to do a *few* things well than *many* things marginally well.

5. Volunteer.

Organizations are always looking for volunteers. Charities, animal shelters, hospitals, parent-teacher associations—these and other similar organizations can do a tremendous amount for your career! They can help you make wonderful connections. (We already learned what a good thing that can be!) They look great on a resumé, they can help you narrow down the field you want to work in, and they can teach you valuable skills.

So what are you waiting for? Resign yourself to the fact you are responsible for your own success! Nobody is going to make things happen for you!

And while it's easy to recognize the steps you have to take, it's often much harder to take them—that is, unless you have the right goals, the right motivation, and the right expectations. How providential it is the next chapter was written to help you with that!

The Least You Need to Know

◆ Being young doesn't have to prevent you from achieving business success.

◆ Determine your biggest strengths and showcase them at every opportunity.

◆ Be a keen observer of others. Watch how people do things and ask lots of questions.

◆ Find a mentor. Use them to critique your work, help you solve problems, and introduce you to others.

◆ Commit to your personal development by reading business books and trade journals.

◆ Work hard not to damage your reputation. It's one of your most valuable assets.

Chapter 2

Success Comes from Within

In This Chapter

◆ Finding your internal motivation

◆ Setting the right goals

◆ Cultivating reasonable expectations

◆ Embracing the G.A.M.A. formula for success

◆ Keeping your focus

Goals and motivation are inextricably linked. You need motivation to set and reach goals, even as reaching goals supplements your motivation. This chapter helps you figure out what motivates you, teaches you to set productive goals, and provides you with tools that keep you motivated!

If there is one chapter in this book that lays the foundation for your future success in business, this is it!

External vs. Internal Motivation

The difference between internal motivation and external motivation could be likened to the difference between driving a car and having it towed.

While both may be effective for getting a vehicle from point A to point B, the first is clearly preferable.

You're likely no stranger to both types of motivation. Most parents condition their children to respond to external, or extrinsic, motivation at an early age by bribing them with rewards in exchange for good behavior. This type of motivation originates with sources that are outside of ourselves. Good examples of external motivators are report cards and paychecks.

Internal, or intrinsic, motivation on the other hand, comes from the satisfaction or happiness one gets from engaging in a certain activity or completing a certain task. This type of motivation is demonstrated when you go out of your way to do an outstanding job on something because you want to experience a sense of pride and accomplishment. While you may not receive anything material for your extra effort, you exert yourself because you are motivated from the inside.

Why is this important to understand? Because external motivation—while important—can only get you so far. To accomplish great things requires that you be driven from the inside.

Key areas of external and internal motivation include:

- Career development, success, achievement
- Problem solving
- Recognition, praise
- Money, possessions
- Teaching, helping others
- Status, prestige, reputation
- Social affiliation, popularity, acceptance
- Family, home, security
- Recreation, relaxation, comfort
- Knowledge, learning, discovery
- Leadership, influence
- Health, vitality

While not generally productive, there are even negative motivators such as fear, terror, and anxiety.

Find Your Internal Motivation

When you have a job you hate, a paycheck alone won't keep you happy or make you a star performer. To be truly successful, you must do something you enjoy.

So what drives you? Here's a quick self-test that can help you answer that question. Get out a piece of paper and write down your answers to the following questions.

1. What do you love to do?

2. If you could do absolutely anything, what would it be?

3. Twenty years from now, what do you most want to have accomplished?

4. If you had access to unlimited funds, what would you do with your time and money?

Finish the following:

5. In my spare time, I like to …

6. I mostly think about …

7. I feel proud when I …

8. I want people to know me as …

Now analyze your answers. What do they reflect the strongest desire for?

♦ A sense of accomplishment

♦ Helping others

♦ Learning new things

♦ Thrill seeking

♦ Recognition

♦ Being creative

Don't be surprised if more than one of the preceding choices applies to you. Most likely, one outweighs the other as your primary motivation, leaving a secondary motivation to complement it. It's not unusual for our behavior to be determined by a combination of motives.

Let's say, for example, you are primarily motivated by a desire to help others, and secondarily motivated by thrill seeking. If this is the case, you would probably do well as a rock climbing instructor or even a firefighter.

While not completely definitive, this brief self-analysis should help you determine to a certain degree what is most important to you. If you are interested in probing deeper, there are a number of organizations that provide personality tests to help you determine your optimum career. A few of these are listed in Appendix A for your convenience.

Once you understand what motivates you, you are well on your way to choosing a career that brings a deep sense of satisfaction. More than just choosing a career, though, you also need to decide where you want that career to take you and what you expect to get out of it. Goals are what help you do this.

Goals! Goals! Goals!

Even in the worst of storms, a well-placed lighthouse can guide a sailor and his crew through dangerous shoals and reefs into the safety of harbor. Effective goals work in much the same way.

What Makes a Goal?

A goal is roughly similar to a purpose, aim, or objective. It is something you intend to achieve or acquire within a specific period of time. For a goal to be effective, it needs to be comprised of the following four main elements:

- ◆ **Specific**   Goals shouldn't be vague or obtuse. Rather, they should be detailed and unambiguous. An example of an indistinct goal would be, "I want to be famous." A more specific goal would be, "I want to be a famous actor on Broadway within the next 10 years." Notice the separate elements to this goal. It answers what (famous actor), where (on Broadway), and when (within 10 years).

- ◆ **Measurable**   If you can't measure a goal, how will you know when you've reached it? Considering the goal we just mentioned, you likely agree the word "famous" is relative. Famous in comparison to what? To whom? A good question to answer that would make this goal measurable is, "What qualifies me as famous?"

◆ **Achievable**   Most goals are achievable, but not all. It would be unrealistic to have a goal of being on Broadway if you are completely tone deaf and can't dance, for instance. While you shouldn't be quick to dismiss a goal because others say you can't achieve it, you do need to make sure your goals are realistic.

◆ **Time constrained**   Did you notice how our example included the qualifier, "within 10 years"? This is an extremely important element to any goal. If you don't set a time limit for yourself, it's easy to lose your sense of urgency and get stuck in a rut. Having a specific date helps you avoid procrastination.

Think Short to Go Long

Goals usually consist of two main types: short-term and long-term. While both types are distinct, they are equally important. Like stepping stones, short-term goals make long-term goals attainable.

Let's say your long-term goal is to open your own Italian restaurant. What are some short-term goals you might set to help you reach your long-term goal? How about working at an Italian restaurant, working in different positions within that restaurant, taking restaurant management or cooking classes, maintaining a positive credit score, and so on? All of your short-term goals should contribute toward reaching your ultimate objective. This enables you to step back at any moment and evaluate career choices in light of whether or not they help or hinder you from reaching your long-term goal. Each short-term goal you set also needs to be specific, measurable, attainable, and time constrained.

Occasionally, you encounter barriers that threaten to impede or even stop your progress. When this happens, you can set specialized short-term goals in place to overcome such barriers. Whatever you do, be determined not to give up on your long-term goals! By the same token, however, if you recognize a particular goal is no longer contributing toward your success or is not important to you anymore, you should be willing to let it go. Doing so allows you to devote more energy toward goals that are of real value.

Write Your Goals Down

Block one evening out of your schedule for goal setting. Go to a place where you are comfortable and free from distractions. You can use paper or a computer to make a chart like the following.

My Personal Goal Worksheet

		Specific	Measurable	Attainable	Time Frame
My Long-Term Goal Is:	Own a Five-Star Italian Restaurant in Manhattan	X	X	X	15 Years
To reach my long-term goal, my short-term goals are:					
1	Research financial aid for enrolling in culinary arts school	X	X	X	Tomorrow
2	Pick up 10 applications from local Italian restaurants	X	X	X	1 Week
3	Start working at an Italian restaurant	X	X	X	60 Days
4	Work as a cook at an Italian restaurant	X	X	X	6 Months
5	Enroll in culinary arts school	X	X	X	1 Year

If you don't already have a long-term goal to work on, let your imagination go wild. Just for practice, come up with a few potential goals and then think about the short-term goals that help you reach them. Make sure each goal measures up to the four main criteria, and then prioritize it.

This exercise aids you in determining if your long-term goal is realistic and helps you establish what steps you need to take toward reaching that goal.

Writing your goals down accomplishes two things. First, it helps you visualize your goals, and second, it instills a personal commitment to reaching them. Keep your list in a common area where you can refer back to it regularly. This could be anywhere from the refrigerator to the bathroom mirror—just make sure you see it often. Rewrite your goals from time to time, refining and visualizing them each time. Goals that aren't written down aren't really goals, they're just dreams. Writing your goals down is the first step toward making them come to life.

Evaluate Your Progress

Have you ever watched a rodent on a running wheel? A person could easily find him- or herself in nearly the same pointless pursuit. Expending energy. Wasting time. Running and running. Getting nowhere.

If you set goals but never look back to evaluate your progress, you, too, get nowhere. Life is hectic. There are thousands of diversions that can rob you of time. If you don't *make* time for reviewing your progress and deciding on needed adjustments, your goals gradually fall by the wayside.

Evaluating your progress doesn't have to take a lot of time. You can do it daily, weekly, or even monthly depending on the type of goal. I personally choose to review my goals daily. I start thinking about them when I get in the shower and continue thinking about them while I drive to work. When I get to work, I review the list I keep on my computer, make needed revisions, add new goals, delete any I've reached, and start my day. You might choose a completely different method, and that's fine. Just do *something!*

Best Practice

View vacation as an opportunity to review your goals. Peaceful settings away from the hustle and bustle of everyday life are ideal for self-analysis, brainstorming, and planning. This is the reason many companies host annual retreats.

A Dose of Reality

Every so often, obstacles will thwart your ability to achieve certain goals. When this happens (notice I said *when*, not *if*), it can be disheartening. Seeds of doubt may cause you to lower your expectations about what you can actually achieve. You might be tempted to slow down or even give up.

To help with such negative thoughts, try not to think of success and failure as opposites, with one being acceptable and the other unacceptable. Instead, consider them complementary to one another.

In the world of economics, a complementary good is a good that is consumed in connection with or because of another good. Examples of this would be computers and monitors, MP3 players and digital music files, and hamburger patties and hamburger buns. Generally speaking, one isn't good without the other. The same is true of success and failure.

Occasional failings are part of the growth and learning process. If you succeeded at everything, it would mean you never learned anything because you already knew everything. View your missteps as little triumphs that make you smarter, tougher, and better!

Navigating your way to business success is like climbing stairs to the top of a high skyscraper. If you trip and fall back a couple steps every few flights, it's no reason to go back to the ground floor and start over. It's also no reason to spend the rest of your life in the stairwell. If reaching your goal takes longer than you expected, this, too, is okay. Your main objective is not to give up on reaching the top floor.

Heads Up!

Goal setting can become an obsession that leads to burnout and disappointment. Remember, attaining goals is not good or bad in itself. It is simply a means to accomplish something that is important to you. The goals you reach are not a good estimation of your value as an individual.

A Formula for Success

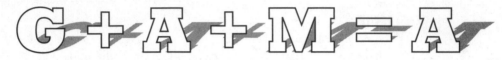

So let's package this chapter all together. Everything we've discussed so far can be nicely summarized with the simple formula above. The long version looks like this:

Goal + Ability + Motivation = Achievement

G.A.M.A. Is Important

All three elements of this equation are equally important. If you have all the right goals and all the ability in the world, but you aren't motivated to action, your achievement will be zero—never more and never less.

G.A.M.A. Is Scalable

Just like any good equation, G.A.M.A. is scalable. If you have 50 percent goal, 50 percent ability, and 50 percent motivation, you will reach 50 percent of your potential for achievement. If any of the first three elements are zero, your result will be zero. The higher each respective element, the higher the overall result.

G.A.M.A. Is Reliable

You can always count on this formula to help you improve your lot in life. Its effectiveness isn't limited to business. Let's say you are interested in buying a home. First, you need a goal—what type of home you want, where, when, and so on. Second, you need the ability—things like a down payment and a good credit score. Third, you need motivation. Buying a home requires you exert the effort to look through listings, make phone calls, and visit potential locations. The end result will be the achievement of home ownership.

G.A.M.A. Helps You Succeed

If G.A.M.A. is the only concept you remember from this book, I guarantee it will repay the cover price hundreds of times over. Why? Because living by it ensures you surmount obstacles, stay focused on your objectives, and set goals that are attainable.

Suppose you would like to acquire something, change something, or that you aren't happy with some situation. It could be in your personal life, on the job, or related to something completely off the wall. What can you do about it? Simple! Shoot some G.A.M.A. rays at it!

Try to come up with an actual situation and then ask yourself the following questions related to it:

◆ Do I have any *goals* I'm working toward? If not, what goals can I set?

◆ Do I have the *ability* to reach the goals I've set, or am I certain to fail? Is this something that is completely out of my control? If so, what *can* I control?

◆ Am I *motivated?* If not, why not? What motivates me?

Obviously, your answers to each of these questions only helps you identify what ingredients you are missing. The next step is to provide the missing ingredients. If you know you'll never possess a certain ingredient, you need to find a different objective. You can't bake bread without flour.

If, however, you realize you do have the ability to muster all the ingredients, all you have to do is set about gathering and mixing them. Once you do that, the results come automatically!

Stay Focused on Your Objective

Following the advice in this chapter requires a tremendous amount of determination and focus. Many of the suggestions I've shared are easier said than done. But is there anything worth doing that doesn't require a degree of focus?

It's interesting what happens to runners when they take their eyes off the track to look at the crowd. They actually slow down! Have you ever seen a runner cross the finish line while eyeing the stands? Certainly not! Instead, the look you see on a runner's face is one of steadfast determination, concrete resolve, and unbreakable focus. The focus required to achieve success in business is no different! How focused are you?

You can do several things to boost your level of focus.

Prioritize

Don't let yourself get distracted by activities that seem important but actually aren't.

The business world is filled with trivial distractions that rob you of time and energy. Instead of getting sidetracked, prioritize your activities based on the amount of time they take in comparison with the reward you receive. When faced with a decision whether or not to do something, ask two simple questions:

- How long is this going to take me?
- What am I going to get out of it?

While you can't use these two questions to decide everything, you'll be surprised by how helpful they can be for prioritizing tasks. This type of decision-making process helps you stay focused on what is most important.

Visualize

I once read a fitness magazine that suggested you can enhance motivation to exercise by visualizing yourself walking down the beach with a perfectly toned body while everyone gawks at you in amazement. While this may seem over the top, it nicely illustrates the power of imagining your accomplishments.

Before you ever become successful, you should already be successful in your mind. When your visualization seems so real you can taste it, your desire to achieve it becomes extremely powerful. In your mind, you are creating your own success.

For instance, let's say your dream is to run your own company from anywhere in the world so you can travel to exotic destinations. If this is the case, you should visualize yourself on the beach, laptop at your side, headset in your ear, Corona in the sand. The more details you can summon, the stronger your desire becomes. Really try to make your dream live!

The reason doing this is so effective is it reminds you how badly you want something and moves you to work harder to attain it. It also convinces you to push through any temporary pain you might experience on your way to achieving your dream.

Best Practice _____

To build your confidence that you can achieve something extraordinary, visualize it first. Making something real in your mind is the first step toward making it real in your life.

Reward Yourself

The proverb "all work and no play makes Jack a dull boy" has a remarkable ring of truth. If you achieve goal after goal but never reward yourself, what's going to recharge your batteries? Burnout can rob you of focus faster than anything.

To keep yourself from burning out, attach rewards to the realization of landmark goals. Rewards could include a day off, a vacation, a new pair of shoes, a new suit, a long lunch, or an extra drink with friends—anything that makes you feel good and that gives you an opportunity to celebrate your accomplishments.

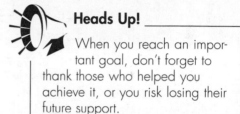

Heads Up! _____

When you reach an important goal, don't forget to thank those who helped you achieve it, or you risk losing their future support.

Stay Positive

Try not to think of success in terms of absolutes. If you shoot for a three-pointer, miss it, catch the rebound, and shoot a two-pointer, did you fail? Of course not! You may have missed the shot you originally intended, but you still made a shot. A two-point shot is worth celebrating, too!

Think of how often business people reach out for something but fail to achieve it. Profitable mergers fail because shareholders vote against them. Deals are lost because someone bids too high. Projects are stopped because funding runs out. Such is simply the nature of business.

Even the worst of blunders can still be valuable learning experiences. There's a lot to be said for the expression, "I'll never do *that* again!"

Always focus on what you have accomplished and what you still desire to accomplish instead of what you failed to accomplish. You need to have an optimistic attitude to keep yourself pressing on toward business success!

Surround Yourself with the Right People

Peer pressure is a powerful force! Whether consciously or unconsciously, the people we surround ourselves with mold our thinking, attitudes, and actions. Social pressure has motivated people to put an end to bad habits, start exercising, work harder in school, give to charity, and a number of other good things.

Run your associates through the following checklist:

The people I surround myself with are:

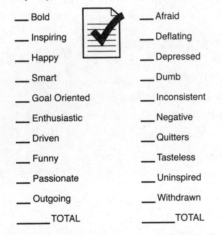

___ Bold	___ Afraid
___ Inspiring	___ Deflating
___ Happy	___ Depressed
___ Smart	___ Dumb
___ Goal Oriented	___ Inconsistent
___ Enthusiastic	___ Negative
___ Driven	___ Quitters
___ Funny	___ Tasteless
___ Passionate	___ Uninspired
___ Outgoing	___ Withdrawn
_____ TOTAL	_____ TOTAL

Is it time to look for new associates?

Rather than discourage you from reaching your goals, successful people hearten you to reach for even greater ones. They inspire you, support you, and set a good example for you.

Winners keep you focused on winning. They teach you to think like a winner, act like a winner, and win like a winner!

The Least You Need to Know

- ◆ External motivation, while important, can only get you so far. To accomplish great things requires you to be driven from the inside.

- ◆ It's important to understand what motivates you personally.

- ◆ For a goal to be effective, it needs to be specific, measurable, achievable, and time constrained.

- ◆ Write your goals down and review them often.

- ◆ Occasional failings are part of the growth and learning process. View your missteps as little triumphs that make you smarter, tougher, and better.

- ◆ Remember G.A.M.A.: Goal + Ability + Motivation = Achievement.

Navigating the Career Highway

In This Chapter

- Choosing a career
- Recognizing when you're in the wrong field
- Changing careers
- Taking a look at the career "big picture"

A career is a journey. Like any journey, it can be packed with excitement or fraught with obstacles. In most cases, it will be both.

Much of how your career turns out depends on the choices you make now. This chapter was written with the goal of helping you make these choices wisely. We discuss how to choose a career that is right for you personally, how to gain your bearings if you are lacking direction, and how to determine if it's time to make a change in the direction you are headed.

What Is a Career?

Put simply, your career is what you do.

Your career can change many times. You can even have more than one career simultaneously. While the word career usually refers to one's paid employment, many people also have unpaid careers such as in the fields of art or music. A career may refer to an entire lifetime of work or even to a shorter period of time such as, "I had a brief career as a server."

The word *career* stems from the Latin *carrus*, which basically refers to a wheeled vehicle. This is rather interesting because just like a career, a wheeled vehicle continually moves, changes directions, and eventually comes to a stop.

The 1950s concept of a career is long gone. It used to be the most successful measure of a career was retiring after 40 years with the same company to receive a gold watch and a pension. Today, however, it's not uncommon to have six different careers before you graduate from college.

Whatever the case, career planning should start before you take your first job and shouldn't end until you retire. It involves choosing a career, finding a job in your field, growing at that job, changing jobs, and sometimes even changing careers.

FYI
A growing trend is to have multiple careers at one time. Examples of this could include doctor/writer, teacher/artist, paralegal/fitness instructor, and so on. The reasons for this vary, but commonly include a need for additional income, to experiment with career options, or to find fulfillment.
This type of career diversity presents an excellent way to gain experience, to develop professionally, and to ease into a new career without a major upset.

Deciding on a Career

If you can't decide on a career, don't worry. You are not alone! Many people face this challenge and overcome it. Be assured there is a career out there for you—a great career! With some effort on your part, you *can* find it!

Great careers typically share three characteristics: They are challenging, fulfilling, and lucrative. You probably want to find a career that is all three of these things. How can you? First, you need to give serious thought to what we discussed in Chapter 2. Understanding your internal motivation is key to finding fulfillment in your career. If you choose a career as an accountant when your primary motivation is thrill seeking, you're likely to be very disappointed—unless of course you happen to land a job at the next Enron. Otherwise, don't skip this vital first step!

To help you choose a career that is right for you, pay close attention to the following do's and don'ts.

Do Assess Yourself

Self-assessment plays a central role in career planning. Why? Because it helps you better understand your personality, work style, values, and what type of environment you are suited for. Potential employers look for clues that expose these traits in a person, and you should be looking for them in yourself.

A self-assessment tells you if you are introverted or extroverted, whether you need variety in your work, whether you should have contact with the public or work alone, how well you adapt to change, and so on. Comprehensive assessments also provide you with a list of advisable careers. Several career assessment resources are listed in Appendix A of this book for your convenience. If you're enrolled in school, you may also want to check to see if they offer any resources. Career and guidance counselors can usually help you with this.

Do Make a List of Potential Careers

From the results of your assessment, pick at least five careers you would like to research further. After that, add any other options you want to explore that weren't already listed. Don't be afraid to put something on your list just because it seems out of reach. Remember, this is a list of career *options*. You still have to research each one.

Do Research

You don't necessarily have to work in a career to know if you'll like it or not. As you research your alternatives, try to find out about entrance and education requirements, available training, job duties, environment, and advancement options.

Search books and periodicals from your fields of interest. Browse the Internet for industry news and trends. Talk to people who work in those fields. Review position profiles featured on job-hunting websites. Dig as deep as you possibly can. If you dig deep enough, you will unquestionably discover things you like and don't like.

By taking these steps, you should be able to narrow your list substantially. For an even tighter focus, you can consider taking a course based on a position or skill within your primary industry of interest. If temporary positions or internships are available, these are also a superior way to feel out an industry.

Don't Let Someone Else Choose Your Career

Family members, teachers, college professors, and creators of "top jobs" lists won't have to live with your career choices—only you will. A career needs to be tailored to your personality, interests, and natural abilities—not someone else's opinion.

Even if you have the opportunity to work for a family business, view this as a career option rather than a requirement. If you try it out and love it, great! If not, you always have a skill you can fall back on.

Don't Discount Your Hobby

Not only will a career based around your hobby be extremely fun, but also very rewarding. What's more, you are likely to be especially good at your hobbies. Many people have become tremendously successful because they built their career around a hobby. Jewelry and clothing designers, builders, mechanics, gamers, and others are among them.

If you can't find a job that allows you to pursue your hobby, you may be able to create one. Chapter 20 teaches you how to do this.

Heads Up!

Before you accept a job working for family or friends, scrutinize it just as you would any other opportunity. If you accept a position as a favor or to avoid hurt feelings, you are likely to regret it in the future. Sentimentality is a bad reason to choose a career!

Don't Choose Based on Money Alone

Although money is an important thing to take into consideration when choosing a career, it shouldn't be the only thing. Countless studies have shown that a high salary doesn't necessarily contribute to job satisfaction. I can personally attest to this fact.

When I was in high school, I considered majoring in education because I love to teach. At the time, I discounted this as an option because I didn't think the compensation was adequate.

Over time, I realized I would never be truly satisfied with my career unless I used my ability to teach others. My consulting company and books like the one you are reading represent the outlet I finally discovered. Even though I made a considerable amount of money in other ventures, I still had to satisfy my need to teach.

Just because something pays well doesn't mean you will like it, be good at it, or stick with it.

What If You Made the Wrong Career Choice?

In June of 2008, the United States Bureau of Labor Statistics released a labor market activity report that indicated the average American holds 10.8 jobs between age 18 and 42, with nearly two thirds of these jobs held before age 27. Twenty-five percent of respondents held more than 15 jobs during this time.

Why do I cite this report? Because changing careers isn't just tolerated, it's expected!

If you aren't happy with your current employment, you've still got plenty of time to turn things around. If you're reading this book, you must be under 40. And even if you're 39, you still have a good 25 years to build a new career!

Remember what we said earlier about a career being a journey? Well, the experience you have gained is prone to have provided you with valuable transferable skills that help you on your journey.

What are transferable skills? They are skills you can use in just about any job. They can include things like the ability to communicate effectively, an understanding of office etiquette, computer skills, marketing knowledge, self-confidence, salesmanship, and a host of other things. What transferable skills do you have? Would you have all those skills if you hadn't worked the places you have? What you think of as a wrong choice may have actually been a critical step to prepare you for the road ahead.

 Best Practice

When interviewing with a prospective employer, focus more on skills than titles. While titles may be industry-specific or nondescript, skills are universal. This is especially important when changing fields. Try to help others see you as someone with multiple skills, not someone with multiple titles.

The other good news is that everything we've discussed in this chapter about choosing a career also applies when you are changing careers. Before you make a career change, you need to go through all the same steps. The only difference is you are a little older and wiser, which increases your chances of success.

Clues It Might Be Time to Go

On a literal highway, there are many hazards. Just as drivers look out for warning lights and warning signs indicating dangers that could impede their progress, so astute professionals remain alert to the signs around them. The last thing you want to experience is an unexpected breakdown on your career highway. Following are a few things to look out for.

Engine Pressure

Like engine pressure, stress can push you to the brink of failure. Besides affecting job performance, there are significant risks of developing cardiovascular disease, psychological disorders, drug and alcohol dependency, musculoskeletal disorders, and more. Any career that pushes you to these extremes is better off avoided.

If you think you can't afford to make a change, consider this: according to the *Journal of Occupational and Environmental Medicine*, health-care expenditures are nearly 50 percent greater for workers who report high levels of stress. The truth is you can't afford not to make a change!

Some jobs are inherently stressful, but just because one person finds a stressful environment okay doesn't mean you will. So if you recognize your emotional well-being is threatened, don't be afraid to pull the plug. Everybody is different. Life's too short to live frazzled!

Flat Tires

Feeling a little deflated? Tired of going into work every day? Not interested in your job anymore? You could be a victim of boredom or even burnout. Boredom can affect your attitude, the quality of your work, and can manifest itself in absenteeism or tardiness.

Thankfully, this isn't necessarily a sign you need to change careers. Maybe you just need to work for a different company in the same field. Or, maybe you need some new projects to break up the monotony. For some, all it takes is a change in schedule to shake things up. If none of these things work, it might be time to consider a career change.

Road Blocks

On the career highway, certain obstacles may arise that you can't just ease around. While none of these obstacles have to put a stop to your career progress, they may require taking an alternate route. Included among such obstacles can be:

◆ **Scheduling conflicts.** If your personal life calls for allowances in your schedule that can't be met by your employer, you may need to find other work. During my brief stint in retail (I've changed careers a few times, too), I had an employee who requested every Saturday off to spend with her children. I didn't fault her for putting her children first in her life, but Saturday was our busiest day. The compromise we made was to give her every other Saturday off. In this scenario, we both compromised. If, however, you and your employer can't work out an acceptable compromise, you'll have to decide what is most important to you. It's worth mentioning that in this example, the employee's unwillingness to work on Saturdays disqualified her for a management spot.

◆ **Issues with pay.** Everyone has a certain amount they need to survive. If your job isn't providing that amount for you, one of two things has to give: either the amount you spend or the amount you earn. But before you go marching into your boss's office to ask for a raise, read the section on pay in Chapter 8. What we're talking about here is situations in which you've earned a raise, asked for a raise, and need a raise, but your company won't give one to you. If you don't have a spending problem but find yourself getting deeper and deeper in debt every month, what's the point of working? Eventually you'll have to tap out anyway. You might as well do it while you still have something left.

◆ **Impossible bosses.** If someone in a position of authority is insistent on keeping you down and there is nobody above their head willing to help you out, you're probably better off moving on. Before you do, though, try to apply the suggestions in Chapter 10.

 Heads Up! _____

Don't be too quick to throw in the towel when obstacles arise. Before you decide to change jobs or change careers, make sure you've exhausted all possible means to overcome them. If you get in the habit of running from problems, you'll never be respected, and you'll never get ahead in business. Sometimes you just have to toughen up.

Dead End

The proverbial dead-end job can be a real career killer. How do you know if you're in one? The real key is to look around you. Find the answers to these questions, and you should be able to determine if it's time to move on.

◆ How big is the company? Is there any room to grow?

◆ How long has the average worker been employed here? Have any of the workers been promoted?

◆ Does my company promote from within? Do they really, or do they just say they do?

◆ Where did most of the management come from? Were they promoted from within, or hired from the outside?

◆ Am I being taught new things or cross-trained on a regular basis? If not, is there a good reason for it?

◆ Have I been here longer than two years but received no additional responsibility even though I'm capable?

Some human resource experts argue there is no such thing as a dead-end job, only a dead-end worker. This is a mistaken viewpoint. While there are dead-end (unpromotable) workers, there are also dead-end jobs. The only way a dead-end job is valuable is if it provides you with skills and experience you can take with you when you leave. Just make sure you recognize when that time comes. Dead-end jobs have a way of sucking you into a career vortex.

Dangerous Curves Ahead

Like a big yellow sign warning you to proceed with caution, financial troubles and massive layoffs within your company or industry can signal it's time to move on. At the very least, they should prompt you to keep in touch with your contacts and update your resumé.

It's better to look for a job while you are still employed because you can be more selective. If you wait until after you've been laid off, desperation might tempt you to jump at the first thing that comes along.

Look Before You Leap

When it comes to deciding on a job or career change, it's prudent not to be too hasty. There are times when you are better off sticking things out. Because every situation is unique, you have to use good judgment when making a decision to leave.

The five or so areas we've just discussed are clues, not rules. Again, every situation is different.

If, however, after weighing all the factors you decide it is time to move on, Chapter 18 can help you make a smooth transition.

The Journey Matters, Too

Imagine for a minute you are planning a road trip to your favorite vacation destination. You've been saving money for a whole year to pay for the trip, and it's finally time to leave. The reservations are made, the car is packed, and it's a beautiful day.

Suddenly, as you're loading the last-minute items, clouds roll in and the sky turns dark. What now? Do you cancel your trip? No! You load up and hit the road. What if you get a flat tire partway through your journey? What if you come to a road block? Do you quit? No! You address the problems and get back on track. What motivates you to continue despite obstacles? It's the fact you know where you are headed. You know what's waiting for you at the end of the road.

When you finally arrive at your destination and reflect on your trip, are you going to wish you'd stayed home just because you had to face some hindrances along the way? Certainly not. The journey was made more memorable because of them.

The course your career takes is much the same. If you keep your destination in mind and keep driving toward it, the obstacles won't really matter. They'll just make your journey interesting.

So be determined to press on! Savor the journey and learn from every experience! Don't let anything keep you from achieving your goals, and don't let anyone discourage you. You can navigate the career highway with success!

The Least You Need to Know

- ◆ Career planning should start before you take your first job and shouldn't end until you retire.

- ◆ If you can't decide on a career, you are not alone. Many people face this challenge and overcome it.

- ◆ Complete a comprehensive career assessment, and then make a list of 5 to 10 career options and research each option thoroughly.

- ◆ Choosing a career is a personal decision that cannot be based solely on monetary rewards; don't forget to look at your personal interests and hobbies for inspiration and know it's okay to change careers.

- ◆ Things like stress, boredom, burnout, company financial trouble, and massive layoffs can signal that it's time for a career change.

- ◆ Before you make a career change, weigh all factors carefully to ensure a wise decision.

Part 2

Getting on the Right Path

The degree of business success you achieve depends greatly on how you present yourself. If you want to obtain the best jobs and get introduced to the best opportunities, you have to understand and practice specific behaviors. This part is designed to help you do that on paper and in person!

It shows you how to create a resumé and cover letter that gets noticed, equips you with dynamic interview skills, and teaches you to make outstanding first impressions that last.

More than that, it trains you to maximize every opportunity you encounter. In this way, you will be able to turn even the most insignificant of experiences into valuable stepping stones on the pathway to business success.

"I'll be great for this company, sir, because I have no partner, kids, or social life, so you can transfer me wherever you like, work me 24-7, and pay me as shamefully as you can stomach."

Chapter 4

Job Hunting 101

In This Chapter

- ◆ Conducting an effective job search
- ◆ Preparing for a job search
- ◆ Writing a job-winning resumé
- ◆ Drafting a dynamic cover letter

An effective job search is characterized by getting the best job in the shortest amount of time. To accomplish this requires you to launch the finest personal marketing campaign possible. In fact, you should try to think of your job search as just that—a way to market yourself.

What do large companies do when they want to launch a new product? They market it everywhere—television, radio, Internet, billboards, magazines. While you may not have access to such a wide array of media, you still need to take advantage of every opportunity to get your name out there. You also want to make sure your marketing collaterals (resumé, cover letter, etc.) are top notch. This chapter addresses these areas and more.

Conducting Effective Job Searches

There are essentially two ways to go about a job search. You can look for individual jobs and apply for them, or you can make yourself visible to potential employers and let them find you. The best results come when you do a combination of both.

Online

In recent years, the Internet has become the most popular job search venue. According to a 2007 survey by The Conference Board, the Internet surpassed newspaper as a favorite with job seekers 73 percent to 65 percent, respectively. It's also the primary tool big companies use to find quality candidates.

You can use the Internet to do research and gather information, apply for jobs, post resumés, create a professional profile, and more. Here are a few examples of online job hunting resources:

- **Monster.com** Post you resumé online; apply for jobs; research potential employers; get career advice; and participate in online job fairs.

- **Jobfox.com** Create a profile; find jobs matched to your skills and personality; view potential matches; and request introductions.

- **LinkedIn.com** Build a professional profile and indicate you are interested in being contacted with job opportunities; network with all your contacts and request introductions to people in their network; and keep your network informed about changes or openings in your career.

- **VisualCV.com** Online resumé tool that allows you to include video, pictures, and a portfolio of your work; and securely share different versions of your resumé with employers, colleagues, and friends.

Refer to Appendix A for links to other great career building resources online.

Heads Up!

Posting personal information about yourself online puts you at risk for identity theft. Only use websites you are familiar with or that are recommended by this book and other reputable sources.

Job Fairs

Job fairs are like giant hiring frenzies. If you're looking for employment and there is a job fair in your area, don't miss it! Bring 30 to 50 copies of your resumé, expect to fill out applications on the spot, and be ready to participate in brief interviews without notice. Try to summarize your strengths, skills, and experience into a two-minute blurb you can give to potential employers, and then practice until it flows naturally.

In advance of the event, decide which employers you are most interested in and visit their booths first (while you're fresh). Dress your best, wear comfortable shoes, and arrive early. And don't forget to smile!

Contacts

Often, the best jobs come from word of mouth. When you're in the market for a job, make sure to let everyone know you're looking. Include family, friends, business associates, college professors, and anyone else you can think of. This doesn't require a lot of effort but it can reap hefty dividends. One of the best ways to do this is with a brief phone call. The call doesn't have to be long or complicated. In fact, it should generally be brief. Done well, it should go something like this:

"Hey, Jim! This is Robert. How are you?"

"I'm fine, Robert. How are you?"

"Great! Thanks for asking. I know how busy you are Jim, and I really appreciate your taking my call! I promise to be brief."

"No problem. What can I do for you?"

"Well, I've decided to take a new direction with my career and I wanted to let you know in case you hear of any openings."

"Sure! What are you looking for?"

"As you probably know, I just got my degree in marketing, and I'm looking for something that allows me to put it to good use. If you hear of anything ..."

"Sure, Robert. I can do that for you."

"Great, Jim! I really appreciate that. Would you mind if I give you my contact information so you'll have it handy?"

Don't worry about getting into too many specifics at this point. The main idea to stress is that you want to know if they hear of *anything*. Even if you have very specific requirements, it's your responsibility to weed out the bad leads.

Best Practice

Most states and nearly all major cities provide free access to job listings, resumé building tools, and even basic job placement services. Check with your school, local library, and chamber of commerce to see what is available in your area.

As soon as you hang up the phone, send a follow-up e-mail or handwritten note thanking the person for their time. This shows your appreciation and is a good reminder for them. Lastly, don't forget to thank them for any leads they send your way.

Over time, as you build a network of contacts and your reputation, job hunting becomes less necessary. Skilled professionals with large networks usually have more job offers than they can take advantage of. There'll be more about networking in Chapter 12.

Professional Staffing Agencies

If you aren't having any success finding a job on your own, you may wish to solicit the assistance of a professional placement agency. Among the benefits of using this kind of service is having a full-time team of individuals working to find you a job. It is also beneficial to use a staffing service if you are still employed and don't have time to conduct your own job search, or if you are looking for a high-level position that may not be advertised. Other benefits include access to "temp-to-perm" positions that let you test the water before you accept a full-time position, and professional representation, which can impress some employers.

One drawback of working with a headhunter is it will probably cost you something. While some recruiters charge the candidate up front, most charge the employer, which means the pay may be somewhat limited initially. Either way, the relationship with the staffing agency is usually temporary, which can allow you to renegotiate your compensation after your contract expires.

Using a staffing service won't prevent you from conducting your own search simultaneously, and it may provide you with some additional options.

Preparing for the Hunt

Imagine a hunter decked in camouflage and trekking into the woods for a kill. Gun in hand and prey in sight, he prepares to shoot when he realizes he's forgotten his ammunition.

Such is the plight of unprepared job hunters. All dressed up, resumé in hand, employer in the sights, when suddenly they find themselves saying: "Oh. You need that? I didn't bring that with me. Can I drop it off tomorrow?" And just that fast, they've damaged the quality of their first impression.

How can you make sure this doesn't happen to you? Spend a little time gathering some basic elements.

The Basics

First, pull together all your contact information. This should include a working phone number with voicemail, an address, and an e-mail address.

 Heads Up!

If you don't have a professional-sounding e-mail address, use a free service like Yahoo! or Gmail to set one up. Try not to include anything more than your name and maybe a number if necessary.

I once had a candidate apply for a job using the e-mail address kinkymamma4u. Needless to say, I didn't call her in for an interview.

You'll also want to track down contact information for your previous employers. Names, addresses, phone numbers, and dates of employment are all important. Almost every application you fill out is going to ask for this information. Giving someone an incomplete application is a sure way to get turned down for the job you want.

The next thing you need to do is pull together all your personal documentation. This should include a current driver's license, Social Security card, diplomas, proof of any certifications you have, letters of recommendation, and so on. Rather than carry these items with you on an interview, make a few quality copies to give out. Just the fact you have copies on hand will be impressive.

If you are applying for a design job, you should have samples of your work in a portfolio or on a disk. If you are applying for a position as an administrative assistant, bring along copies of letters you've written or forms you've created and so on. Having these things handy gives you an excellent opportunity to showcase your skills and set yourself apart from other candidates.

References

Once you have the interest of an employer, they're probably going to ask you for a list of professional references. Rule number one when it comes to references: Don't list someone as a reference unless you've asked their permission first. Rule number two is to make sure you know in advance what they are going to say about you. Just because someone agrees to be a reference doesn't mean you're going to like what they have to say. Be sure to use people who know your strengths. Tell them what kind of a job you're applying for so they can focus on the right things. If you're tactful, it's even okay to coach them a little.

When choosing your references, try to use solid professional contacts like former bosses, co-workers, and customers. If you don't have any professional references yet, you can use personal or character references, but these should be used sparingly. Examples of good character references are teachers, coaches, clergy, well-respected community members, and the like.

After you've collected your list of references and made sure their information is current and accurate, put four or five in the form of a reference list. Include each reference's name, title, company, address, phone number, e-mail if you have it, and the nature of your relationship with the person. Put your name and contact information at the top of the list.

Best Practice

Before you change jobs, ask your supervisor for a letter of recommendation. Over time, it's easy to lose track of people, but a good reference letter can sing your praises for years.

If the person you ask says he is too busy or he isn't a good writer, offer to provide him with sample letters and a list of your skills to help him out. Some employers may even agree to let you write your own letter for them to sign.

Get Organized

The wider your job search gets, the more important it is for you to stay organized. The last thing you want is for a prospective employer to call you about a position and for you to say, "Who is this? What company?"

You might want to consider using a spreadsheet to keep track of your job search. Include things like the company name, name of the contact person, their contact information, the position you applied for, and the method you used to apply. You should also include the date you applied so you'll know when to follow up.

If you prefer to use an online service for this, check out www.jibberjobber.com.

Writing a Resumé

Writing a professional resumé isn't as daunting as you might think. It's basically just a description of your professional background, and nobody knows your background better than you. Once you gather all your current and previous employment information, half the task is complete. All that remains is to list your skills and add a few job descriptions. If you use a program like Microsoft Word, formatting is a snap, too. Trust me, you can do this!

Types of Resumés

Resumés are typically organized in one of three ways: chronologically, functionally, or a combination of the two.

The chronological format is by far the most common of the three resumé styles. It starts by listing your work history in order from newest to oldest and typically includes a brief description of your duties and accomplishments at each job. Many employers prefer this type of resumé because it is concise and easy to follow. It is a good format to use if you have a solid work history without significant gaps.

When writing a chronological resumé, be sure to include a paragraph or two at the beginning that summarizes your strengths. This should be the very first item on the page before you list your work history. Think of this as a mini advertisement that showcases your best qualities. Keep your sentences to the point and use strong, active verbs like *achieved*, *directed*, *enhanced*, and *produced* when describing your past achievements. Use powerful adjectives such as *skilled*, *driven*, *determined*, and *committed* to describe yourself.

A functional resumé places more emphasis on your skills than on the chronology of your work history. If you have a record of bouncing between jobs, or if you have large gaps in your employment, this type of resumé is preferable. You might also use a functional resumé if you recently graduated and lack sufficient work history to showcase. Keep in mind this format might lead prospective employers to ask more questions about your work history because they may wonder what you are trying to conceal.

A combination resumé includes a summary of your skills at the outset and then follows up with your chronological work history. This type of resumé works well in situations where your previous employment lacks relevance with the job you are applying for, because you can showcase your transferable skills up front.

Samples of each resumé type are included in Appendix C.

FYI
A *curriculum vitae* (Latin for "the course of one's life or career") is essentially an advanced resumé. It is typically used when seeking scientific or academic positions. It is also fitting to use a curriculum vitae (CV) if your professional credentials include an advanced degree, residencies, internships, or if you have a lot of publications. CVs are usually requested when applying for grants as well. International CVs are used when applying for positions overseas. They typically include a measure of personal information such as date of birth and nationality.

Putting It to Paper

After you've gathered all your information and decided on the format you are going to use, the next step is to put your qualifications in writing. Don't be concerned about making your resumé fit on a single page. It's more important to be thorough and accurate. Your goal should be to focus on strengths that are most relevant to the position for which you are applying.

When deciding what to focus on, think about what impresses a potential employer. Sales increases, system enhancements, policy improvements, and things that can be quantified by percentages and dollar amounts are especially desirable. If you faced a problem that you were able to address and overcome, this is another point to feature. Simply listing tasks doesn't carry the same kind of weight as specific, measurable results.

A likely scenario is your resumé is going to find itself in a stack with a hundred others. When an overworked HR person with tired eyes picks up your resumé and gives it a 20-second scan, what is going to stand out? What makes your resumé different from all the rest? These are important questions to keep in mind while you are writing your resumé because you need it to make an impact!

Heads Up! _____

Relying on spell-check and grammar-check to proof your resumé is risky because software won't usually catch every mistake. Sometimes it even suggests inappropriate changes. It is better to have your resumé proofed by at least two people prior to distributing it. Nothing gets your resumé discarded more quickly than grammatical and typographical errors.

In addition to having a traditional paper resumé, you may also want to consider maintaining a digital version of your resume online. Many large companies accept only digital resumés so they can scan them for keywords relevant to the position they are looking to fill. Digital (or online) resumés also make it possible to showcase a portfolio of work. Websites such as those mentioned in this chapter and in Appendix A allow you to create such resumés with ease. One note of caution: if you decide to create an online resumé—something I highly recommend doing—make sure you also have a paper version to complement it.

A Note for Recent Graduates

If you're reading this and thinking, _This is all well and good if you have experience, but I just graduated and the only experience I have comes from waiting tables_, don't fret. You can still put together an excellent resumé!

All you need to do is focus on your skills. A resumé that is academically focused can include more than just your area of study. Think of the skills you have developed from completing classroom projects and labs, practicum, internships, and volunteer work. Do you have any computer skills? Hardware? Software? Are you good at doing research? Enumerate all of these. What personal qualities do you have? Are you customer service oriented? What academic awards have you received? All such things are relevant.

Refer to Appendix C for two excellent examples of student resumés.

Five Resumé No-No's

Avoid the following resumé mishaps:

Lying. Just because a lot of people lie on their resumés doesn't mean it's a good idea. Besides sacrificing your integrity, you are also likely to get caught. Any company worth working for is going to check your references and background before they hire you. When they discover your deception, you might not even get a chance to explain yourself. Besides, if you don't get a certain job because you lack the qualifications, it probably isn't the right job for you.

Too much information. When writing your job descriptions, keep them concise and relevant to the job for which you're applying. Elaborating on every job duty and task more than likely crosses someone's eyes than impresses them. There's always time to go into greater detail during an interview. Avoid sharing salary information, grievances with previous employers, and reasons your employment was terminated. All these things are better discussed in person, if at all.

Over personalizing. Despite your strongest urges, say no to glitter, sparkles, neon paper, clipart, gigantic scrolling fonts, and sprays of your favorite fragrance!

Granted, when tastefully done, minor personalizations can be a nice touch. What is considered acceptable? A professional headshot of yourself is a nice way to set your resumé apart. Another option is to put your name in a color font and use high-grade paper. You can even feature the logos of companies you previously worked for, as long as there are no restrictions on their use. The idea is to make your resumé look professional, not flashy!

Gaps. Large gaps in employment history are viewed unfavorably by most employers because they can reveal a lack of drive or dedication. If the gaps are related to personal problems, some employers are afraid the same problem will arise again in the future.

Rather than leave gaps on your resumé, try to fill the time between jobs with career-related endeavors such as increasing your education. If this is not possible, you may want to address any gaps right up front by explaining them in your cover letter.

Multiple short-term positions. If you've averaged more than one position every two years, potential employers generally view this as a red flag that you won't stick around. To compensate for this, write the most dynamic skills-based resumé possible and hope for an interview so you can explain yourself.

You can also list your employment in terms of years instead of months and years (i.e., 2007–2009 instead of November 2007 to January 2009).

If you notice you're trending toward short-term, unrelated positions, you should be selective about your next position and plan to stay there for at least a few years.

Resumé Checklist

- ❏ Includes current contact information
- ❏ Is accurate, thorough, and free from typographical errors
- ❏ Is visually appealing and easy to read; uses at least a 9.5 pt. font
- ❏ Includes a summary of qualifications relevant to the position requirements
- ❏ Focuses more on accomplishments than job duties
- ❏ Uses action words and a lively tone
- ❏ Includes at least 10 years of employment history where available
- ❏ Lists all education and specialized training received, including professional certifications and associations

Writing a Cover Letter

Effective cover letters enthusiastically convey your interest in a position and outline your relevant skills. Think of a cover letter as a one-page, professional introduction to you and your resumé. If you are submitting your resumé in person, a cover letter isn't necessary. However, if you are submitting a resumé online, by fax, or by mail, a cover letter is essential. Your cover letter should do such a good job of introducing yourself that the reader is eager to read your resumé.

The tone should be mildly assertive, professional, and should focus on what you can do for the employer rather than what you expect the employer to do for you.

There are two basic types of cover letters. One responds to a known job opening, and the other seeks to find an unadvertised position. Before you sit down to write a cover letter, you first need to know what you are trying to accomplish.

Responding to a Known Job Opening

The first paragraph of a response letter should include the title of the position and where you heard about it. It should also affirm your interest in the position. Following is an example.

"Your advertisement for an Administrative Assistant on Monster.com appears to be a perfect match with my qualifications. I am confident my skills and background meet your requirements, and I am anxious to speak with you about the position further."

Prospecting for an Opportunity

The first paragraph of a prospecting letter is handled differently because it is unsolicited. For this reason, it needs to be especially engaging. Here's an example:

"I have been following your company in the news for some time, and I am impressed with your recent expansion! I have a Bachelors of Science in Business Administration and feel confident my experience as an intern at XYZ makes me uniquely qualified to fill a position at your company. I would welcome the opportunity to discuss any openings you have available."

The Body

The next step is to explain what you have to offer.

A list of four to six bulleted points works best because they stand out and are easy to read. Each point should relate to the position you are applying for and should highlight elements that could otherwise get lost in your resume. You can list specific accomplishments, personality traits, education, or awards you have received.

View each point as a personal selling feature. Focus on things that are related to the position you are applying for; that are unique to you; and that convey your ability, motivation, and acumen.

Here are a few examples:

Heads Up!

When writing your cover letter, don't copy terminology directly from your resume. When information overlaps, it's better to expound on it or put it in different terms.

- I am highly skilled at developing new systems. During my employment at XYZ, I created a customer loyalty program that increased sales by more than 20 percent.

- Your advertisement indicated you are seeking someone with strong customer service skills. I received an award for Outstanding Customer Service during my work at ABC.

- Graduated Magna Cum Laude.

◆ You indicated you are looking for an experienced leader. In my resumé, you will notice I have held three leadership positions in recent years. I am highly adept at getting results through the efforts of others.

The Final Paragraph

The last paragraph of your cover letter should include a reaffirmation of your interest in the position along with the action you plan to take. Your action could be to wait (i.e., "Thank you for reviewing my resumé. I eagerly anticipate your response."), or to follow up (i.e., "I will contact you by phone to arrange a convenient time for us to meet."). Either way, make sure you leave the door open.

The samples in Appendix C nicely demonstrate how to write the first paragraph, the body, and the final paragraph of a cover letter.

Is That All?

Applying the suggestions in this chapter makes you like a fisherman who baits his line, casts it in the water, and then gets some nibbles.

Your next challenge is to hook a fish and reel it in. Chapter 5 shows you how.

The Least You Need to Know

◆ View your job search like a personal marketing campaign. Take advantage of every means at your disposal to get your name out there.

◆ Before you actively search for a job, take time to gather essentials like the contact information of previous employers and a list of professional references.

◆ Use a spreadsheet or a service like www.jibberjobber.com to help you keep your job search organized.

◆ If you have large gaps or multiple short-term positions in your employment history, use a functional resumé.

◆ When writing your resumé, avoid lying, giving out too much information, and over personalization.

◆ A cover letter should enthusiastically convey your interest in a position. It ought to be professional yet mildly assertive in tone, and should focus more on what you can do for the employer than what the employer can do for you.

Chapter 5

Close the Deal: Getting the Job You Want

In This Chapter

- ◆ Making your first contact count
- ◆ Preparing for your interview
- ◆ Identifying the many types of interviews
- ◆ Answering tough questions
- ◆ Mastering the art of interview etiquette

I'm going to let you in on a little secret from the other side of the desk: finding quality employees is no easy task!

Candidate one doesn't complete his application and is rude to your receptionist. Candidate two is smacking gum and her cell phone keeps ringing. Candidate three can't stop berating his last employer. Candidate four is in a micro mini, and candidate five won't answer your questions. Screening applicants can be downright grueling!

Why am I telling you this? Because what usually happens sometime during this process is that a well-dressed, poised, and qualified candidate walks through the door and gives a top-notch interview. The contrast between this new super-candidate and all the others becomes strikingly evident, and you know this is the person you want to hire!

How can you become that person? You don't have to be the best, the smartest, or the most charismatic. You simply have to understand what employers are looking for and then package yourself accordingly. This chapter teaches you how to do that!

Make Your First Contact Count

As the word implies, "screening" is designed to let favorable candidates through while keeping unfavorable candidates out. To even get a shot at an interview requires you pass the initial screening process, which usually works something like this: Someone—an HR person, an assistant manager, or a decision maker—has a stack of applications on their desk and starts going through them one at a time. Each application or resumé gets a 15- to 20-second scan to determine the applicant's suitability for the position. If nothing unfavorable jumps off the page, the applicants' information goes in a pile that survives to the next step. At this critical point in the screening process, you can't afford to make any mistakes that get your resumé discarded.

Follow Instructions

If you can't follow instructions during the application process, why should anyone believe you'd follow instructions on the job? Few things peeve a hiring manager faster than an applicant who doesn't follow the company's process. If an ad says, "please e-mail your resumé to hiring@abcinc.com," that is exactly what you should do. Don't think for a minute overnighting your resumé to the company president is going to solicit a favorable response.

Another common misnomer is that you can cut through the hiring red tape by hand-delivering your application and requesting an interview on the spot. While this may work at some small businesses, it's not likely to work at most companies. *If* you even get past the receptionist, the person doing the hiring is more likely to be annoyed than impressed.

Cross Your t's and Dot Your i's

Incomplete applications get a one-way ticket to the paper shredder. In the eyes of a potential employer, they either mean you're lazy, or you don't care about getting the job. Either way, you're confetti.

Best Practice _____

If you've submitted your application or resumé and haven't heard anything back for over a week, it's okay to follow up with a phone call. The goal of this call is twofold—to make a favorable impression and to verify your information was received. Respectfully ask how long before you can expect to hear something, and don't call again until after that time has passed. Keep the call brief and friendly. If you have to leave a message, don't call back inside of a week.

Avoid this snarc by getting all your information together in advance so you'll have it handy when you start on the application. Take your time filling out any employment paperwork. Recheck each page to make sure you don't miss anything. Make sure all the information on your application matches what is on your resumé, be thorough, and write neatly. Double-check the spelling on any words you're unsure about.

I've interviewed a lot of people who thought if something was on their resumé, it didn't have to be on their application—this notion is false. Many applications even have a notice that says, "Please answer *all* questions. Resumés are not a substitute for a completed application." Remember, employers rate applicants on how well they complete their application.

To complete a job application, you will need:

Personal:

- ◆ Name
- ◆ Address
- ◆ Phone number
- ◆ E-mail address
- ◆ Proof of eligibility to work in the United States
- ◆ Details about criminal convictions
- ◆ If under 18, working papers/age certificate

continues

continued

Education:

- Schools/colleges attended

- Dates attended

- Major

- Degree/diploma

Position:

- Title of position you are applying for

- Hours and days you are available to work

- Date you can start work

Previous Employment:

- Names, addresses, and phone numbers of previous employers

- Previous supervisors' names

- Dates of employment

- Compensation

- Reason for leaving

References:

- At least two personal and two professional

- Names, relationships, addresses, and phone numbers

Be Nice to *Everybody!*

When applying for a job in person, it is especially important to be nice to everyone you meet! I've been in charge of hiring at several companies and have interviewed hundreds of people. Among those I've turned down for positions were some of the best-dressed and most qualified candidates. Why? Because they were rude to my staff.

Whenever it comes time to hire a new staff member, I always put my front office staff on high alert. I encourage them to introduce themselves to the candidates and let me know what they think. Sometimes, our receptionist tells me a candidate was late, rude, or came unprepared. Any input that comes from my staff is heavily weighted.

Some companies have even been known to place an employee in the lobby disguised as an applicant. While this may seem over the top, it shows you should try to make a favorable impression on everyone you come in contact with when you are applying for a job.

Another great practice is to write down the name and position of anyone you come in contact with. This way, if you come back a second time, you can call people by name. I remember one occasion when we were torn between two candidates and I asked my staff what they thought of each one. Not surprisingly, they all viewed one candidate more favorably because she was friendly and remembered everyone's name. Can you guess which candidate we hired?

How to Prepare for Your Interview

Once you have an interview scheduled, what's next? Throw on a suit, grab a copy of your resumé, and hit the door? Not quite. Going to an interview unprepared is no different than taking a test you haven't studied for. In fact, preparing in advance for an interview is just as important as showing up for it. So how can you make sure you are well prepared?

Research! Research! Research!

Earlier, I used the analogy of fishing to describe the process of job hunting—trying to *hook* and *reel in* a good opportunity. Likewise, researching a prospective employer is like researching what bait to use. Different kinds of fish respond to different types of bait; similarly, each company responds to a different type of candidate.

To become the right type of candidate, you have to understand what is important to the organization you are targeting. To do this, read everything about the company you can get your hands on! Be sure to review company literature, its website, current news about it, and any recent press releases. Look the company up on Yahoo!, Google it, and if it is publicly traded, look up its financials. Find out everything you can about its culture, mission, values, and issues. The more you know, the better equipped you will be for your interview.

> **FYI**
>
> Doing research about a prospective employer can protect you. I was recently offered a job with an unusually high salary. Although the salary was tempting, I soon learned the company was facing extreme financial difficulty. The reason the company offered me such a high salary was because it was gambling I could help it raise its sales. The more I research I did, the more evident it became that its business model and product were fundamentally flawed. In light of my research, I decided to turn down the position. Shortly thereafter, the company laid off 70 percent of their salaried staff, and eventually closed the entire division. Had I failed to do proper research, I might have made a costly decision.

Another reason to do research is that, invariably, a skilled interviewer asks you the big question: "What do you know about our company?" If you really want to impress them, ace this question! I can probably count on one hand the number of times I've gotten a good answer to this question, and I hired everyone it came from. The only way to answer this question properly is to do research in advance.

Get Ready for the Tough Questions

Beads of sweat form on your forehead and passing seconds feel like hours. You try to come up with an answer, but the best you can muster is a recital of, "um's." Is this a nightmare or a job interview?

Hopefully, you've never found yourself in a scenario like the one I just described. And with a little advanced planning, you'll never have to. The three keys to answering tough interview questions are as follows:

◆ Be well prepared for your interview.

◆ Anticipate some of the questions you are likely to be asked and formulate compelling responses in advance.

◆ Focus on the *questions behind the questions* instead of on the questions themselves. In other words, what are the questions really designed to find out about you?

Of course, there is no way for us to address every possible question you could face in a job interview, but we can concentrate on five of the big ones.

Best Practice _____

To help you prepare for interviews, read a book that contains common interview questions and suggested responses. Doing so puts you in the proper mind-set for giving clear, concise, and thoughtful answers that can mean the difference between getting a job and not getting it. *The Pocket Idiot's Guide to Interview Questions and Answers* by Sharon McDonnell is one of the best.

What Are Your Goals?

Other ways it could be asked:

> Where do you see yourself five years from now? Ten?

> What do you hope to accomplish in your career?

What they are really trying to determine:

> Are you goal-oriented?

> Do you have realistic expectations?

How to answer:

Know what your goals are in advance, and don't be afraid to share them. Make sure they're specific, measureable, achievable, and time-constrained. Focus on career goals, but share one or two personal goals as well. Briefly explain the thought process behind your goals and why achieving them is important to you.

What Is Your Greatest Weakness?

Other ways it could be asked:

> What do people most often criticize you for?

> When I call your previous employers, what will they tell me is your greatest weakness?

> If there is one thing you could improve about yourself, what would it be?

> What personality traits do you possess that tend to interfere with your work?

What they are really trying to determine:

> Are you self-aware?

> Are you committed to personal and professional development?

> Do you have a realistic view of yourself?

How to answer:

Don't be afraid to mention an actual weakness. Then, as soon as you've stated your weakness, explain what you have done, or are doing, to compensate for it. Don't berate yourself or share more details than are necessary, but answer honestly. Pick a weakness you have taken realistic steps to overcome. Try to turn a negative into a positive. Here's an example:

"Because I am somewhat of a perfectionist, I tend to be very critical of my own work and the work of others. At times this has caused me say things about other people's work that hurts their feelings. To compensate for this tendency, I always try to focus on the positive aspects of others' efforts before I make suggestions for improvement, and I work hard to be very tactful."

Why Should We Hire You?

Other ways it could be asked:

> Tell me why you are the most qualified candidate for this position.

> What can you do for our company?

> Convince me to hire you.

What they are really trying to determine:

> Do you understand the requirements of the position?

> Are you quick on your feet?

> Do you have salesmanship?

> Did you give thought to why this is the right job for you?

How to answer:

Show them you understand the job description and have matched it with your skills. Focus on specific ways you meet the position requirements. Mention positive things you have accomplished for previous employers. Tell them what you like about their company and be enthusiastic.

What Questions Do You Have for Me?

Other ways it could be asked:

> The floor is yours.

> It's your dime.

What they are really trying to determine:

> What is important to you?

> Have you really thought about this position in advance?

> Did you prepare for the interview?

> Are you rational and thoughtful?

How to answer:

Contrary to what some may believe, this is not your chance to interrogate the interviewer with dozens of questions. Instead, pick five to seven quality questions you need answered to make an informed decision. Try to use questions that express your desire to understand the position and the company better. Here are some examples:

> How would you describe your company culture?

> What are some of the most important traits you are looking for in the person you want to fill this position?

> Who would I be reporting to? How would you describe their management style?

> What is the typical career path for this position?

> If I think of more questions later, is it okay if I follow up with you? May I have your business card?

> Based on what I have seen so far, I feel confident I would be an excellent addition to your company. What do I need to do so I can move to the next step?

Tell Me About Yourself.

Other ways it could be asked:

> Describe yourself.

> Tell me about your background.

What they are really trying to determine:

> What is important to you?
>
> What are your priorities in life?
>
> What is your personality?
>
> Are you driven?
>
> What career path have you taken?

How to answer:

This question is not an invitation to give a dissertation on your life history. Keep your answer to 45 seconds or less.

Avoid retorting with another question, like, "What do you want to know?" or "Do you mean personally or professionally?"

This is definitely a question you need to give some advance thought to. Some things to include in your answer are: a few of your most shining accomplishments, a summary of your career path, and a couple well-chosen tidbits about your personal life if it seems appropriate. Focus strictly on positive aspects of your background and keep your tone upbeat. Again, be prepared for this question. Almost every interviewer asks it, and it's likely to be the first question out of the gate. Make your first answer your best answer!

As you review the questions above and try to formulate your answers in advance, don't become overly preoccupied with the exact wording you would like to use. Focus instead on the thoughts you would like to convey. By honing in on the thoughts instead of the words, your expressions will come across naturally and won't sound rehearsed.

What to Wear? What to Wear?

Don't wait until the morning of your interview to decide what you are going to wear. At the very least, do it the night before. Check to make sure everything is neatly pressed, free from holes, stains, animal hair, or other unsightly distractions. Try each garment on to make sure it fits properly, and shine your shoes.

How you dress for a job interview is unquestionably one of the most important things to focus on. When forming an opinion of you as a candidate, most interviewers rate your dress and grooming higher than any other single factor.

FYI

Illegal interview questions include those about race, sex, religion, national origin, birthplace, age, disability, marital or family status, and so on—basically anything that doesn't pertain to the job or your professional background.

If you happen to be asked an illegal question or two, don't be too quick to take offense. Most likely the interviewer is just ignorant about the law, or made a mistake. I remember one occasion when I interviewed a woman with a charming European accent. In friendly conversation, I innocently asked her where she was from. By the time I realized I had just asked an illegal question, it was too late. Instead of making me feel like a jerk, she just responded with a pleasant, "Wales." Later, after I hired her, she kindly reminded me I shouldn't have asked that question. In hindsight, I appreciate that she didn't use the opportunity to skewer me.

If you feel comfortable with the question, go ahead and answer it. If you don't, try to answer the *intent* of the question. If the question is blatantly illegal and you don't feel comfortable, change the subject.

Proper interview attire is especially important if you're under 30 because most professionals automatically assume you lack experience. Not only that, but you also have to contend with media stereotypes that peg your generation as unprofessional and slovenly. Don't let yourself be grouped with an unfair stereotype. Be determined to stand out in a positive way!

 Heads Up! _____

Don't let your pride get in the way of your job prospects. If you happen to be someone who thinks you're entitled to "express yourself" with an edgy style, you're right. But (and this is a big *but*) don't think it isn't going to affect your shot at getting the job you want. A job interview isn't the time to showcase your unique sense of fashion.

For job interviews, choose conservative over trendy!

So, what should you wear for a job interview? Here are three basic principles to keep in mind. (We discuss professional dress and grooming with even greater detail in the next chapter.)

Appropriate for the job. Traditional business attire is not appropriate for every interview. If, for example, you are applying for a job as a welder, you wouldn't wear a suit and tie. A good rule of thumb is to consider what you are likely to wear on the job and then take it up a notch. If the job calls for jeans, wear khakis. If it calls for a button-up shirt, wear a button-up shirt and tie. If it calls for a shirt and tie, wear a suit.

The same principal applies for ladies. If the job calls for jeans, wear khakis. If it calls for khakis, wear a skirt. If it calls for a skirt, wear a suit. If it calls for dress sandals, wear heels.

Your personal best. I used to work for a heavy-hitting executive who would say, "Pay attention to what they look like now, because it's the best you're ever going to see them." I can't tell you how many times this has proved itself true, and now, it's a hiring principal I live by. All prospective employers expect you to interview with your best foot forward.

Conservative. When dressing for an interview, your goal should be to compliment your professionalism, not distract from it. No plunging necklines. No micro minis. Cover any tattoos. Avoid heavy fragrances. Don't wear anything too trendy or flashy. Don't wear anything controversial.

This doesn't mean you have to dress stuffy—it's good to be in style—but before you decide what to wear for an interview, put it on, take a hard look in the mirror, and ask yourself: What does my attire say about me? Do I look like a true professional? Better yet, ask a friend whose opinion you can trust.

Pre-Interview Checklist

Interviews are stressful enough. Reduce that stress (a little bit, anyway!) by completing the following checklist:

❏ Extra copies of resumé

❏ Cover letter (when applicable)

❏ List of professional references with contact information

❏ At least two character references with contact information

❏ Contact information for all previous employers

❏ Samples of work

❏ Letters of recommendation

❏ Driver's license

❏ Social Security card

❏ Professional certificates and diplomas

❏ Have reviewed industry news

❏ Did research about the company

❏ List of questions to ask

❏ Prepared to answer tough questions

❏ Good directions to location and name of contact person

❏ Good night's sleep

❏ Appropriate dress

❏ Pad of paper

❏ Pen

❏ Extra pen

❏ Breath mints

Types of Interviews

A common practice in the NFL is to review footage of plays made by an opposing team during the week leading up to a game. In some cases, each player is given a DVD that features a unique perspective he needs to study. Knowing how the opposing team could respond in certain situations can give the player a considerable advantage.

Just like coaches in a football game, employers can use a number of strategies when conducting job interviews. Let's talk about a few of the "plays" they might run so that you, as a player, can be prepared.

Telephone Interviews

If your resumé makes it past the initial screening, the next step is likely to be a telephone interview. Telephone interviews are used to screen large pools of applicants into smaller pools of candidates who will be invited for face-to-face interviews.

When it comes to telephone interviews, the main thing you need to be aware of is that they can surprise you at any time. In order to combat this challenge, you should make it a practice to always have a copy of your resumé handy.

As soon as you realize the call you just picked up is a telephone interview, there are a few things you need to do. First, you need to stop whatever you are doing. Turn off the TV, the video game, and the radio. Spit out your gum. Lock up your pets. If you're driving, pull over. If you need a minute to get yourself organized, ask for it. It's better to request a brief hold than to give your interviewer the sense you are distracted.

The next thing you need to do is grab a copy of your resumé to reference and a pen and paper to take notes. Take a deep breath, and try to relax. Telephone interviews are usually short and don't tend toward a lot of details. Most of the questions should be relatively easy to answer. Respond to the interviewer's questions with succinct answers. Try to speak slowly and clearly. Never interrupt! Keep your tone upbeat and positive.

Your main goal on a telephone interview is to secure a face-to-face interview. At the close of the call, thank the interviewer for his time and ask if it is possible to meet in person. Follow up the call with a handwritten thank-you note.

Best Practice

Telephone interviews are a type of screening interview. Screening interviews can also be held in person, and are used to prequalify candidates before they meet with an official hiring authority. Often, they are conducted by HR department personnel or members of management who are not in a position to make final hiring decisions.

If you have the opportunity to participate in a screening interview, you should work just as hard to be prepared and deliver a professional interview. Your chances of getting a second interview hinge on the screener's assessment of you, regardless of what position they hold.

Group Interviews

A group interview normally includes a presentation about the company conducting it, along with a question and answer session. Group interviews provide the perfect opportunity for you to size up a company because you can discern how organized they are and how serious they are about what they do.

You main objective at a group interview is to stand out in a positive way. At risk of sounding like a broken record, I'm going to say it again: come well prepared! Being prepared is the single most powerful thing you can do to get yourself noticed at a group interview. Why? Because 90 percent of the candidates won't be prepared! When it comes time for Q&A, be the one with all the best questions. Research the company thoroughly so what you ask is relevant. And of course, dress to impress.

Some group interviews take things to another level by arranging for group exercises based on work-related or hypothetical situations. During such exercises, you are likely to be observed and scrutinized by company management. If you find yourself in such a scenario, try not to let it make you nervous. The key is to get as involved with the group as you can. Take the lead when possible. Interviewers are looking for candidates who express their leadership, interpersonal, and communication skills well.

Heads Up!

On one occasion, I was invited to a group interview for a "Management Training Program." Instead of a genuine group interview, it was really just a sales pitch for a pyramid scheme. Some unscrupulous companies use so-called "group interviews" to trap unsuspecting victims into doing dirty jobs. If the entire focus of a group interview is on how much money you can make selling a "miracle" product, watch out!

Panel Interviews

If there's one type of interview that can seem downright intimidating, the panel interview is it! Take comfort in the fact that fundamentally it's not that different from a regular interview.

Panel interviews are generally comprised of the applicant and two or more interviewers who take turns asking questions. The key, again, is to be well prepared. Because the questions are likely to come in quick succession, you need to have your qualifications well in mind. Remember, the interviewers are trying to determine how well you handle stressful situations, so stay calm and collected.

When answering a question, proper etiquette is to respond to the interviewer who asked it. At the same time, you should also address the group as a whole. To help you do this, begin your address by making comfortable eye contact with your questioner. Then, as you are talking, move your focus from one set of eyes to the next while pausing for a few seconds on each. As you conclude, you should again focus on your original questioner.

Dinnerviews

Lunch and dinner interviews present a unique set of challenges. Used to size up candidates' social graces, dinnerviews call for a brush-up on your table manners. Don't forget this important first step!

Besides minding your manners, here are a few other ABC's:

♦ Don't order alcohol. Opinions vary on this, but unless alcohol happens to increase your reaction time, I wouldn't recommend it.

♦ Stay away from messy food. Items like ribs, overloaded chili-burgers, and snow crab legs are a big no-no. Order food that can be cut into manageable bites.

♦ Take small bites. Enough said.

♦ Don't order the most expensive item on the menu. Don't order appetizers or dessert unless your host suggests it.

♦ Be extremely nice to the restaurant staff, and especially to your server. Don't complain about anything, and don't send your food back unless it's clucking, if you get my drift.

♦ Let your host pick up the tab and the tip. They invited you, and they are planning to pay.

Interview Etiquette That Impresses

Going on a job interview is a lot like going on a first date. You want to look your best, and act your best. You want to talk your best talk, and walk your best walk! Let's review some basic behaviors that go a long way toward impressing a potential employer.

Calm and Confident

Job interviews are inherently stressful, but it's important not to let stress overcome you. How can you convey the impression you are confident and in control? First, resist the urge to respond to questions hastily. Try to speak slowly and deliberately. Avoid unnecessary interjections like "uh" and "um" by replacing them with brief pauses while you collect your thoughts. Demonstrate your confidence by engaging your interviewer with thoughtful questions.

While you should be careful not to become overly comfortable or casual, it's still important to express yourself naturally. When you act naturally, you automatically put others at ease and make them feel comfortable with you. The more comfortable they are with you, the more likely they are to hire you.

Finally, regardless of how desperate you may be to find a job, don't let it show. Try to give the impression you are highly interested, but still have other options. If you are asked how your job search is going, respond that you feel very optimistic, and are trying to be selective as you evaluate each opportunity.

Nonverbal Cues

Studies have repeatedly shown nonverbal communication sends a message that is five times stronger than the spoken word. In other words, what you say is less important than how you look when you say it.

While interviewing, be careful not to get distracted by things happening around you. Maintain eye contact with the interviewer and pay close attention to their questions. Hold a relaxed posture, and lean slightly forward to show your interest. Don't lean back in your chair, don't slouch, and keep your feet on the floor in front of you. Steer clear of nervous ticks like tapping your fingers or twirling your hair.

Heads Up!

Two of the most common interview flubs I've seen are ringing cell phones and gum chewing. Both are disruptive, rude, and betray a lack of professionalism.

Make it a practice to turn off your phone and spit out your gum before you enter any business meeting. Anything less can damage your first impression.

Topics to Avoid

On your initial interview, it's not appropriate to breach the subjects of pay, overtime, or benefits unless the interviewer brings them up. Even though these things are important, it's better to discuss them on later interviews when you are close to being hired. On your first interview, show the employer you are more interested in the job and the company than in the compensation.

You also want to avoid badmouthing previous employers or managers. Even if you have been treated unfairly in the past, you will fare better on an interview if you focus on the positive. If you have been fired from a job and are asked about it, simply explain the facts of the situation and try to leave feelings out of it. If you were wronged in some way, explain the actions that were taken against you, but don't blame specific people or the company as a whole.

To Talk, or Not to Talk?

Another interview proficiency involves how much to talk. Talk too much and you'll get tuned out. Talk too little and you'll appear timid. So what's the right amount?

First, you should only answer questions you are asked. Take a second to formulate your answer before you start to talk, and be careful not to ramble about unrelated subjects. Just answer the questions.

Generally, you should keep your responses to 45 seconds or less. Doing so keeps your interviewers attention and interest. If you are asked a question that requires you to explain or describe a complicated subject, it's okay to talk a little longer, but watch your interviewer to make sure you're holding their attention.

If your personality is such that you tend to be quiet or abrupt, be especially vigilant about answering every question thoroughly and completely.

Follow Up

Think about our date analogy from earlier. If you go on a date with someone and are really excited about how it went, but you don't call them later to express your interest, what are they likely to conclude? Surely they will conclude you aren't that interested in them. The same is true when it comes to interviews.

If you go on a great interview and are excited about how it went, send a thank-you note reiterating your interest in the position. Thank the person for their time and let them know you hope to hear from them soon.

Sending a follow-up note after an interview is a professional courtesy that only takes a second and sets you apart from other candidates.

Evaluating a Job Offer

Imagine you are shopping for a new car. What features are most important to you? Leather? Sunroof? Navigation system? Now consider what each item costs. Can you afford to get every feature you want?

The more likely scenario is that you weigh your wants and needs until you decide on the best option for your budget.

Shopping for a job can be similar. You might settle for less pay because there is an opportunity for rapid advancement. Or you might drive farther to get to work because you love the environment.

When it comes to pay, for example, there are two figures you need to know before you accept a job: 1) The minimum you can survive on, and 2) the amount you reasonably expect to earn. Once you have these amounts in mind, you can narrow your choice down to jobs that fall in that range.

Weigh other factors like access to group health insurance, 401(k), scheduling needs, traveling restrictions, and so on. Make a list of pros and cons to ensure emotion doesn't cloud your judgment. Ask yourself if accepting the job helps or hinders your future career prospects.

Decide what is important to you and only accept jobs that meet your criteria. As with any other business proposition, you should meticulously calculate whether to accept a job.

The Least You Need to Know

◆ When applying for a job, be sure to follow all instructions and make sure there are no errors or omissions on your application.

◆ Research a company before you interview. Learn everything you can about its culture, mission, and what is being said about it in the news.

◆ Prepare your answers to difficult interview questions in advance.

◆ Dress conservatively, appropriate for the job, and wear your personal best. Try each garment on to make sure it fits properly, and shine your shoes.

◆ During an interview, convey the impression you are calm and confident. Don't talk too much, and be yourself.

◆ Follow up every interview with a handwritten thank-you note.

Chapter 6

How to Make Positive and Lasting Impressions

In This Chapter

- ◆ Making the most of your one shot
- ◆ Dressing like a professional
- ◆ Mastering the initial interaction
- ◆ Preparing your elevator speech

When it comes to business, impressions mean everything! Whether you're going on a job interview, attending a conference, or stepping into an important business meeting, you've got to look and act your best! Let's face it: everyone prefers doing business with people who are well put together. So how can you make an impression that really counts for something? This chapter shows you!

The First Three Seconds

That's right! You only get three seconds to make your initial impression. How can someone draw so many conclusions in such a short period of time? As humans, and especially as professionals, we have adapted to quickly read certain cues that help us determine whether or not a person is worth our time. When it comes to business, our initial impression generally involves drawing one of three basic conclusions in our mind:

◆ This person appears to be above me in business or social status. I should probably try to make a good impression and cultivate him as a contact.

◆ This person appears to be on the same level as me in business or social status. I would probably enjoy interacting with this person.

◆ This person appears to be below me in business or social status. There is most likely no benefit in interacting with them. I'll be friendly but keep them at arm's length.

Snap judgments are common in the animal world, too. When the male Six-Plumed Bird of Paradise is trying to woo a mate, his intricate mating ritual involves a recital of hulalike dances on an area of jungle ground that he carefully cleans of all dead leaves and other debris. If his bachelor pad is untidy or his dance is sloppy, he doesn't get any second chances. The female is swiftly on to another prospective mate, and it's no lovebirds in paradise for him. Human nature can be remarkably similar.

The fact is your demeanor, body language, posture, mannerisms, hair, makeup, shirt, tie, blouse, skirt, shoes, briefcase, watch, and on, and on, and on—all say something about you.

It's Even More Important for Young Professionals

As a young person, you have to work even harder than others to get all these cues right. Why? Because the tendency of many seasoned professionals is to view younger colleagues as less responsible and reliable. You can't afford to do anything that supports this notion.

If you're honest with yourself, you'll realize you are often guilty of making the same kind of snap judgments about others. To illustrate, let's imagine that you are going in for a presurgery consultation with a new doctor. As you're waiting, a friendly looking young office assistant with cartoon-bedecked scrubs opens the door to the lobby and calls your name. If she appears to be 20 years old, as they often do, would it bother you? Probably not. Why? Because all she's going to do is open doors and print invoices. For the most part, her work doesn't affect you.

But change the scenario a little and imagine that you're in the exam room waiting for your doctor. As the door opens, you notice that this new doctor of yours appears to be in his 20s and is wearing cartoon scrubs also. Now does it bother you? Do you automatically deduce that this person may not be your best choice of doctor? That maybe you'd like someone with a little more experience and a more professional appearance? If you're anything like me, you probably do.

Why is it different for the office assistant than it is for the doctor? Because when someone appears to be younger or less experienced than ourselves, we automatically balk at the idea of giving this person full reign. At best, we question a younger person's authority more readily. Although they may actually be the most capable person in the world, our first impression can often be unfair.

Because you can't trade your sprightly young body in for an older model (and hopefully don't want to), you'll have to learn how to make your youth work to your advantage. Instead of meeting people's expectations, you've got to dash them to itsy bits. If your appearance and the first words out of your mouth are far superior to what they expect, you're on the way to gaining the respect you deserve.

Dress for Success

Take a look around and you're likely to conclude that the term "dress for success" is more or less outdated. The explosion of Internet commerce and the popularity of casual Fridays can make it seem as if it doesn't matter how you dress for work anymore. This idea, however, couldn't be farther from the truth. For a young person in the business world, how you dress is arguably more important than for anyone else.

Naturally, the way you dress depends largely on your industry, your position within that industry, the area you live, and so on. In any case, whether you're a man or a woman, the key thing to remember is that it's more important to be professional than fashionable. Always choose the conservative over the flashy, the timeless over the trendy, and the modest over the provocative.

Best Practice

Of utmost importance when choosing your attire is to consider the occasion. If you were going to visit the President of the United States, would you wear tennis shoes? Likely not.

Dressing for the occasion may require advanced planning on your part. If you're going somewhere new and you aren't sure how to dress, consult with someone who has been there or do research online.

Traditional Business Dress for Men

When choosing a suit, stick with a conservative cut in solid or pinstripe. You can't go wrong with black or navy, but brown and gray are fine, too. When it comes to pinstripes, make sure they're not too wide and bold or you start looking more cocky than confident. If you decide to dress up your suit with a pocket square, think neat and solid over puffy and flashy.

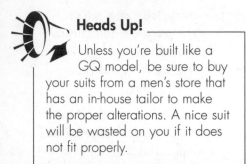

Heads Up!

Unless you're built like a GQ model, be sure to buy your suits from a men's store that has an in-house tailor to make the proper alterations. A nice suit will be wasted on you if it does not fit properly.

For shirts, I suggest the polished, traditional look that a white or blue neatly pressed button-up provides. If you must wear patterns, make sure they're muted.

You've probably heard all the rhetoric about "power ties" and making bold statements with your tie, but here's the rule: simple and subtle. Your goal is to draw attention to your professionalism, not your clothes.

Shoes should be black or chocolate brown and well polished. Lace-ups are usually best. Don't underestimate this detail. Many people look at your shoes before they look at your face.

Belt should match the shoes, socks should match the pants, and suspenders are for firemen.

Limit your jewelry to an understated watch and a wedding band if you're married. Save the triple chronograph for the weekend. If you're going to wear cufflinks, make sure they're subtle or you risk looking pretentious.

If you want to seal the deal, keep your briefcase and portfolio looking good, too. Oh, and trust me on this one, buy a nice pen. Nothing is worse than getting all dressed up, sitting across the table from a high-powered executive, and pulling a pen out of your pocket that says BOB'S FROZEN MEATS.

Finally, remember that your grooming says more about you than anything else. Your girlfriend may think your scruff is cute, but the businessman across the table from you won't. Keep your shave close, your hair neatly trimmed, and your sideburns under control.

Traditional Business Dress for Women

For the most part, the rules of business dress are the same for women as they are for men. Choose classy and conservative over trendy and flashy. As much as you may love the latest fashion trends, remember that traditional workplace attire doesn't usually reflect them.

For the most professional look, select a skirted suit. Pants suits are generally acceptable as well, but less so in certain industries. If you choose to wear a dress, be sure to compliment it with a matching jacket.

When it comes to the length of your skirt, you unequivocally need to keep it just below or just above your knee. More than 2 inches in either direction and you go from sensible to excessive. Resist the urge to wear low-cut tops as well. Low necklines give others the wrong impression. You want to be acknowledged for your professionalism, not your sexuality.

When dressing for business, remember that your face should be the focal point. To accomplish this, avoid wearing any single item that draws attention away from your overall look. Keep jewelry to a minimum as well. A good rule of thumb is one ring per hand and one earring per ear.

Too much perfume or makeup can also become an unwanted distraction, so use both sparingly.

Low heels are considered more professional than high heels, and sandals or flats are a definite no-no. Always wear neutral- or flesh-colored hose, and keep an extra pair in your purse for the occasional snag that eats nail polish for breakfast.

Best Practice

You need to give consideration to your attire no matter what industry you work in. Even if you work on a construction site, you can still wear clothes that are neat and well kept. If you hope to become a foreman, dress like a foreman!

A plumbing company in my hometown advertises, "All our plumbers are clean and crack-free!" How their plumbers dress clearly affects their job prospects and their reputation in the community.

If you think you've heard all this before, you're probably right. Most of it's not new. But trust me when I tell you that you can't overestimate the importance of these details when you're the little fish in a big pond. When others observe what a "together" young professional you are, they'll start viewing you as the much sought-after exception to the rule.

The Next Three Minutes

If someone tells you that you only have three seconds to make a first impression, they're not giving you the whole story. The first three seconds get your foot in the door; the next three minutes give you the chance to show if you can back up that impression.

First, Smile

Few things will complement you better than a smile. In a world of road rage and auto-mated tellers, a smile translates to warm and fuzzy feelings. Some psychologists say that a smile can even make you feel better about yourself. Millionaire Andrew Carnegie was famous for his cheerful smile. He was so celebrated for his smile that you could almost call it his trademark. Combine a killer product with a killer smile, and you've got your-self a recipe that's hard to beat. Just be sure not to smile so much that you look like the Cheshire cat, or people might start wondering if you're working with a full toolbox.

Be on Time

Show up five minutes late for an important meeting, and it won't matter if you're dressed like one of the royal family and smiling like Andrew Carnegie. Being punctual shows respect for people's time and demonstrates you're reliable in other areas, too. This is the first major step you can take to establish your character as a real professional.

Heads Up!

When it comes to punctuality, be early, but not too early. Show up more than 10 minutes early and you appear overeager and risk having others conclude that your time isn't valuable.

Shake Like a Pro

In the United States and most places abroad, the handshake is the kick-off for nearly all business interactions. Get it wrong, and you'll have a lot of ground to make up.

If your hand is too limp or your grip is too soft, you send the signal that you're timid and uncertain about yourself. Grip too tight or shake too vigorously and you give the impression that you're overeager and domineering.

The best handshake includes a dry, medium-firm grip and a quick pump with the hand once or twice.

Best Practice

If you're the type of person who gets sweaty hands when you're nervous, carry a handkerchief in your pocket or purse to dry them. You may even wish to use a restroom to wash your hands before a meeting. It may seem extreme, but if you're trying to make a first-rate impression, it's worth the effort.

Body Language Speaks Volumes

A heavily quoted study by UCLA Professor Albert Mehrabian outlines three basic elements of face-to-face communication. It's often referred to as the "7%-38%-55% Rule," and basically says that your words (7 percent), tone of voice (38 percent), and body language (55 percent) are what communicate your feelings and attitudes. Whether or not the percentages should be taken literally has been debated, but the valuable thing we take away is that body language counts … a lot!

To ensure your body language instills confidence, always sit or stand up straight with your shoulders back. Shoulders that are hunched forward send the message that you lack self-assurance and poise. Even if others in the room are slouching or crossing their legs, it's better to maintain good posture with your feet in front of you on the floor. There'll be time for kicking your feet up after you nail your first impression.

Even if you're nervous, be sure not to fidget with your hair, clothing, feet, or hands. The last thing you want is to appear restless or distracted. Your goal should be to remain attentive to those around you and maintain positive eye contact. In so doing, you'll send the message that you're intelligent and you mean business.

Small Talk Matters

Just because it's called small talk doesn't mean it's not important! I vividly remember a time early in my career when I joined a local networking group in an effort to uncover sales opportunities. The basic premise of the group, like other networking organizations, was to make connections that would eventually translate to extra business.

Every month when the Tuesday breakfast would roll around, I dreaded the idea of attending. Why? I never took the initiative to meet anyone. I was bad at small talk and I knew it. All I ever did was arrive alone, set my brochures on the table by the door, eat alone, and pick up my brochures on the way out. I never made any connections and I never got noticed.

This experience taught me a valuable lesson: if you're going to make a good impression on people, you have to be good at small talk.

Listen More Than You Talk

Do you enjoy conversing with someone who does all the talking? How long does it take before you tune them out? If you talk too much, you risk giving others the idea that you're self-absorbed, overconfident, or at best nervous.

Try this instead: Learn to ask positive, open-ended questions that will get the other person talking. The difference between an open-ended question and a close-ended question is that an open-ended question can't be answered with a yes or no answer. For example, if you ask close-ended questions, your conversations are likely to go something like this:

"So, you're in marketing?"

"Yep."

"Do you like it?"

"Sure do."

"Has business been good for you this year?"

"Yep."

"So, are you interested in taking a look at my products?"

"Not really."

And that is often about as far as you'll get. Why does this happen? Because we fail to get others talking about things that are important to them.

I've heard it said that there's no sound sweeter than the sound of your own voice. Although I'm not sure if I totally believe that, I do know that people generally like to talk about themselves. I also know that if you listen to what people are saying while they're talking about themselves, you can gain remarkable insights into what makes them tick. This in turn helps you cultivate a stronger relationship more quickly.

Ask Appropriate Questions

Learn to ask questions like these, and you can keep somebody talking for hours:

> Tell me about what you do.
>
> What do you like best about what you do?
>
> What kind of challenges do you face in this line of work?
>
> How did you get into this industry?
>
> What are your plans for the future?

Notice that none of these questions can be answered with a yes or no.

If you master the art of asking open-ended questions, the other person gets to warm up the conversation by doing most of the talking, and you get to demonstrate what a good listener you are. Eventually, they'll return the favor by listening attentively to you. And, after all, isn't that what you really want?

Heads Up!

Asking personal questions about someone's marital status, whether they have children, and the like are best reserved for later conversation. During the initial interaction, it's best to stick with business-related topics.

Become an Active Listener

We've all seen the movie where the thief is trying to make his big score by picking the combination lock on a safe filled with gold bars, stock certificates, and diamonds. Can you imagine a robber listening to a safe with one ear while an iPod is blaring in the other?

If you can picture that scenario in your mind, you understand what good listening is all about. The next time you're in a conversation with someone, try to think of the information they're sharing as treasure. Often a person's thoughts can be just as valuable as literal gold bars or diamonds. This is especially true if you are trying to land your dream job or close a profitable deal. Listen carefully and you may be able to pick up the perfect morsel of information to help you reach your goal.

So how can you show others you are a good listener? First, resign yourself to the fact you are going to really listen, not superficially listen. Have you ever caught yourself nodding as if you were listening but really you were only waiting for the other person to take a breath so you could talk again? Or maybe someone is rambling on and on about something you have no interest in until finally you find yourself fixating on their nose hair and praying that they'll take a breath so you can excuse yourself.

The key to countering this anti-listening behavior is to view the other person as more important than you. Do you appreciate it when someone views what you have to say as important? So does everyone else. Even though humility is a rare quality these days, it is nonetheless worth cultivating. If you can develop this trait, it will prevent you from making all kinds of conversation blunders. Think about it for a second: If you sincerely view what someone is saying as important, will you interrupt them? Will you be checking out the good-looking guy or girl who just walked in? Answering your cell phone?

Granted, good listening isn't something you can fake. But, if you actually make this part of your mind-set, you will come across as down to earth and trustworthy—not to mention, it will make you a better person.

Listen with More Than Your Ears

Being a truly good listener also involves listening with your eyes. You can doubtless recall a time when someone was looking everywhere but at your face while you were talking to them. If you're a woman, I know you can. So, if you ever find your eyes drifting around the room while someone else is talking, it's good to remember how it feels when others do it to you. Keep in mind that positive eye contact reinforces the notion that you are focused, intelligent, and serious about what you do.

Good nonverbal cues that let other people know you are listening include nodding your head when you agree, raising your eyebrows when they say something interesting, and smiling or laughing when they say something funny.

Best Practice

Some experts contend that you should even go so far as to mimic another person's posture and body language as he speaks to you. While not overdoing it, this subtle effort can put the other person at ease with you on a subconscious level. Examples of this could include crossing you leg when his leg is crossed or leaning forward when he does.

If you don't see yourself as this type of active listener, I suggest you use every opportunity to practice your listening skills. It may be uncomfortable at first, but you'll get better with time. If you start your practice at home, it may even help you improve your relationships there.

When in Doubt, Confirm

Human communication is extraordinarily complex. Because this is the case, nonverbal cues can often be misread. The solution to avoiding misunderstandings is proficient verbal communication. To illustrate the point, consider an example:

On September 10, 1939, British Submarines HMS *Oxley* and HMS *Triton* were patrolling off the coast of Norway. The subs had been in regular contact with each other when *Triton* spotted an unidentified submarine in nearby waters. Believing it might be *Oxley*, the *Triton* crew sent a number of signals and challenges, but the ship didn't respond (to this day, no one knows why). *Triton* therefore concluded that it was a German U-Boat and fired two torpedoes. Both torpedoes struck the submarine, sending her directly to the ocean floor.

As *Triton* closed in on the area, they only found three survivors—all were British. *Oxley* had been out of position. All it would have taken to prevent this disaster is a few friendly words of confirmation.

The case can be similar with face-to-face communication. Because of differences in age, background, culture, and the like, people may misread our "position." The surest way to prevent this is to repeat what is said to you.

The thought of doing this may call to mind a childhood game of copycat, but I assure you that's not what I'm talking about. Can you imagine two professionals engaging in a game of copycat?

"We've had a great year."

"You've had a great year, huh?"

"That's what I said. Sales have been excellent!"

"Excellent sales, huh?"

"Yes. We've been selling the new Widgets."

"You sell Widgets?"

"That's what I said."

Anyway, you get the point. The idea isn't to repeat everything that is said, but to restate general ideas as confirmation that you understand. A better example would be the following:

"Sales have really been down this year."

"They have, huh? I'm really sorry to hear that."

"Thanks. I'm not sure what we're going to do. I was thinking about closing one of our divisions."

"That sounds pretty drastic. Which division are you considering closing?"

"Our Widgets division."

"That's a pretty important division, isn't it?"

Doubtless you can see the contrast between these conversations. You may have also noticed that the final statement in the last snippet of dialogue was a question. Asking clarifying questions is another way to let people know that you are sincerely interested in what they have to say and prevent misunderstandings. When in doubt about what someone said or meant, it's always best to ask.

For instance, imagine you're on a job interview and someone asks if you're proficient with Microsoft Excel. Let's say you've used the spreadsheet feature of the program for years and feel extremely comfortable with it. You quickly answer, "Yes!" and the interview moves on.

Without asking additional questions to clarify what they mean by "proficient," you may soon discover that their definition is considerably different from your own. A good follow-up question might be, "What features of the program am I expected to be proficient in?" If the answer is, "Statistical and engineering formulas and graphing." you could save yourself a lot of embarrassment in the future!

So now that we've got you looking first class and communicating like a professional, the last thing to address is attitude.

It's All About Attitude

Like it or not, your attitude will show through in everything you do. Even your body language is controlled by your attitude. Subtle changes in your facial expressions and posture start speaking about you before you even open your mouth. They tell others about your self-confidence, attitude toward life, view of the future, and so on. If you maintain an enthusiastic, upbeat manner and avoid negative topics, people will naturally feel drawn to you and view you as likeable. Sounds like a good first impression to me!

The Elevator Pitch

Assuming everything has gone well so far, the next logical step is that someone is going to pass the baton to you. They're going to want to know more about this polished, young professional they've just met. "Tell me about yourself," someone says.

What are you going to do now? You've been such an attentive listener! You look so sharp! If you only knew what to say!

When I used to get this question, I would usually blurt out the name of the company where I worked along with my official title and then nod and smile like an idiot while I waited for someone to ask me another question. What I didn't realize is that titles don't really tell anyone about what you actually do or who you really are. Besides, fancy titles are a dime a dozen. Start looking around and you'll notice that everyday jobs are assigned baffling titles to make them more palatable. I think our local librarian bears the label of Chief Information Officer.

So what are your options? What can you say that will leave the impression you want?

The General Idea

In the business world, there's a well-known concept called the elevator pitch. Its basic premise is that you should be able to deliver a concise and compelling speech about who you are and what you have to offer in about the same length of time as an elevator ride. Get it right, and the person you are talking with will be mentally engaged and anxious to hear more. Instead of using perplexing titles, technical terms, and fluff, the elevator pitch focuses on the big picture and the unique benefits of your service, product, or you as an individual. To do this effectively should take no more than 100 to 150 words.

The paragraph you just read is 112 words.

Creating Your Pitch

How can you develop your own elevator pitch? First, consider your audience. Is your ultimate goal to land a job, get an appointment, close a deal, or make a contact? Depending on the circumstances, your choice of what to focus on should vary.

Next, decide on the main points you want to get across. These points should be unique, appealing, and of course, truthful. Your objective should be to capture the person's interest as quickly as possible.

Think for a minute about your best qualities. Are you energetic? Hard working? Persistent? Do you have a high level of integrity? Are you an innovator? Have you accomplished something impressive in your career? Include these things in your elevator pitch.

A Model to Follow

Consider Jason: by age 23, Jason had developed a special brand of anti-virus software that would eventually come to revolutionize the market. The product could be downloaded for free, and had numerous advantages to conventional solutions already on the market. He knew he had a great product, but he needed financial backing to get it off the ground.

As he was riding the elevator down to the lobby of the hotel where he had been staying for the annual technology exposition, a professional looking middle-aged man in a turtleneck and blazer suddenly struck up a conversation:

"Are you here for the Technology Expo?"

"Yes. And you?" Jason replied.

"Sure am. My business partners and I are looking for a few good ideas we can invest in. What are you here for?"

This was the chance Jason had been waiting for. What could he say to capture this man's interest? If he stated plainly that he "was a developer of anti-virus software," would that be compelling or motivating enough to get this person's attention? Would it make him stand out from the other 3,000 developers at this conference? He knew it wouldn't.

Thankfully, Jason read a book about the elevator pitch and had prepared one for an opportunity just like this.

"Thanks for asking!" he said. "Actually, I personally developed an extremely effective form of anti-virus software that blows everybody else out of the water! You know how most anti-virus programs cost a lot of money and require constant updates?"

"Yes."

"Well mine can be downloaded for absolutely free, never needs updating, and works 100 percent of the time! I can even guarantee it! The other great thing is that even though it's initially free, it generates huge profits on the back end. I'm just getting it off the ground and still need a few savvy investors. Would you be interested in taking a look at it?"

How do you think Jason did? Are you sold on his idea?

You may have noticed that Jason didn't ramble on and on about the countless features and technicalities of his software. Instead, he succinctly covered the most appealing points and then passed the baton back with a well-placed question designed to lengthen the conversation.

Jason's enthusiastic and well-prepared pitch may have just landed him the promising meeting he needs. And he did it in just over 100 words. With a little forethought and practice you can do the same thing!

An Important Final Thought

Does what you've read in this chapter sound like too much to be concerned about? Does it seem like you couldn't possibly focus on all these things and still be comfortable? Still be yourself?

If so, try to view the foregoing topics as guidelines rather than rules. You could liken them to gutters on a bowling lane. Between gutters, there is a huge area for the ball to move in. Keep it as close to the center as possible and you increase your chances for a strike. Move it a little toward the edge and you may still get a strike if your technique is right.

Remember that mastering the first impression takes time and practice. If you can apply even half the things we've discussed here, you are noticeably ahead of your peers and well on your way to gaining the respect and acknowledgement you deserve!

The Least You Need to Know

♦ You only get three seconds to make your initial impression, so always try to look your best.

♦ When it comes to professional attire, choose the conservative over the flashy, the timeless over the trendy, and the modest over the provocative.

♦ Your body language speaks volumes about you. Stand up straight with your shoulders back. Don't slouch. Don't fidget. Pay close attention to those around you and maintain eye contact.

♦ Learn to ask positive, open-ended questions to get other people talking and then listen attentively. Ask clarifying questions to prevent misunderstandings.

♦ Your attitude shows through in everything you do. By improving the way you feel on the inside, you will improve the way you look on the outside.

♦ Make time to develop a concise and compelling elevator pitch that holds people's attention.

Chapter 7

Off on the Right Foot

In This Chapter

- ◆ Embarking on day one
- ◆ Mastering your first week
- ◆ Choosing your associates wisely
- ◆ Establishing your value

Runners know the first six seconds of a race usually determine its outcome. If a runner isn't in ready position for the starting signal, and if he doesn't get off on the right foot, his weak start translates to a weak finish.

When you start a new job, your first days and weeks have a lot to do with your long-term success. What can you do to make sure you get off on the right foot? This chapter shows you!

Before You Start

Before a race, runners stretch to warm up their muscles. They also adhere to a strict diet and get the proper amount of rest. Taking such measures ensures they are in tiptop shape for their race. Like a runner, there are a number of things you should give attention to before you start a new job.

First, make it a point to take a couple weeks off. A brief hiatus from work or school can do wonders for your frame of mind. It can also give you the opportunity to get personal errands, doctor appointments, and procrastinated items out of the way so they don't interfere with your new job.

Use some of your time to do in-depth research about your new employer. Ask if you can get a copy of the company policy manual or employee handbook and read it before you start. Gather as much information as possible from the company website and read about what is happening in the industry.

If you have a lengthy commute, try driving it a couple times during the hours you will be traveling to and from work. Act shrewdly by choosing alternate routes you can take in the event of an unexpected traffic jam.

Take time to go through your closet and choose an outfit for every day of your first week. Then, get them professionally cleaned and pressed. If you aren't sure what to wear, choose the most conservative items first. There will be plenty of time for you to express your personal style once you get a feel for what is acceptable to the company culture. For more specific guidelines, review Chapter 6. And don't forget to ask if your company has a casual Friday or anything similar you should know about. It would be a shame to show up in a suit when everyone around you is in jeans.

Best Practice

If your job requires a uniform, ask for it in advance. This gives you a chance to make sure it fits properly, and ensures that you look like a company fixture from day one.

Day One

You're full of nervous excitement, and you hope—more than anything else—your first day goes just as smoothly. You can't help imagining what your new job is going to be like, and you long to make a good impression. Will it be everything you expect? Not a chance!

Check Your Expectations at the Door

When it comes to finding your way in a new workplace, predetermined expectations lead to disappointment. Even if your notions are based on input from a company insider, they are likely to be skewed by that person's individual perception. If you're going to set expectations, you're better off setting them for yourself. At least then you can control them.

Arrive Early

I feel like I shouldn't even have to say this, but don't be late on your first day! You're better off waiting an hour in the parking lot than being two minutes late. Get up extra early. Eat a balanced breakfast extra early. Get ready extra early. Leave for work extra early.

Heads Up!

Because you never know what to expect on your first day, it's wise to pack a lunch and some snacks.

If you're a smoker and you're not sure what the company attitude is toward smoking, you may also want to bring a pack of nicotine gum. Since some employers are strongly against smoking, asking where the smoking area is on your first day could leave an unfavorable impression.

Ever consider quitting? It's likely to help your career.

Like at First Sight

I'm not talking about romantic attraction. In the context of business relationships, it's the kind of feeling that makes you walk away saying, "I really like that guy!" or "She seems really great!" It's exactly the kind of impression you want to make on the people you meet your first day.

From the moment you arrive, make eye contact and smile at everyone. From the person who cleans the toilets to the person who signs the paychecks, give everyone you pass a friendly acknowledgment. If you happen to be sitting or standing beside someone, take the initiative to introduce yourself and tell them it's your first day. Ask them what they do and what department they work in. Do your best to remember their face and their name. Even if you are naturally shy, this is the time to step out of your comfort zone!

Use body language to convey a confident demeanor. Keep your chin up, shoulders back, and spine strait. Walk briskly and with a sense of purpose.

Mind your manners by saying please and thank you at every opportunity. Hold doors. Avoid swearing. Each mannerly act you perpetuate benefits your reputation tenfold.

If you have questions, don't be afraid to ask for help. People generally like helping others and will immediately feel obligated to make you feel at home. Asking for help, accepting it graciously, and showing appreciation for it is one of the most effective ways you can forge relationships from day one.

One More Thing

Between completing your employment paperwork, taking a tour, and getting your work area in order (if you get to do that much), your first day is likely to be a blur. Regardless of what it consists of, don't let it pass without thanking the person who hired you for the opportunity and letting them know your first day went well. Even if you have to leave them a voicemail, this gesture goes a long way in reassuring them they made the right hiring choice!

Week One

If day one is the first six seconds of a race, week one is the first lap. By your second day, there will probably be a measure of buzz among your new colleagues and managers. "Have you met the new hire yet?" will be the question of the day. Everyone will be trying to size you up and share their observations with each other. Now is the worst time to trip over your shoelaces!

Arrive Early and Stay Late

Until you discern what is appropriate, plan to arrive at least a half hour before your shift and stay at least a half hour late each day. Doing this sends the message you like your new job and you aren't a clock watcher. It may also give you the chance to learn something about the company culture. If you were to show up at our office just in time for your shift, you'd miss the "coffee chats" we have from 8:15 to 8:45. Often, these comprise some of our best meetings!

Best Practice _____

During your first week, why not bring a dozen bagels or some fresh fruit to share with your new workmates? It's amazing how fast you can make friends with free food!

Stay Busy

Unless you work at a large company with specialized training and shadowing programs, your first week may not be as structured as you'd like. Many small- and medium-size businesses provide a limited amount of direction and then expect you to make your own way. If you find yourself in such a situation, your primary concern should be to stay busy!

Take the initiative to do anything that needs to be done. If you aren't sure what to do, ask your colleagues if there are things you can help them with. If you notice a cluttered supply closet, offer to organize it. If you see a dirty rug, shake it out. If your boss won't give you any assignments, make a list of options and ask them which would be helpful. Approach one of your colleagues and ask them if you can pull up a chair and observe them for a while.

FYI

If you start a position as a new manager and aren't given specific instructions, it could be a good sign. For one thing, it means you won't be micromanaged, and for another thing it means you are trusted to take the direction you see fit. Use your first week primarily to observe and get to know your employees. Ask lots of questions and take good notes. Be alert to problem areas but avoid making waves too quickly. We address this subject with greater detail in Chapter 15.

Be a Sponge

Like a sponge in a bucket of water, immerse yourself in the company culture. If there's a softball team, join it. If everybody frequents a certain place for lunch, join them. Take advantage of every opportunity to make new connections.

Observe everything happening around you and try to learn from it. How do people act? What do they look like? What pace do they work at? What method of communication do they prefer? Understanding such nuances makes it easier for you to fit in.

 Heads Up!

When you start a new job, be careful not to settle into a clique. The most accepting individuals may not always be the ones with the best reputation. In the beginning, you are better off getting to know everyone in a professional, arms-length sort of way. Be friendly and personable, but spread yourself around!

Bite Your Tongue

"When I worked at Wonder Widgets, we did it like this and it worked a lot better! Maybe you should try it like this."

"Well this isn't Wonder Widgets, and you're an idiot!"

To avoid scenarios like this one, spend your first week as a learner and not a teacher!

One of your greatest assets when you start a new job is you look at things with a fresh set of eyes. Use this to your advantage by keeping a notebook of ideas and suggestions you can share at a future time—"future" being the operative word! Speak too soon and you'll give others the impression you're a know-it-all. Besides, you never know if things are done a certain way for good reason.

A similar pitfall is talking about things you're not familiar with. This is especially common among people who are hired for their expertise or who are expected to know a job because they've done it at another company. Be careful not to discredit yourself in the beginning, or it could take a long time to earn back trust. If you aren't sure about something, save yourself the embarrassment and admit it!

Avoid controversial subjects like religion and politics, too. Don't tell dirty jokes or make sarcastic comments. Keep away from negative topics and resist the urge to criticize people or their work.

Mind Your Manners

If your mind is sharp enough to remember elementary school, you can probably recall the class rules: "Keep hands, feet, and objects to yourself"; "Tidy up after yourself"; and "Quiet hands only." I'd wager my kindergarten teacher, Miss Jackson, still has them stuck to the wall of her classroom.

While they may not be pasted to the wall, each workplace has its own set of unspoken rules. Violate these rules of office etiquette and you'll quickly become an unwelcome addition.

Electronic device protocol. Keep your cell phone on silent or vibrate at all times while working. Wait until breaks to return voicemails or exchange text messages. When making personal calls, find a private place away from your co-workers (not the bathroom) to talk. Don't bring your phone with you to meetings. Don't assume you can listen to music at your workstation unless someone approves it in advance, even if it's on your iPod.

Best Practice _____

It's discourteous and unprofessional to use company property for personal business without permission. This includes blogging, micro-blogging, checking your e-mail, banking online, or anything else via your work computer. Before you sully your reputation with a presumptuous act, ask your manager if such activities are allowed. You might find them more accommodating than you expect.

Ask permission. Don't take undue liberties such as eating food that doesn't belong to you, barging into offices without knocking, interrupting conversations, or borrowing office supplies. Only take breaks that are scheduled in advance, and ask permission before you step out. Until you understand your boundaries, consider everything off limits.

Clean up after yourself. Show everyone you are clean and organized by keeping your work area presentable. Remove trash at the end of each day and put things away in their proper place. Clean up all your messes! If your food splatters in the microwave, wipe it out. If someone else's food splatters in the microwave, wipe it out.

What Now?

Once you get your first week behind you, you'll probably feel pretty good about your new job. You may even be settling in, making friends, and understanding your role clearly. Don't let yourself get too comfortable! To earn respect as a young professional, you've got to work extra hard—especially during your evaluation period. Like a runner who finishes her first lap with a substantial lead, you can either ease up or run even harder to make sure you hold your position. The latter is clearly your best option!

FYI

Most companies have a 90-day evaluation or "probationary" period that gives them an opportunity to assess the quality of your work and see if you fit in. At the end of this period, they have three options: extend your probation, terminate you, or make you a permanent employee. For information about your legal rights, visit the Department of Labor at www.dol.gov.

Choose Your Associates Wisely

The people you surround yourself with have a profound impact on your thinking and influence others' opinion of you. While you should be friendly to everyone, don't get too close until you know who you can trust and you understand the company hierarchy.

To be successful at a new job, seek out those who are the best at what they do and get to know them. Figure out who the influential people are and then look for a reason to work with them. One of the best people to reach out to is your own boss! Review Chapter 10 for suggestions on how to do this.

Keep an ear to the company grapevine, but don't contribute to it under any circumstances! Listening to the chatter can protect you from forming alliances with the wrong people, but chiming in will not benefit you! When forging new business relationships, remember that respect is more important than friendship.

Establish Your Value

If you always give your best, people notice and speak well of you. You will quickly develop a reputation as someone to be trusted and respected. And while it's important to put your best foot forward in everything you do, when you start a new job, it's particularly critical! To ensure you're meeting the expectations of your new employer, do the following:

Get your goals in writing. To do anything well, you have to know what you're working toward! No matter where you work, it's reasonable to ask for a list of goals or objectives. If one hasn't been provided for you, ask your boss for a few minutes of his time and get him to outline them. Once you know what your goals are and you have them in black and white, you'll know what to focus on!

Confirm. When given a new assignment, take good notes and then confirm you understand the instructions clearly. A simple "So what you mean is …" will suffice. When you are finished doing something for the first time, ask someone—a manager is best—to double-check your work. After you've done this once or twice, you should be confident enough to proceed on your own.

Request deadlines. Until you learn what takes priority, request deadlines with your work. When you're given something to do, ask "When would you like this back?" or "When is this due by?" If you are given multiple tasks at once, ask your manager to put them in order of importance for you.

Communicate with your manager. If something is taking longer than you expect to complete, or you get stumped, let your manager know immediately. If you put it to the side because you're afraid to ask for help, you'll be perceived as a procrastinator instead of a proactive team player.

Triple-check. You're apt to make more mistakes in the beginning, so always check your work more than once! Think twice before you click Send or Submit, and before you announce you're done.

Don't complain. No matter what you're asked to do (within reason), do it without complaining. Just assume everything requested of you is for good reason and say "my pleasure" with a smile. It's not always good to be a yes man, but until you really settle in, it's the safest bet!

The Long Haul

Look at your new job like a long-distance marathon rather than a sprint. Running fast in the beginning isn't enough. Carry the principals of hard work and professional courtesy with you everywhere you go. If you do, you'll find you never have to go looking for success because success will come to you!

The Least You Need to Know

- Before you start a new job, take at least a week off to get all your affairs in order so nothing interferes with it.

- A new work environment isn't likely to be what you expect, so be prepared to go with the flow.

- From the moment you arrive on your new job, make eye contact with everyone, be friendly, and exude confidence with your body language.

- Don't get too close to anyone in the beginning. Figure out who's influential and good at what they do, and then look for a reason to work with that person.

- Get your goals in writing and make reaching them your chief concern.

- In the business world, respect is more important than friendship. Doing quality work and being reliable speaks for itself.

Chapter 8

Get the Most Out of Your Job

In This Chapter

- Learning how to negotiate salary
- Asking for a bonus
- Arranging a flex schedule
- Making the most of your fringe benefits
- Utilizing all training opportunities
- Establishing contacts to open doors

To be successful in business, you need to squeeze every drop out of every opportunity! If you approach each job determined to maximize its potential, you can build wealth, a powerhouse of skills, and a network of connections that propel you toward business success!

In this chapter, we look at six specific areas and show you how to capitalize on each one.

Get Paid!

Believe it or not, the amount you earn is directly connected to your future business success. Why? Because the more you make, the more your work is perceived to be worth. Designer products are a good example of this principal in action. Why can designers demand such a premium for their products? In some cases, it's because they use better materials, but that's not always the case. Isn't it true some inexpensive products are just as well-made as their designer branded counterparts? Certainly! So why do people pay more for a designer label? Because they see other people are willing to pay more.

If your work history shows frequent raises and above average compensation, potential employers assume your accomplishments justified them. To that end, each time you accept a new position, make sure you are earning more than you did in your previous position. Each time you're eligible for a raise, make sure you get one. Is this a pipe dream? No! It just requires effort and some good negotiating skills.

Negotiating Your Salary

Negotiating salary with a potential employer can be intimidating, but is definitely worth the effort! Even one extra dollar per hour can mean an additional $2,000 in your pocket at the end of the year.

FYI

As we talk about salary negotiation and asking for pay raises, it would be easy to assume every job presents you with such opportunities. Unfortunately, this is not the case. Many entry-level positions and highly structured corporate environments have specific pay grades that are non-negotiable. Early in your career, it is likely you will have to accept a job (or jobs) that have limited upside potential. Don't be discouraged by this! In such situations, your main focus should be to understand the system of compensation available and leverage it to the best of your ability. Once you have built a track record of performance, you can justify higher levels of compensation from future employers.

Keep in mind as you approach any salary negotiation that your goal is not to win. If you win, it means your employer has lost, which leaves a bad taste in their mouth. If they walk away feeling like they paid too much for you, it sets the stage for ill will and resentment. Instead, try to achieve a compromise that leaves both of you feeling satisfied. How can you do this?

The timing of your discussion has a lot to do with it. If you march into an interview and hastily begin salary negotiations, you probably won't get what you want. It's much better to agree on the job itself before you talk about money. If you establish your value in the outset and convince the company you're the only person for the job, negotiating your price will be easy!

Best Practice

Wait until you receive a formal offer to begin salary negotiations. If you make the first offer, you could bid too low and miss out on thousands of dollars, or bid too high and cut yourself out of the running.

To get the ball rolling, you could ask, "Based on what you know about my salary history and my abilities, why don't you make me an offer you think is fair and then we can talk about it?"

Letting your employer make the first offer creates a starting point for the negotiations and gives you insight into their thinking. From there, you can only go up.

The next thing you need to do is figure out what you're worth. To make an accurate estimation, don't compare yourself with friends or other people you know. Such comparisons don't usually take all the proper factors into consideration. Things like the job itself, your work experience, the geographic area, the state of the economy or industry, and so on are what really matter. Don't forget when you are applying for a job, you have competition willing to work cheaper than you, so you need to be fair. To come up with a reasonable salary range, use a service like Salary.com or Payscale.com. Being able to justify your salary on paper can go a long way toward getting you the pay you deserve!

Once you know what you're worth, you also need to decide the minimum you are willing to accept. That being said, paying the amount you "need" isn't your employer's responsibility. For them, the amount you need is equal to fair market value for the position. If you discover the amount you need is more than the amount you're worth, you either have to change the way you live or choose a different career.

Once you've laid all your cards on the table and you get your first offer, don't accept it. Simply say you appreciate the offer, but need some time to think it over. This action alone sometimes solicits a better one.

Wait no more than a day or two to get back with your answer. At this point, you either need to accept the offer or justify a better one. If you decide to fight for a better offer, make a list of all the reasons you deserve it and be prepared to make a presentation of them. These reasons could include special education, examples of money you have saved or earned for companies in the past, or evidence you deserve better compensation based on a salary report like the ones mentioned earlier. If you aren't happy with the response you get, you can repeat the process as desired. Just try to be flexible!

Bear in mind your counteroffer doesn't necessarily need to be a higher salary. You could negotiate for a future raise based on performance during a set period, or for a sign-on bonus. You could even ask for extra vacation time or a bigger office. All these things should be considered part of your overall compensation package.

Asking for a Raise

When you decide to ask for a raise, it should be because you've earned one, not because you want one. Simply put, the key to getting a raise is performance!

Most companies evaluate employees for raises annually based on individual performance. Others allow for out-of-cycle raise requests, but have certain guidelines you must follow to be considered for one. If you are unsure how it works at your company, consult your employee handbook or immediate supervisor.

If you are confident a raise is justified, follow these three steps:

1. Make a list of all the reasons you deserve a raise. Include goals you've met, money you've earned for the company, additional responsibilities you've taken on, or important tasks you've completed.

2. Decide on the amount you are going to request and run a report on Salary.com or Payscale.com to justify it.

3. Request a meeting with your immediate supervisor to discuss the matter. This gives him or her an opportunity to consult with HR or other managers who have a say in the matter. Whatever you do, don't break the chain of command!

After you get the meeting you requested, be straightforward. Let your employer know you are requesting a raise of $X amount based on contributions you have made, and be prepared to explain them. Nerve-wracking? Yes! But once you speak up, the worst they can say is "no."

If "no" is the answer you get, don't leave it at that. Instead, ask what you can do to make yourself eligible for a raise in the near future. You could even offer to take on additional responsibilities to justify it.

Get a Bonus!

If part of your compensation comes from performance-related bonuses, leverage them to the best of your ability! Structured bonus programs are designed to motivate employees to focus on the most important aspects of their job. When you maximize your bonus potential, it means you are doing a great job and getting paid more. It also makes you a model employee and gets you noticed!

If, on the other hand, the best bonus you can hope for is a turkey at the end of the year, the following suggestions might help you put some extra cash in your pocket.

Keep a Log

As time passes, it's easy to forget what you've done to help your company. And if it's easy for you to forget, imagine how easy it is for your boss to forget! To justify your request for a bonus, keep a list of the most important things you accomplish each week. Include items that show how you went above and beyond the call of duty rather than simply doing things that are part of your job. After all, you already get paid for doing your job.

I once had a receptionist whom I charged with the responsibility of ordering our office supplies. At the end of the year, she came to me with a list of all her purchases and the amount she saved our company by clipping coupons. I never asked her to clip coupons, mind you—I only asked her to do the ordering. When I realized she saved us over $2,500 for the year by taking some extra initiative, I gave her a bonus of $1,000 and agreed to split the savings with her every year from then on. Documenting your accomplishments works!

Ask for It!

Sitting around and hoping for a bonus isn't likely to get you one. If you really want a bonus, you need to ask for it! How should you go about asking? At the beginning of the year, try having the following conversation with your boss.

"I really enjoy working here, and I'd like to make sure I'm focusing on the things that are most important to you! I'd also appreciate the opportunity to earn a bonus this year. Do you think it would be possible to set some specific goals for me and then agree on a bonus I could receive if I reach them?"

If you're a good worker, your boss is reasonable, and your company is profitable, they should be willing to give you a bonus.

Best Practice

When your employer agrees to give you a pay raise or a bonus, ask for signed documentation. Even if you trust them, you should still ask! Because details fade from memory over time and managers come and go, having an agreement in black and white will prevent future misunderstandings.

Your Schedule

It's remarkable how many expressions there are about time. *Time is money. Time is your most precious possession. Time is of the essence.* Whatever the case, one thing is certain; people appreciate the value of time!

Even if you can't get your boss to agree on a pay raise or extra bonus, you may be able to get some additional time off. Don't underestimate the value of such time! A flexible schedule can make it possible for you to pursue extra schooling, to improve your physical health through exercise, to volunteer, to start a side business, or to do any number of worthwhile activities. So how can you negotiate a better schedule? T.I.M.E.!

+ Think

+ Initiate

+ Monitor

+ Evolve

1. Think

Before you initiate a conversation with your employer, take inventory of your workload and your personal responsibilities. Ask yourself: Is it possible to handle my current job duties in less time? Can any of my work be done from home? If I am granted extra time off, what will I do with it? When emergencies come up, how will I handle them?

Once you answer all these questions and conclude your idea is realistic, decide how much time you can feasibly be away from your job. Next, write a proposal outlining your duties and desired schedule. Make sure you are prepared to justify why the changes will be good for the business and not just good for you personally!

2. Initiate

Approach your employer to discuss your request, but don't expect them to jump up and down with enthusiasm. While flexible schedules are becoming more popular, they still aren't the norm. If your boss bristles at the request, just ask them to give it some consideration. You could even request to try it on a temporary basis and see how it goes.

3. Monitor

If you get the green light from your employer, you've only won half the battle. Your next challenge is to make the schedule work. From the perspective of your boss and your colleagues, there should be no hiccup in the quality or reliability of your work. This is key! You have to monitor the feedback from everyone around you and work harder than ever to be attentive to everyone's needs. The last thing you want is for your workmates to get the impression you're letting things slip and say something to the boss.

Make sure everyone has your contact information, and check your e-mail and voice-mail regularly. To thrive on a flexible schedule, you have to keep in touch! To that end, I encourage you to have all your work e-mails and voicemails forwarded to a Smartphone or other handheld device, and that you respond to them promptly.

4. Evolve

Working a flexible schedule requires making constant adjustments. If your employer agrees to be flexible with you, return the favor! Because the world of business doesn't revolve around your personal life, be prepared to make allowances for emergencies that arise. If you're needed at work during a time when you are supposed to be off, don't balk! You can always take off during slower times to make it up.

If you notice something is creating a frequent conflict, figure out a way to correct it. Don't wait for someone else to bring it to your attention. As you make improvements over time, your schedule should become easier to manage.

FYI

People sometimes are not sure of the difference between part-time employment and flex time. Part-time employment offers fewer hours than full-time and usually pays less. Part-time jobs seldom offer benefits.

Flex time allows employees to choose when they want to work as long as the work gets done. Flex time usually offers standard rates of pay and benefits. In some cases, employees are required to work a core number of hours each day, week, or month, but can do so at any time they see fit. In other cases, they are required to work between certain times each day (i.e., from 11 A.M. to 3 P.M.) with the remainder of the day being flexible.

Fringe Benefits!

It would take an entire book to review every type of employment benefit along with its pros and cons. Not to mention, such benefits vary greatly from company to company. To keep things simple, I suggest you find out what is available where you work, make sure you understand it, and know its value.

Health insurance, for example, can be very confusing. Just because you are offered health insurance doesn't mean it's good insurance. It could be the premiums are too expensive to afford, or it doesn't provide adequate coverage, which means more out-of-pocket expenses.

Use a chart like the following to help you calculate the value of your benefits. Every benefit counts, no matter how small! Even free soft drinks and bottled water can add up to hundreds of dollars a year. All benefits should be considered part of your total compensation package.

If a benefit is especially important to you but your employer doesn't offer it, use the same negotiation principals we discussed earlier in this chapter, but ask for benefits instead of pay or bonuses.

Benefit Description	Total Annual Value	-	Annual Cost to Me	=	Total Net Value
Health Insurance	$1,800.00	-	$900.00	=	$900.00
Life Insurance	$600.00	-	$0.00	=	$600.00
Dental Insurance	$360.00	-	$360.00	=	$0.00
Vision Insurance					
Short Term Disability					
Long Term Disability					
Vacation Pay	$960.00	-	$0.00	=	$960.00
Sick Pay	$384.00	-	$0.00	=	$384.00
Holiday Pay	$192.00	-	$0.00	=	$192.00
401(k)	$960.00	-	$0.00	=	$960.00
125 Benefit Plan					
Non-Production Bonuses					
Child Care					
Company Vehicle					
Tuition Reimbursement					
Health Club Membership					
Product Discounts					
Food or Beverages					
Other Perks					
TOTALS	$5,256.00	-	$1,260.00	=	$3,996.00

> This figure represents the amount you should add to your base pay to get a more accurate estimation of your overall compensation.

Calculating the value of your benefits.

Get Trained!

Money comes and goes, but good training sticks with you forever! Like an annuity that never gets depleted, good training pays dividends over and over again.

On-the-Job Training

On-the-job training is the oldest kind of training in the world. Before our predecessors established schools of higher learning, everyone learned this way—and it's still one of the best ways to pick up new abilities! Even if your training is sporadic and unplanned, do your best to take advantage of it. Don't let the fear of extra work prevent you from taking on new assignments or volunteering for special projects. To be truly successful in business, you have to live outside your comfort zone!

If a colleague asks you to help with something new, rather than saying, "I don't know how to do that" why not ask, "Can you show me how to do that?" Every skill you pick up makes you a more seasoned and efficient worker. So commit to your business success by being a constant learner!

Schooling, Certifications, and Licensing

The American Society for Training and Development estimates U.S. companies spend more than $109 billion on training and developing employees every year. How much of that is being spent on you?

If your company offers specialized training, talk to your human resources department about how you can get involved. Whether its industry specific licensing or a tuition reimbursement program, take advantage of it!

If your company doesn't offer any training programs, consider asking them to make an exception for you. Most businesses know good training promotes employee satisfaction and loyalty, so all you have to do is convince them providing you with special training will be good for the bottom line. Try to come up with reasons like these:

- I will be able to take on additional responsibility (which saves money for the company).

- I will be able to do more work in less time (which saves money for the company).

- My training will enhance the company image, which translates to more sales (which makes money for the company).

- Paying for my training will be cheaper than hiring someone who already has the training and paying that person more (which saves money for the company).

If the company grants your request, it may ask you to sign a contract agreeing to stay with the company for a specific amount of time. Such a request is reasonable, but make sure you review the terms carefully. Be sure you can comfortably answer these questions:

- After my schooling is complete, is there a minimum time period I'm required to stay with the company?

- How will the tuition be paid? If by me, how long will I have to wait for reimbursement?

- If an emergency forces me to stop attending school, what happens and will it affect my reimbursement?

- Is a there a minimum GPA requirement to be eligible for reimbursement?

Heads Up!

Some companies may expect you to wait up to a year or more to receive reimbursement for your expenses, and some may require that you pay for books and other supplies out of your own pocket. Make sure you understand the financial obligations of any tuition reimbursement agreement before you enter into it, or you could find yourself in a costly and embarrassing situation.

There's nothing like real-world, roll-up-your-sleeves training to make you successful in business! The vast majority of employers will take a seasoned industry professional over a fresh college grad in a heartbeat! So take advantage of every opportunity to beef up your credentials. Down the road, you'll be glad you did!

Contacts

If the people you work with like, trust, and respect you, it pays off down the road! The top job spots and the best business opportunities usually come by word of mouth—often from former colleagues. By forming solid contacts at work, you put yourself on the receiving end of countless business opportunities! Because establishing contacts is easier said than done, Part 3 is devoted entirely to this subject.

The Least You Need to Know

- To be successful in business, you need to maximize every opportunity!
- Each time you accept a new position, make sure you are receiving better overall compensation than in your previous position.
- Before you try to negotiate for higher pay or bonuses, justify your request with a track record of performance.
- If you ask for a flexible schedule, explain why it is good for the business and not just good for you personally.
- Take advantage of every training opportunity available to you.
- The top job spots and the best business opportunities usually come by word of mouth, so make good contacts at work.

Part 3

It's All About Relationships

Dale Carnegie said: "You can make more friends in two months by becoming genuinely interested in other people than you can in two years by trying to get other people interested in you." I believe this quote captures the essence of this part.

To build relationships with others, you have to reach out to them, take an interest in them, and offer them a piece of yourself. When you put forth the effort to build strong and mutually beneficial relationships with the people around you, you earn their trust, respect, and support. As a young person in business, there's arguably nothing you need more.

In Part 3, we review effective conflict management techniques, show you how to communicate with power, how to network with influential people, and how to create a dynamic personal brand that draws others to you.

"Well, wouldn't you know it, Mr. Gundzik—
I just happen to have a brochure of my product line right here!"

Chapter 9

Capitalize On Co-Worker Relationships

In This Chapter

- ◆ Embracing your co-workers
- ◆ Building your relationships a little each day
- ◆ Setting boundaries
- ◆ Playing politics
- ◆ Surviving the inevitable conflicts

We used the word *capitalize* in the title of this chapter for a good reason. Besides just meaning "to take advantage of," the word *capital* can also relate to wealth. And in the context of co-worker relationships, both meanings apply. You see, if you "take advantage of" co-worker relationships, they help you advance your career and build wealth. How so? This chapter explains. In addition, you find out how to build healthy working relationships, navigate the sticky world of office politics, and resolve conflicts.

You Need Each Other

Symbiotic relationships are commonly seen in the animal world, where contact among species is beneficial to life. An outstanding example of this is the relationship between the Ocellaris clownfish and the Ritteri sea anemones, as delightfully portrayed in the Disney classic movie *Finding Nemo*.

It's truly remarkable how these species complement one another! The clownfish is extremely territorial and makes its home in the anemone, protecting it from fish that would otherwise eat it. The anemone in turn protects the clownfish from its predators with stinging tentacles. Wouldn't it be nice if all working relationships were so complementary?

When dealing with difficult co-workers, it can be easy to forget that building good relationships with them contributes toward your own business success. In what ways? For one thing, people who are known for getting along with their co-workers get promoted faster than the ones who are involved in conflicts. And if you think about it for a minute, you'll probably realize there are things you need your co-workers for. Do they cover your shift when you're sick or on vacation? Do they handle responsibilities you don't like or aren't good at? Do they possess skills you don't? Chances are you answered "yes" to at least one of these questions.

I can personally attest to the power of good working relationships because one of the most lucrative job opportunities I ever accepted came from a co-worker who I initially had a hard time getting along with. Thankfully, we worked through our differences and, when he left to start his own company, he offered me a great position.

Keep in mind how much time you spend with your co-workers—probably more than you do with family or friends. If you have to be together, you might as well make the time as pleasant as possible!

Build a Little Each Day

Good working relationships aren't formed overnight. Like all relationships, they develop over time. What starts out as like eventually grows to trust and respect. Let's consider three building blocks of such relationships.

Respect

If you're going to share space for eight hours a day or more, an environment of respect is essential. When the people you work with realize you respect them as individuals and as professionals, they respect you in kind. Of course, respect can be expressed in a number of ways, but actions speak louder than words! Your focus should be on showing others you respect them, not just saying it.

The key to showing respect is to treat others the way you want to be treated. Let's say, for example, part of your job involves completing a form that gets passed to your co-worker for processing. Let's also assume that if you leave part of the form blank, your co-worker has to complete it, making more work for her. Now ask yourself, "If I were her, would I want to receive an incomplete form?" The simple answer is no. So in this case, showing respect would involve completing your share of the work. When you work diligently and complete all your activities, your co-workers conclude you are serious about your job and respect you for it. Be trustworthy, reliable, and honor your commitments.

Heads Up!

A quick way to lose the respect of your co-workers is to violate the rules of office etiquette. For a review of common workplace blunders, see Chapter 7 under the heading "Mind Your Manners."

Another way to show your co-workers you respect them is to take responsibility for your actions. When you make a mistake, it usually costs your workmates a measure of grief. If you gloss over your mistake, it gives the impression you don't care about anybody but yourself. And letting someone else take the heat for you is even worse! When you own up to your blunders, you send a powerful message you are mature and secure.

You also show respect to your co-workers when you share credit for accomplishments. Imagine a member of management stops by your department to congratulate you for something you did well. You remember you had help from your teammates, but you fail to mention their help as the boss is showering you with praise. It may feel good to take all the credit for yourself, but guess where your peers will be the next time you need help? If you fail to give credit where credit is due, you lose the respect of your co-workers. Instead, praise them for a job well done whenever possible—especially in front of management. What bad can possibly come from such a respectful approach?

Those who go out of their way to demonstrate respect for others can expect the same treatment for themselves. There is likely no greater force that can catapult someone to success in business than the respect of those around them. Such respect is clearly worth cultivating.

Support

When you support your co-workers, they support you. And let's be honest—we all need support sometimes! All team sports require players to pick up slack for one another from time to time, and the workplace is no different. If you see co-workers are buried under work and you're not busy, offer to lighten their load. Be a listening ear if they need to vent. Offer to swap shifts if they need it. Go out of your way to be helpful.

Avoid pointing fingers at co-workers when things go wrong. Even when the mistake is someone else's, use wording like "What went wrong?" instead of "What did you do?" Ask "What we can do to fix this?" instead of "What are you going to do about this?" Include yourself in the solution by offering to help when you can.

If your co-worker makes a mistake, discuss the matter with that person privately before you blindside them in a staff meeting or tell a supervisor. Such professional courtesy encourages others to trust you and look out for your interests in the future.

Best Practice

One way to turn co-workers into allies is performing random acts of kindness. I'll never forget the time when one of my co-workers walked in my office with a big, shiny apple, placed it on my desk, and said, "I stopped by the store on my way to work and these looked so good I had to share. Thanks for your hard work!" With a single act that only cost a few cents, she made me like her.

You can accomplish the same thing by bringing a few extra lattés, smoothies, or bagels in the morning; leaving a card when someone is sick; offering help; picking up shifts; or whatever else seems appropriate.

Communication

In the hustle and bustle of a workday, it's easy to overlook communication as a vital aspect of successful relationships. Frequent communication is important because it helps you avoid conflict. Much like oiling the gears in a motor, regular communication keeps things running smoothly and prevents friction from building up.

If you take a little time out of each day to show personal interest in your co-workers and to talk with them about potential issues, you will find small

> **FYI**
>
> The fourth cornerstone of healthy working relationships is trust. Trust follows naturally when you respect, support, and communicate with your colleagues.

problems rarely become big ones. You will also find it fosters an environment of tolerance and trust.

For a detailed discussion about communication, see Chapter 11.

Business Is Business

It's much easier to deal with co-workers if you keep in mind why you are at work in the first place. Most of us don't go to work to make friends or find life partners. In fact, work isn't an especially good place for cultivating close, personal relationships. Work is a place to make money. You can certainly have fun while working, but that shouldn't be your objective.

Workplace relationships need boundaries. There's a big difference between friendly and overly friendly, interested and overly interested, personal and overly personal.

Here's what happens when you get too close to your workmates without setting appropriate limits:

◆ A friend does something unethical but you don't feel comfortable reporting it because he's your friend. Later on, your friend gets caught and someone tells management you knew about the behavior. You look bad.

◆ You develop a romantic interest in someone at work and he starts visiting your cubicle every day. He's known to slack at work and is frequently seen chatting with you. Your name comes up for a promotion and one of the management team says, "I always see him goofing off and flirting with so and so. I don't think he's that serious about work." You miss an opportunity.

 Heads Up!

You are better off avoiding office romances altogether. Why? They can distract from your job, problems at home can trickle into your work, and break-ups are complicated when you work together.

If you can't deny your feelings and you decide to pursue a romantic relationship despite the risks, at least keep it secret. Putting your romance on display only creates chatter for the company grapevine and could damage your reputation.

◆ One of your friends starts expressing major grievances with a supervisor. You don't personally have an issue, but you witness something that she asks you to come forward about. You don't think it's that big of a deal and prefer not to make waves. You stand your ground, but lose a friend.

This isn't to say you can't have friendships at work; it just means you have to be careful how you go about forming them. If you become close with someone at work, make sure she understands your work life and your personal life are separate. You can't afford to let personal feelings interfere with your work! It takes a mature and professional individual to maintain proper limits.

 Heads Up! _____

> If you join your co-workers for drinks after work, be careful how many you have, and be even more careful how you act! No badmouthing the boss, no sharing company secrets, and no karaoke. If you hope to be respected as a professional, you need to maintain your dignity.

Playing Politics

Office politics can be hard to identify until they affect you. And while the connotation associated with "playing politics" is generally negative, when people find themselves on the receiving end of helpful politicking, they usually don't complain. So what are office politics anyway? Put simply, the term refers to how people use their power to affect things—either positively or negatively—in the workplace. Some people use politics to influence others. Some use them to gain control of property or to land positions. Whatever the case, politics can affect your job.

Rules of the Game

To experience the positive side of politics and avoid the negative, do the following:

♦ **Be likable.** When people like you, they won't talk bad about you or try to hurt you. In some cases, they'll be inclined to use their power in your favor.

♦ **Earn trust.** Office politics are played under the radar. There's no rulebook and no referees. The basic structure of an interoffice political network is private conversations. So if you hope to stay in the loop, people have to trust you first. The best way to earn such trust is to never repeat anything you are told privately.

FYI

It's common for people to confuse the company grapevine with office politics. While the two are related, they are not the same thing. The grapevine can consist of simple chatter and rumors, but politics affect actions. Consider some examples:

Politics: You submit a request to someone who has a grudge against you and he takes longer to process your request than he would for someone else.

Grapevine: You hear a colleague might be fired. Whether or not it happens is irrelevant. As far as you're concerned it's just a rumor.

Politics: You hear about a job opening but you don't meet all the qualifications. A friend in the department recommends you and you get the interview.

Grapevine: Everyone is talking about a new office romance.

Always listen to the company grapevine, but don't contribute to it. And while the rumor mill may provide you with valuable information that doesn't come through other channels, take what you hear with a grain of salt.

- ◆ **Stay neutral.** Rather than throw your two cents into every controversy, stay neutral whenever possible. Once you take sides on an issue, you automatically alienate people on the other side. Unless you have a compelling reason to take a stand, you're better off saying, "That's really none of my business."

- ◆ **Don't gossip.** When it comes to harmful gossip or malicious rumors about the personal life of others, you should make it your aim to never be the source. In so doing, you will develop a reputation as a pleasant person and keep yourself out of paltry office rivalries.

- ◆ **Avoid taboos.** Keep yourself from becoming the subject of gossip by avoiding topics at work that involve religion, politics, sex, health problems, problems at home, or grievances with superiors. All of these are private matters.

When You Become the Victim

Someday you just might find that, despite your best efforts, someone has decided to make you their target. If this happens, approach the instigator and try to resolve the problem. You could say something like, "I noticed you seem upset with me. Did I do something to offend you?" Sometimes, such an approach cause them to open up about their issue. In other cases, just the fact that you confronted them causes them to stop making trouble. If the problem persists, you may have to take additional measures.

Best Practice _____

One key to dealing with difficult co-workers is mastering the art of assertive communication. For a detailed discussion, see Chapter 11 under the heading "Assert Yourself."

When Conflicts Arise

Conflicts aren't always a bad thing. Often, the best solutions and the strongest relationships are born from conflicts. Look at the United States and the United Kingdom, for example—once great enemies, now powerful allies! What really counts is how you deal with conflict when it arises.

Remember Your Objective

When conflicts occur, our natural inclination is often to try to prove we are right or to see the party at odds with us "put in its place." Such thinking is counterproductive, however, because it drives a bigger wedge between the ones involved. Instead of focusing on *winning*, try to focus on *resolving*. If you enter a discussion with the goal of reaching an agreement, your tone, body language, and choice of words you use sets the other person at ease. Think *discuss* rather than *debate*.

Think Before You Speak

Of course, a discussion involves listening as much as talking. Don't be so quick to justify your own point that you fail to listen. Many conflicts stem from nothing more than minor misunderstandings. Once you let the other person explain himself, you may find you were missing important details.

Before hurling accusations, it's good to pause and ask yourself questions like:

◆ Is this totally his fault, or should someone else share the blame for this problem?

◆ Do I personally share some of the responsibility for this disagreement?

◆ Was the conflict caused by any circumstances that were out of this person's control?

◆ Was this person lazy and careless, or is he just inexperienced and in need of training?

Asking questions like these help you determine the best way to approach the issue and gives you time to cool off. When tempers are flaring and emotions are stirred, it's easy to overreact.

What If You Can't Resolve It?

If you've addressed an issue multiple times but there's no improvement, what then?

- ◆ **Let it go.** If it's not especially serious and doesn't affect your ability to do your job, letting go is the best option! Not only does it help you develop thicker skin, but it demonstrates you are flexible and easy to get along with.

- ◆ **Distance yourself.** If your duties aren't inextricably linked, why keep suffering? Simply separate yourself from the other person. It's better to let the issue go if you can, but in extreme cases, this is a tolerable alternative.

- ◆ **Talk to the boss.** Talking to your boss about a problem with a co-worker should be done only as a last resort. Unless an issue reflects negatively on you or looks bad for the company, try to resolve it through your own efforts. Doing so is the mark of a true professional.

    Even if it's common for the people around you to vent their anger, hold grudges, or hide from issues, don't play their game. Stand out as refreshingly different. Be diplomatic. Working to resolve conflicts rather than adding fuel to the fire pays off in the long run.

The Least You Need to Know

- ◆ Building good relationships with co-workers contributes toward your business success.

- ◆ The cornerstones of healthy working relationships are respect, mutual support, communication, and trust.

- ◆ Workplace relationships need well-defined boundaries or they can get messy.

- ◆ Listen to the company grapevine, but don't contribute to it.

- ◆ Stay on the positive side of office politics by being likable, earning trust, staying neutral, and avoiding gossip or controversy.

- ◆ When conflicts arise, do everything in your power to resolve them amicably.

Chapter 10

Connecting With Management

In This Chapter

- ◆ Turning your boss into a powerful ally
- ◆ Earning management's trust
- ◆ Breaching the management-employee barrier
- ◆ Getting friendly with your boss
- ◆ Handling disagreements with your boss

How would you rate your relationship with management? Good, bad, or ugly? If you really want to excel in the workplace, your answer needs to be *outstanding!*

Unfortunately, building outstanding relationships with your superiors can be very difficult to do. Many people feel uncomfortable around members of management. Others let formalities or a lack of confidence get in their way. And a number of bosses are unapproachable, unfriendly, or even rude. So how can you build the right kind of relationship with management—especially your direct supervisor? How can you handle disagreements when they arise? How can you earn your boss's respect? All these questions and more are answered in this chapter.

A Powerful Ally

Until you run your own business, you always have someone to answer to—and even then you're accountable to customers or shareholders. Ultimately, it's these people to whom you're accountable that determine whether you move up, down, or out. And while you benefit from the support of everyone around you, the support of your boss is most important—especially when you're young!

As a young person trying to get promoted, people tend to doubt your ability. The best remedy for such doubt is the endorsement of an influential manager. When your boss says, "I know she can do the job! Trust me on this one. You won't be disappointed!" people will listen!

Best Practice

Although this chapter focuses on building a strong relationship with your direct supervisor, the principles are useful for building relationships with all members of management. Apply the techniques in this chapter when you deal with any superior. If there's one thing better than the approval of your boss, it's the approval of an entire management team!

When the higher-ups are trying to decide whom—you or one of your colleagues— to promote, will your boss rave about what a superstar you are? Will they offer their glowing recommendation? They will if you apply the suggestions in this chapter!

What Counts the Most

Your boss goes to work every day for the same reason you do—to make money. The only difference between you and your boss is you have different jobs to do. Regardless of what your particular responsibilities entail, it's your boss's job to make sure you do them well. When you support your boss by doing your job well and following direction, you earn trust and approval.

Support by Word

Rule number one: don't say anything bad about your boss. This can be challenging at times, especially if your boss happens to be incompetent. But even if the boss's faults are plain for everyone to see, don't draw attention to them. Even if you talk to a co-worker in confidence, you can't be sure that person won't repeat what you've said. Once your co-worker does, your words are bound to end up twisted.

If you have a legitimate concern about the way your boss is handling matters, your obligation is to talk to your boss directly, to one of their superiors, or to a member of HR—not to fellow employees!

When you focus on your boss's positive qualities and draw attention to these instead, you can't go wrong.

Support your boss by avoiding the tendency to correct her when others are present. This saves you embarrassment if you happen to be wrong, and keeps them from resenting you if you happen to be right. Once you become a manager, it's especially important to do this because, as a management team, you should always present a united front.

This is not to say you should agree with everything your boss says and does. Doing so is a sure way to lose the respect of your colleagues, and maybe even your boss. Be confident enough to drop words of advice or caution when you're sure of yourself, but do so only in private and even then, do it sparingly.

Heads Up!

Don't post negative comments about your boss on blogs, social-networking sites, or any public forums. It's not unreasonable that your boss could be following your online presence.

Best Practice

Don't be afraid to toot your own horn from time to time. If you do something that deserves commendation, find a tactful way to mention it to your boss. As long as you aren't known as a braggart, some modest self-promotion can do you good.

Cite good things you've done in a matter-of-fact and informative style, as if you think it's something they need to know. If they respond with a thank you, you've accomplished your objective.

Another great way to demonstrate how supportive you are is to touch base with your boss at the end of the day and ask how his or her day went. If the boss landed a big contract or accomplished something to be excited about, it gives you a chance to commend them. If the boss had a bad day or lost a big sale, it gives you a chance to be a sympathetic ear. Either way, you demonstrate you are interested in their success. Showing such a personal interest goes a long way toward turning your boss into an ally!

Naturally, though, no amount of support by word can ever take the place of support by action.

Support by Action

Imagine how quickly you would tire of using a software program that lost information, froze, dropped reminders, and miscalculated. How long before you'd replace it? This aptly illustrates the type of support—or rather, lack of support—many employees give management. To achieve business success, you need to show your support by action:

◆ **Do your job.** Enough said!

◆ **Always present potential solutions when you bring up a problem.** The more issues you can resolve on your own, the more useful you become. Before you jump out of your seat and run to your boss for answers, think the problem through on your own and come up with one or two options to correct it. This sends the message you are self-motivated and resourceful—two traits of any good leader.

◆ **No surprises!** Bosses don't like surprises. If something comes up that could bite them, don't let them hear about it from someone else. If you make a mistake, own up to it! Go to them with an admission, solution, and pledge it won't happen again.

◆ **Keep track of everything.** If you're given something to do, make sure your boss never has to follow up on it. Your boss should have the utmost confidence that once they pass something to you, it's as good as done. If your boss ever asks about it again, you should know the answer or know where to find it quickly.

◆ **Have a good attitude.** A person who strives to maintain and project a positive outlook can boost the morale of the entire department and the boss. When everyone is complaining because health insurance costs are going up, be the person who says, "Thank goodness we have great coverage and that the company picks up half the cost!" When you're friendly and upbeat, your boss enjoys work-ing with you.

◆ **Maintain good relationships with your co-workers.** Your boss would much rather be doing other things than mediating conflicts among staff members. If you're frequently involved in disputes, management won't favor you, and it's unlikely they'll promote you.

Get on the Same Page

You can't support your boss if you don't understand what is expected of you. If your duties aren't clearly spelled out, request a meeting to review them. You could say something like, "I'd really like to make sure I'm meeting all your expectations. Would it be possible for us to sit down and review my responsibilities?" It's a rare individual who would decline to accommodate such a request.

Make sure you know what tasks you are expected to handle on your own and what tasks you should request assistance with. One of the quickest ways to sabotage your relation-ship with your boss is to overstep your bounds. Conversely, if you keep asking for help with something you should be doing on your own, you will quickly get a reputation as a pest. It's always best to clarify your boundaries as early as possible when you take on a new position or get a promotion.

> **FYI**
>
> Even if your job comes with a formal job description, it prob-ably doesn't include all your responsibilities. Your boss likely has a number of things that are important to him even though they aren't in print.

You also need to figure out which method of communication your boss prefers. E-mail or voicemail? Text or IM? Get this right and it can make a big difference in how fast your boss becomes comfortable with you. Remember, you're the one who should adapt to your supervisor's preferences—not the other way around.

Another great practice is to request a deadline whenever you are given an assignment. This ensures there are no misunderstandings about when things are due. If you think "as soon as possible" means "this week" and your boss means "this afternoon," you'll be the one who takes the heat. A simple, "When would you like this back?" can save a lot of headaches later.

Whenever you complete a project, ask for a quick evaluation of your work. This accomplishes two things: one, it gives you a chance to develop your skills, and two, it gives your supervisor a chance to verbalize what a great job you did. The more she says it, the more she believes it! One small caveat to this: don't be afraid of criticism. When you apply the guidance offered, you'll be the better for it.

Once you understand what is required of you and are consistently meeting or exceeding the expectations of your supervisor, you only have to stay the course. If you lose momentum or start cutting corners, your boss will notice. The only thing worse than an average worker is an outstanding worker who becomes average.

Breaking Barriers

Managers wear red shirts; employees wear gray shirts. Managers use the lounge; employees use the break room. Managers associate with managers; employees associate with employees. Does it ever seem like there's an invisible barrier between you and your manager? Would you like to develop a more comfortable relationship but aren't sure how? With some minor adjustments to your approach, you may be able to break through the management-employee barrier.

You've got to figure out what makes your boss tick. Start paying attention to how he interacts with his supervisor. (This can be a great indicator of how the boss expects to be treated.) Take note of how often he socializes and with whom. When does he take his breaks? Is the boss introverted or extroverted? Is he dry or gregarious? Does he do his best work in the morning or the afternoon? As you take note of these subtleties, it helps you determine the best ways and the best times to approach him.

Try to reach out to your boss on a personal level. At an appropriate time, strike up casual conversations about his hobbies and interests. Ask him about his weekend or a vacation he took. Use the techniques we discussed in Chapter 6 to get him talking about what's important to him.

One of the best ways to make a connection with your supervisor is by asking him to mentor you. Say something like: "I really admire the things you've accomplished in your career and I think I could learn a lot from you. How would you feel about being my mentor?" If he agrees to mentor you, it can change the way he perceives you. Instead of viewing you like a subordinate, he may begin to view you like a student. Such a relationship could incite him to give you special consideration and attention.

Best Practice _____

If you really want to understand how your boss thinks, ask him for the titles of business books he's recently read. If he recommends them, go pick up copies for yourself. After you've read them it gives the two of you something to talk about. It also flatters him that you value his opinion on reading material.

Once you learn what kind of books he likes, you'll always have a thoughtful gift you can give him. Inscribe a personal note in the front, and every time he opens it he'll think of you.

As you get to know your boss, you can adapt your work style to fit his. If you discern he is detail-oriented, know the details before you present an idea. If he's a big-picture thinker, make sure you can communicate your ideas in a big-picture way. Focus on the things that matter most to your boss. Try to anticipate his wishes and act on them before he asks you.

I used to work for a boss who was tremendously disorganized. Every time I would send him an e-mail or leave a form on his desk to complete, it was like pulling teeth to get it back. Even worse, the way I dealt with the problem made him dread working with me because he felt like I was a nag.

Gradually I learned if I would just step into his office when he had a free minute and say something like, "Hey boss, can you help me with something? It'll be real quick." and then stay there until he was finished, it was a win-win. I got what I needed, and he never felt like I was piling work on him. The other benefit was it gave us a chance to talk. This small change dramatically enhanced my value to him. Capitalize on your boss's strengths and compensate for his weaknesses!

Boss or Friend?

As you age in the workforce, there's bound to come a time when one of your friends becomes your boss. When this happens, new challenges can change the dynamic of your relationship. How should you deal with such a change?

First off, try to be happy for her. If you can cultivate a positive attitude toward the change, it helps you deal with any inconveniences that arise. If she happens to receive a promotion you wanted, try not to let it make you angry or resentful. Such feelings only end up hurting you. The fact she received the promotion instead of you is a good indicator of her value to the company. Talk to her about the change and let her know you respect her and are there to support her!

And keep in mind having your friend as a boss can be good for your career. Although you shouldn't expect special favors, you certainly have a better channel of communication than many of your colleagues. Many people long for such a relationship with their boss but are unable to attain it.

Recognize your relationship at work may change to a degree. It's possible there will be certain information she may not be able to share with you—and you shouldn't expect her to. If you used to confide in her about certain matters, you may need to find someone new to talk to. Be realistic in your expectations and support her just as you would any other manager.

When Disagreements Arise

It's okay to disagree with your boss. Business leaders and professionals disagree all the time. You'll never get ahead in business if you try to agree with everyone. If you want to be recognized as a leader, you have to stand up for what you believe in! Occasional, well-founded disagreements with your supervisor can even help you earn his trust and friendship. However, you must be careful about how you approach things. When you find yourself at odds with your boss, keep the following tips in mind:

- **Know your stuff.** If you decide to verbalize a disagreement, make sure you can back up your reasons for doing so. Wait until you're armed with all the facts and be prepared to explain yourself. Furnish alternative solutions to show you've thought the matter through.

 Heads Up!

Whenever possible, speak to your boss about disagreements in private. If you challenge him in public, he could feel pressured to assert his authority. Such a confrontation would be counterproductive and embarrassing for you.

- **Disagree for the greater good.** Your boss wants to succeed. When you disagree because he has made an error in judgment that could cause problems for your organization, he's likely to thank you for it. You'll also prove you're dedicated to helping your company succeed.

- **Watch your tone.** Approach disagreements in a way that says, "We're on the same team." Use "we" instead of "I." Don't tell your boss he's wrong; just let him know you'd like to try a different approach. Don't threaten. Don't embarrass him. Keep your emotions in check. Be cool and logical!

◆ **Concede when necessary.** If you have a disagreement with your boss but he refuses to see things your way, let him have the last word. Once you've explained your reasons and he decides on another way, offer your full support! And unless new evidence suggests you should discuss the matter again, don't bring it up.

The Least You Need to Know

◆ Having your boss as an ally is critical to your business success.

◆ The most important way to build a good relationship with your boss is to support them by doing your job well and following direction.

◆ Don't talk bad about your boss. If you have a legitimate complaint, talk to them directly.

◆ Reach out to your boss on a personal level by striking up casual conversations about their hobbies and interests.

◆ Learn your boss's preferences and adjust your work style to accommodate them.

◆ It's okay to disagree with your boss, but be diplomatic in your approach.

Communication That Unlocks Doors

In This Chapter

- ◆ Mastering the art of face-to-face communications
- ◆ Asserting yourself
- ◆ Talking on the telephone
- ◆ Putting it in writing
- ◆ Keeping the channels of communication open

Good communication is the foundation of successful relationships. In business and in life, people who are first-rate communicators have a considerable advantage over those who are not.

Depending on the field you are in, one type of communication may be more important than another. The ability to communicate face-to-face may be more important than the ability to communicate in writing, for example, or vice versa. But more often than not, successful business people are good all-around communicators. This chapter outlines the basics of successful communication and has been specifically tailored to focus on things that can be naturally challenging for young people.

Face-to-Face

Have you ever noticed how some people seem to be natural conversationalists? Without even trying, they seem to be able to captivate the attention of a single person or an entire room. Would you like to be able to command that kind of attention? Although some people are just naturals, good communication skills can be learned! Unfortunately, many young people haven't learned this skill because online social networking, video games, and other electronic devices take the place of quality face-to-face interactions. If you find yourself turning to your computer for your social interactions, your success may depend on turning off your electronic devices and tuning in to the person in the room with you.

> **FYI**
>
> Good conversation skills were discussed extensively in Chapter 6 and should be considered in conjunction with the information in this chapter.

The facets of face-to-face communication could fill volumes, but for the sake of this book, we're going to spotlight five actionable areas.

Think Before You Speak

Most people hurl their two cents into a conversation at the very moment a neurological pathway fires it. Effective communicators, on the other hand, collect their thoughts into meaningful expressions and share them at the right time.

Rather than blurting out opinions or conjecture, think through what you are about to say to determine whether it will be meaningful to others. Filter out technical jargon and figures of speech that might be incomprehensible. By waiting to speak until you have something truly meaningful to say, you will come to have a reputation as someone worth listening to.

Listen First

When you listen to others, they will be more likely to listen to you.

The proper way to listen involves maintaining positive eye contact, offering nonverbal cues like nodding your head, and asking clarifying questions. Such a listening style gives others the impression you are thoughtful and courteous. It also gives you insight into the thoughts of those with whom you are speaking. As a result, you will be able to tailor your comments to what is important to your audience.

Eliminate Fluff

Filling your expressions with useless interjections like "uh," "emmm," "like," "y'know," and so on makes you seem uncertain and even immature. If you are about to use a filler word, take a breath and pause instead. A brief silence to gather your thoughts is a hundred times better than mumbling an, "uuuuuh … hmmmmm."

Eliminate slang. When speaking, always keep in mind on whom you are speaking with. Accord others due respect by using language that is acceptable to their generation and status.

Pitch, Pace, Tone, and Volume

You've probably heard it said that, "it's not what you say, it's how you say it." When it comes to communicating professionally, nothing could be more true. If you constantly speak in a fast and elevated tone, you grate on people. If you speak painfully slow and in a monotone, you put your listeners to sleep. Too quiet and they won't hear; too loud and you appear domineering.

Focus on speaking with adequate volume, at a normal pace, and with a confident tone. If you aren't sure how you sound, ask a trusted friend or mentor for his opinion and then make adjustments accordingly.

Best Practice

If expressing yourself in front of a group is naturally difficult for you, try joining a local speaking organization to help you conquer your fear. Many professional public speakers were timid at one time. With effort and practice, you can learn to communicate with power.

Talk Tough

Say what you mean and mean what you say! If you always hedge your comments with fragile opinions and qualifiers, others perceive you as weak. When asked your opinion, avoid expressions like "I feel" and "I like." Instead, focus on solid, specific observations that are based on fact. If you're asked a question but you don't know the answer, fight your urge to wager a guess. Remember, you're a professional—not a politician!

Assert Yourself

It's good to be agreeable, but you can't be a yes man if you hope to get ahead. When problems arise, others disagree with you, or you have an important point to make, you must be able to assert yourself!

Assertive communication could be likened to the middle ground between aggressive communication (bossy and arrogant) and submissive communication (helpless and apologetic). When you communicate in an assertive way, your listeners should get the impression you are sincere, confident, and reasonable.

To communicate assertively, focus on specific issues instead of people or feelings. Make clear, direct requests, and avoid pointing the proverbial finger. Here is a good example of how to use assertive communication when dealing with a difficult co-worker:

> "Sometimes when we get close to a deadline I notice you start rushing me, which makes me wonder if you think I'm incompetent. I can understand why you would get tense, but I'm very aware of my deadlines and I've never missed one before. Obviously we have slightly different ways of doing things, but I think we'll work better together if you trust me to handle my job and I trust you to handle yours. If you'd like, I can give you an update on my progress when we get close to our deadline."

Did you notice how the emphasis was more on the problem and the solution than personal feelings or blame? Assertive communication avoids accusatory statements like "you always" or "you never" and instead directs attention to the effects of particular actions and the solution to them. Notice the use of "I" instead of "you" in the following expressions:

> "Your work is always sloppy." vs. "I would like you to work on your punctuation and spelling."

> "You always finish late." vs. "I need you to start turning your work in on time."

> "You're such a negative person." vs. "I'm having a hard time dealing with some of the negative things you say."

Assertive communication doesn't sidestep issues; it just makes the delivery more palatable. It also helps you achieve your goals, protects you from being taken advantage of, and demonstrates self-esteem.

FYI

One way to be assertive is with body language. When you lean forward and keep your hands on the table during conversation, it sends the message you are engaged.

You can show assertiveness at other times, too, such as when you visit someone's work area. If you pause briefly and place a hand on their desk, it signals you are confident and close with that person.

If despite your best efforts to communicate assertively, you get an unwarranted tongue-lashing, resist the urge to interrupt. Even if much of what someone says is untrue, listen anyway. Once they are finished, restate your case in the same assertive manner. Don't lose sight of your goal, and don't let interruptions or circular reasoning distract you from making your point.

On the Phone

Have you ever been in desperate need of tech support only to reach an unfriendly, unaccommodating customer service rep after what seemed like hours on hold? I'm sure you have! And if you've ever wanted to reach through the phone and shake a sense of service into somebody, you'll appreciate the value of this section.

The way you handle yourself on the phone will give other people a mental picture of how knowledgeable you are, how much you care, and even how you appear. Because you can't use facial expressions or body language to help convey your thoughts, you need to have an appealing phone personality! The elements of an appealing phone personality are outlined next.

A Pleasant Greeting

A call that starts well usually ends well. To get off on the right foot, answer your phone before the third ring. Doing so demonstrates responsiveness!

Make sure the voice you answer with is upbeat and friendly in tone. Start off with a courteous pleasantry that includes your name such as, "Good morning (or afternoon), this is _____. How may I assist you?" Using your full name is considered polite and sets your caller at ease. Adding an expression like "How may I assist you?" lets the caller know you are going to be helpful right from the start!

Proper Tone

Whenever speaking on the phone, keep your tone warm, friendly, and enthusiastic. The easiest way to do this is to smile. If you actually smile, it comes through in your voice, and it's contagious!

Be sure to speak clearly, enunciating all your words properly. Don't speak too quickly, and keep your voice at an even pace.

Think of your voice like a musical instrument. With it you can convey excitement or boredom; confidence or trepidation; peacefulness or anxiety. What feelings does your phone voice convey?

Be Positive

Carefully choose the language you use and keep it positive! Reaffirm you are going to be helpful by using words like *certainly*, *absolutely*, and *definitely*. Notice the contrast:

"You're welcome." vs. "My pleasure!"

"No problem." vs. "Certainly!"

"I don't know." vs. "I'll find out for you!"

"Yes." vs. "Absolutely!"

Heads Up! _____

Just as in regular speech, you should avoid using filler phrases such as "uh" and "um" when speaking on the telephone. Using such fillers creates the impression you are unsure of yourself.

Use Proper Etiquette

The first rule of phone etiquette is to be focused on your call. When you are shuffling papers or talking to someone in the background, it is just as rude as if you were doing so in person. Speakerphones are notoriously bad for picking up background noise and give the impression you are more interested in other things. Avoid using them for important calls.

Be respectful by never putting someone on hold without their permission and by apologizing for any waits they have to experience. Always ask, "May I place you on hold please?" and then pick up the phone every minute or so to let them know you are still on the line.

Adhere to a policy of warm transfers. A warm transfer happens when you first contact the party you are transferring to and make known whom you have on the line and why you are transferring them. This prevents your callers from having to reintroduce and repeat themselves. Never transfer anyone to voicemail without their permission!

Best Practice

When leaving a voicemail, speak at a slower pace than normal. Leave your full name, a brief explanation of why you are calling, and then repeat your contact information twice at the end of the call. Try to keep the total message to 45 seconds or less.

In Writing

In the business world, written communications take hundreds of forms—letters, memos, e-mails, websites, blogs, instant messages, articles, press releases, booklets, brochures, business cards, flyers, and more. Whichever type of written communication you use, the principles that make it effective stay the same. Use the following four-step method to ensure your business communications meet their objective.

1. Consider Your Audience

The tone of your writing, the details you share, and the points you emphasize should take into account your audience.

Imagine you are creating three presentations outlining your company's IT policies. Let's assume one is for the board of directors, one is for the employees, and one is for the clients. Isn't it reasonable to conclude the tone, details, and points that are emphasized should be different in each presentation? Just because the content is essentially the same doesn't mean the material should be developed in the same way.

To get a feel for your audience, ask yourself questions like: How will they interpret and react to what I am about to say? Will they understand the explanations or verbiage I am about to use? Is my goal to impress, inform, commend, or something else? As you write, take the age, social status, income, nationality, occupation, and any other relevant details of your audience into account. Write in a way you think strikes a responsive cord in your readers based on what you know about them.

Heads Up!

Never use chat acronyms or text message shorthand in important business communications like e-mails! Such blunders not only make you look unprofessional, but also increase the likelihood your message gets lost in translation. tm—u shld rlly 86 th shrthnd! :)

2. Organize Your Material

Before you actually start writing, put together an outline of your main points. If the communication is simple, you can do this quickly in your head. If the communication is complex, your time will be well spent if you write it out.

After you have a rough outline, organize it. What do you want to mention first? What do you want to mention last? What do you want to elaborate on? Don't underestimate the importance of putting things in the correct order, which is especially important when you are conveying bad news. It's always better to sandwich bad news in between two pieces of good news. Example: Our sales were up 20 percent this month thanks to our hot new product line! Unfortunately, we sold out of our most popular item yesterday. Thankfully, we expect more to be delivered early next week!

Best Practice

Before you put anything negative in writing, ask yourself if it is something that can be communicated in person. A practice that has always served me well is to put upbeat, positive things in writing where they can be reread over and over again and to reserve negative things for face-to-face communications where they can be quickly left behind. Think "Commend in print, chastise in person."

The exception to this rule is when you have a valid reason to document something.

Making an outline keeps your writing focused on the main points, organized into paragraphs, and free from omissions.

3. Write

Everyone's writing style is different. Don't try to force a style you're uncomfortable with. Instead, let the words flow as if you are having a conversation with someone. You are more likely to get your point across if you communicate in a way that is comfortable for you. A conversational style of writing is also more appealing to read.

Business communications should be clear and to the point! Include relevant details but don't get too wordy. When writing memos or e-mails, it may even be helpful to use bullets for your main points. Doing so makes it easy for the reader to extract the most important information even when they're in a hurry, which business people usually are.

As you write, keep your audience and your objective in mind. Before you start a new paragraph or section, read over what you've already written to make sure it is logical and easy to understand.

FYI

As a child, the first style of writing we learn is creative writing. Creative writing is used to amuse or entertain. Expository writing is used to instruct or educate. With few exceptions, business communications are usually written in an expository style.

With creative writing, you would typically use flowery expressions and vivid word pictures to solicit favorable reactions from your reader. With expository writing, you have to maintain the readers' interest by organizing the material so the content is interesting, useful, and relevant.

You can't turn something boring into something electrifying just by using fancy language. What you can do is make it worth reading because it is well organized and instructive.

---

4. Proofread and Edit

Everything you write tells your reader something about you. It tells them how educated you are, how much you care, and how much you know. Before you click Send on an e-mail or put the stamp on a letter, take time to proofread and edit it thoroughly!

Proofreading can be a tricky process. I can't tell you how many times I've proofread something six times only to miss the same mistake each time. The more time you allow to elapse between the initial writing and the proofreading, the more accurate your proofreads will be. For important documents, I recommend waiting a day or more. Even if you can only wait 10 minutes, your odds of catching mistakes will improve.

And while this may not be the most environmentally responsible idea, I suggest you print important communications and read them on paper before you send them electronically. It's easy to miss things when you proofread on a computer screen.

As you proofread, try to put yourself in the place of the reader. Imagine how you would react if you were reading your words for the first time. Is the tone respectful? Are the relevant details included? Does it look and sound professional? Are there any grammatical mistakes, punctuation errors, or misspellings?

If you really want to be sure you haven't missed anything, ask a friend or colleague to check you work. A fresh set of eyes can do wonders to help polish your writing.

E-Mail Etiquette

Hundreds of billions of e-mails are sent every day, making e-mail the most popular form of business communication. Because it's also a tool that frequently gets abused, here are a few do's and don'ts:

- *Do* use e-mail for informal reminders and memos.

- *Don't* send lengthy instructions by e-mail. These can be overwhelming to the recipient and are usually better explained in person.

- *Do* use e-mail for little notes of appreciation and to put praise in writing.

- *Don't* use e-mail for disciplinary action or performance reviews.

- *Do* use e-mail when you want a permanent record of something.

- *Don't* be sarcastic in e-mail or use it to vent. Your tone can be easily misinterpreted.

- *Do* use e-mail to forward important updates to colleagues.

- *Don't* use e-mail to blast chain letters to your entire address book.

Keep the Lines of Communication Open

Studies have shown regular communication in the workplace translates to higher job satisfaction. Open communication is important because when problems are bottled up, they fester and eventually lead to explosions. Consider the following case in point:

Amanda and Sherri work for a company that sells credit card machines to businesses. Amanda's job is to visit business owners and convince them to let her company do a free evaluation of their credit card processing rates in hopes of selling a new system.

When a prospective client agrees to the evaluation, their statements are faxed to Sherri's desk for analysis. Sherri then analyzes the statements within 15 minutes and returns them to Amanda with a report. When there is a savings, Amanda attempts to close the sale.

Amanda has never liked working with Sherri because she returns reports late from time to time. Because it doesn't happen every time, she hasn't said anything.

One day, Amanda visits a business owner who is extremely interested in her product and has 23 locations. If she closes the sale, she will earn over $4,600 in commission! She collects all the statements and faxes them to Sherri with "RUSH" written on the coversheet.

Back at the office, Sherri receives the fax, immediately notices "RUSH" written across the front, and moves Amanda's report to the top of her pile even though she already has seven others pending. She compiles all the information within 10 minutes and tries to fax it back when she notices that, in her haste, Amanda forgot to include the return fax number. Sherri tries to contact Amanda on her cell phone but without success. Finally, she takes the initiative to look up the company on the Internet, gets its fax number, and sends the report. Despite her best efforts, the report still arrives 20 minutes late. During this time, the business owner decides he can't wait and leaves. Amanda—not realizing her mistake—is seething.

Entering the office later that day, Amanda only manages to flash Sherri a dirty look as she barges into the branch manager's office.

"I can't work with Sherri anymore!" she says. "She's terrible at her job! Every time I'm visiting a prospect, she faxes the reports back late. Today she was 20 minutes late and I probably lost a huge sale because of her. You've got to assign me a different processor!"

The branch manager is totally baffled.

"But Sherri is one of our best processors." he says. "Nobody else seems to have a problem with her. Have you talked to her about it?"

"No. But this happens all the time and I'm tired of it!"

"Well, we just hired a new processor because Sherri has been so bogged down. He hasn't had much training but I guess he can be assigned to you if you prefer."

"I would like that. Anybody will be better than Sherri!"

Amanda leaves the room feeling vindicated. Her manager, on the other hand, is annoyed by her outburst.

Later, the branch manager calls Sherri into his office to let her know she won't be working with Amanda anymore and to give her a verbal warning.

"So what happened today with that client of Amanda's?" he asks.

"I don't know." Sherri replied. "I guess she just got excited in the heat of things and forgot to put the return fax number on her report. She can be pretty forgetful at times, but I try to help her out when I can."

"You mean Amanda forgot to include the return fax number?" the branch manager asks.

"Yes. And then I couldn't reach her on her cell. I finally went on the Internet to get the fax number for that company because I didn't want her to lose the sale. Why do you ask? Did she get the deal?"

"Never mind," the branch manager said. "I just wanted to let you know I've assigned Amanda a new processor to lighten your load a little. Keep up the good work!"

Can you identify all the things Amanda did wrong in this scenario?

She should have talked to Sherri about her concerns the very first time she received a late report. If she had done this, the entire incident would have been averted. Instead, her frustrations grew until she blew up. Secondly, she should have gone to Sherri before she ever approached her manager.

Who would you say ended up looking bad in this example? Did Amanda get a better processor? Did she procure favor with her boss? Was she benefited in any way? What could she have done differently to improve the situation?

The importance of communicating in a regular and open way can't be overestimated. If a little time is taken out of each day to show personal interest in your co-workers and to talk with them about potential issues, you will find that small problems rarely become big ones. You will also find a relationship based on mutual trust and respect will be cultivated.

Success and the ability to communicate go hand in hand. By practicing the suggestions in this chapter, you are well on your way to communicating in a way that unlocks doors!

FYI

Seek out opportunities to communicate. When you interact with people face-to-face on a regular basis about minor issues as well as more important topics, communication comes naturally. Rather than using your lunch break to listen to your iPod and message your friends, use it to reach out to your colleagues.

When it takes just as much time to hand deliver a memo as it does to e-mail it, choose the more personal method. Before you click Send, ask yourself: *Is this something I could communicate just as effectively in person?* By taking the initiative to push yourself away from the desk, you will experience your relationships with the people around you getting stronger.

The Least You Need to Know

- ◆ Filter your speech for technical jargon, conjecture, and useless interjections.

- ◆ When you listen to others, they are more likely to listen to you.

- ◆ To stand out as a leader, you must learn to assert yourself.

- ◆ The way you handle yourself on the phone gives others a mental picture of how knowledgeable you are, how much you care, and even how you appear.

- ◆ Use the four-step method to ensure your written business communications are professional.

- ◆ Always communicate regularly and openly with your colleagues.

Networking: How to Weave Your Web

In This Chapter

- Identifying places to start networking
- Networking with skill
- Maintaining your network
- Avoiding networking no-no's

Networking has been a staple of business for centuries. Archeological evidence shows even the Ancient Egyptians built extensive networks of contact and trade linking them with the Middle East, North Africa, Greece, and Italy. Successful business people always have been, and always will be, good networkers!

So how can you build a network for yourself? Who should be in your network? Where are the best places to network? How can you get started? This chapter answers these questions and more!

Where to Start

The ability to network effectively starts in your mind! Understanding the value of having a network and accepting that you possess the ability to network should be your first priority.

Why Network?

Building a network is an excellent investment in your future! Not only can it provide a steady stream of referrals, jobs, information, and business opportunities, but it can also serve as a resource when you are looking for reliable goods and services.

According to a study called "Professional Networking and Its Impact on Career Advancement," sponsored by Pepperdine University's Graziadio School of Business Management, the ability to network has a direct correlation with income. It also stated that "elite professionals"—those with salaries exceeding $200,000 a year—place an even higher value on networking, viewing it as part of their job. You could say networking is a habit of highly successful people!

Even if you don't need a network right now, you probably will in the future. Imagine if you start your own business or write a book. What if you're looking for a new job? Wouldn't it be nice to have an established network of connections you could look to for support? With a well-organized network, anything you need is just a phone call away!

Yes You Can!

If the idea of building a network is daunting to you, start small. You don't have to be a socialite or a schmoozer, working every room and passing out business cards like candy. You only have to reach out to one person at a time. Look at networking like depositing change in the bank. Even if you only deposit a little at a time, it eventually amounts to big money. In the same way, building a valuable network takes years. You don't have to rush—you just have to start!

It's okay if reaching out to new people makes you nervous and awkward. Networking is challenging! Just be determined not to let apprehension hold you back. Rejection and failure are both part of the process. If you're sitting on the plane next to someone and you strike up a conversation with them, they're either going to reciprocate or shut you down. If they shut you down, what have you lost? If they reciprocate, think of what you could potentially gain.

Most of us aren't natural-born networkers, but we can learn to be! The rest of this chapter shows you the approach to take, and gives you some icebreakers to keep in your pocket. Once you understand how to network, it becomes like any other task. You simply translate what you know into action and get better with time.

Heads Up! _____

If you're naturally shy and have tried without success to overcome your reticence, you might want to seek professional help. A licensed psychologist could provide you with exercises and advice to dramatically change your life. Chronic shyness can greatly limit your potential in the business world.

Places to Network

You can network anywhere. This is an important point to remember! If you reserve networking for conferences and online social networks, you greatly limit your potential. Here are a few other places you might like to try:

- Gym
- Coffee shop
- Work
- Bookstores
- Parks
- Church
- Public transportation
- Cruises
- Casinos
- Hotel lobbies
- Charity functions
- In line at the store
- Festivals
- Sporting events
- Nightclubs
- Parties
- Conferences
- Training workshops

Talk to people everywhere you go and give out as many business cards as you can! You never know if the person you're talking with will offer you a dream job. Once you understand the entire world is your networking playground, you can visit whenever you like.

Best Practice _____

Set a networking goal for yourself. Every time you exchange contact information with someone, pay yourself a dollar. Decide how much you want to "earn" each month and spend the money when you reach your goal. If your goal is $50 a month, you'll make 600 new contacts a year.

People You Already Know

Don't exclude friends, relatives, schoolmates, and former workmates from your networking radar. Strengthening relationships with your existing connections is the easiest place to start! Because you already have a rapport, all that's necessary is to make a phone call or write an e-mail. Ask them how they've been doing, fill them in on what's happening with you, and exchange contact information. It's really that simple!

Look up old friends from high school and college. Inquire about their significant others, their hobbies, and their aspirations. Ask them what they've been doing for a living and let them know you'll use their services if the opportunity arises. Politely ask them to do the same for you.

Within Your Field

Your industry can be a veritable paradise of worthwhile connections. The beauty of networking within your field is you already share a common bond and have an abundance of things to talk about, making introductions easy.

Heads Up! _____

When networking within your industry, be careful not to share privileged information or trade secrets with your competition. The wrong slip could cost your company a lot of money and get you fired.

If you work at a large company, make it a point to meet everyone you can. Find out what department they work in, what position they hold, and what their interests are. Exchange contact information and keep in touch. The bonds you form on the job can last for years after you've moved on. If consultants or visitors come to your office, reach out to them, too!

Most industries have networking or trade associations you can join. Why not become a member? Attend conferences and trainings whenever possible and use these as opportunities to network.

Interest Based

The great thing about networking with people who share your obsession is business and social status become irrelevant. If you join a car club, who cares if the guy next to you is broke or rich? President of a Fortune 500 company or out of a job? The shared interest creates a talking point that can lead to profitable business relationships.

No matter what you're into or how bizarre it seems, there's a good chance somebody else is into it, too—and you never know if that person could be your next great contact. Even if you can only find a community online, make connections there. If you can't find anybody who shares your passion, start your own club and let people find you!

Online

Networking via the Internet becomes more popular every day. And as its popularity grows, so does its effectiveness. Social-networking sites like MySpace, Facebook, and LinkedIn have become staples for millions of eager networkers.

If you fall into the demographic for which this book is intended, I probably don't need to tell you much about how to network online. In fact, you probably came out of the womb with a MySpace account. That being said, when it comes to using the Internet for business-related networking, there are some special considerations.

For one, business networking shouldn't be treated like a popularity contest. It doesn't matter if you have 5,000 "friends" if they don't know who you are, what you do, and aren't disposed to refer you. To build a valuable network online, you still need to make real connections. Do this by personally introducing yourself to each of your contacts online. Let them know what you do and inquire about what they do. Work to establish a meaningful dialogue and get to know each contact on a professional level.

The other thing to keep in mind is there are millions of people on hundreds of networks, which makes it hard to stand out. If you want to keep your network alive, you have to deliver a worthwhile experience and keep your name in front of your "followers." If you establish an account with every social network but fail to actively manage those accounts, people quickly forget about you. It's important to start small and only take on what you can handle. (See the next chapter for information on how to create an appealing online identity.)

FYI

If your intent is to network for business, make sure your profile is dignified and professional in appearance. Don't share links between professional profiles and personal profiles unless you're confident that nothing you've posted discredits you as a professional.

Rather than using a nickname, use your full first and last name to identify your profile. Reserve nicknames, puns, and party pictures for your personal pages and keep these private.

When it comes to business networking, LinkedIn is by far the most respected and widely used tool. Its content is geared for professional use and includes very little personal information.

Networking Basics

Now that we've discussed where to network, let's talk about how to network.

Conversational Quality

Conversations are the foundation of networking. Whether face-to-face, ear-to-ear, or screen-to-screen, all networking starts with a dialogue of one kind or another.

When networking, make it a point to contribute to a conversation without dominating it. Our tendency can be to think we need to tell others as much as possible about ourselves so they remember us. But in reality, it works the other way around. Think of networking like a game of catch. You pass the ball and then you catch the ball. Everybody gets to play and everybody shares. Don't be a ball hog! (Refer to Chapter 6 for more on conversation skills.)

People are rarely given the attention they deserve. If you show a genuine interest and focus on what others are saying, they appreciate you for it. Look them in the eye and avoid touching your hair, face, or looking at your watch. Take time to linger in conversation, and don't be in a hurry to rush your business card onto them. If you just introduce yourself and pass on a card, it probably ends up in the trash.

Be careful not to focus solely on the dominant individual in a group. When several people are talking, it's easy to gravitate toward the most influential or outspoken. When you do this to the exclusion of others, you miss good networking opportunities. While you should introduce yourself to the heavy hitters, it's usually the people around them who turn out to be your best contacts.

When you approach new people, be yourself, be sincere, and be friendly. If you try to put on an air of accomplishment or superiority, you repel rather than attract.

Never apologize for introducing yourself. Instead of saying something like, "Excuse me, I see you're busy, but I just wanted to …" say "Hi. My name is _____. And you are?" Approach with confidence and get right to the point. After your introduction, ask a few well-chosen questions and let the conversation flow.

> **Best Practice** _____
>
> If you're really bad at introductions, latch onto an extrovert and let them do the hard part. Once they break the ice, you can contribute to the conversation. One caution, though; you won't always have somebody with you, so you still need to work on developing boldness.

Network Without Words

If you find yourself in a room full of people, whom do you approach?

    a. The shy-looking guy or girl texting near the exit?

    b. The two executives standing off to the side having a quiet discussion?

    c. A small group of three to five people having a lively discussion?

If you answered C, you're right. In social settings, we all send signals that tell others whether we're open to interacting. Always be conscious of the signal you're sending, or you could be saying no when you actually mean yes.

Make yourself approachable by moving around and talking with a variety of people. Stand up straight with your shoulders back and smile a lot. Make eye contact with as many people as possible and be enthusiastic! All these things send the signal that you are confident, engaging, and ready to interact.

We already discussed the proper handshake in Chapter 6, but when you are networking, you can take things up a notch by doing the two-handed handshake or the quick elbow grab. While not overdoing it, such subtleties draw others into you and demonstrate your eagerness to build a relationship.

Be Memorable

When you leave an event after meeting a hundred people, very few stick out in your mind. The ones who do make themselves memorable in some way. You, too, should make yourself memorable! How can you? First, be determined not to blend. I try to remember "to blend is a dead end."

Almost anything can make you memorable. I've seen people use buttons, wild ties, even props. And depending on the industry you're in, some of these things may prove effective. Generally, though, it's better to be remembered for your professionalism. If you are impeccably dressed and groomed, give others your undivided attention, and radiate positive energy, people remember you!

It's not always possible, but try coming up with a unique phrase that describes who you are, what you do, and where you're from. It should be one easy-to-remember sentence. Once you have this phrase, you can tell people you're, "Debra the accountant from Denver" or "Matt the marketing guy from Madison." This way, if they misplace your card, they'll still be able to find you. It might seem a little cheesy, but it works.

A unique website URL can be another memory aid. The website for one of my companies used to be www.gaingroupinc.com, but once I realized this was too difficult to remember, I changed it to www.startgaining.com. Maybe you could do something similar.

Be Generous

Many people think networking is insincere and selfish in nature. That it's all about peddling wares and pushing products. And while some folks may network strictly for selfish reasons, the reality is good networking is about give and take. The most effective networkers are generous with their time and freely share information. It's the same reason companies give away free trinkets at trade shows and conventions.

Best Practice

Before you go to a networking event, prepare something useful to share. Then, when you finish conversing with someone, you can say: "I've really enjoyed our conversation! I think I have something you would enjoy looking at. Would you mind if I e-mail it to you?" Such an approach keeps the door open and leaves them anticipating your future contact.

Do you have something of value you can offer? What about a marketing tip, some interesting news, a copy of a report? It doesn't have to be much. Even if it's something that is widely available, others appreciate that you directed them to it.

You can also be generous with your words. Make people feel good about themselves by giving them your undivided attention, using their name often, and acknowledging their comments. Reassure them with phrases like:

> I can see you've given this subject a lot of thought!
>
> Your insights are very enlightening!
>
> I really admire what you've accomplished!
>
> I learned a lot from your presentation!
>
> Speaking with you has been a tremendous pleasure!

Of course, you don't want to lie, but if you can find a reason to commend, do so!

If you meet someone who offers a valuable service or product, refer people to them! This is one of the most generous things you can do because it has a direct impact on their bottom line. It's also the thing most likely to garner their appreciation and recip-rocation.

Follow Up

Networking is about more than meeting new people. Even if you make a great first impression, you still need to follow up!

To help you do this, pick one or two things that are unique about each person you meet. Make a quick note on the back of the person's business card or in your PDA once you walk away. It could be a skill, hobby, or topic you discussed—anything you can remember the contact by. Later, when you follow up, you'll have something to refer back to.

Make it a point to follow up on every lead, even if it seems minor. Your follow-up doesn't have to be detailed or time consuming. It could be something as simple as a personal note with your website address that says, "I enjoyed meeting you at the con-ference; let's make sure we keep in touch." If you promised to do or send something, deliver on your commitment as quickly as possible!

If you can establish a connection beyond your initial meeting by inviting someone to an event, a meal, or a special presentation, then you're really cooking! Obviously you won't be able to do this with everyone, but if you sniff out a great lead, don't hesitate!

Heads Up!

Generic mass marketing isn't the same as personalized follow-up. If you subscribe people to your newsletter without their permission, they're more likely to be annoyed than impressed.

If you use mass marketing to stay in touch with your contacts, make a personal follow-up before you add them to your list. You should also mention your intent to do so and give them a chance to opt out.

Maintain Your Network

So you meet lots of people and follow up with them. Now what? Like a freshly planted seed without water, an unattended network will die! You've got to keep your network alive!

First, you need to know your network. Who's in it? What are their interests, hobbies, and professions? If you don't know such things, how can you refer people, forward relevant news, or ask for advice? Don't think of your network as a vague sea of professionals; think of it as an intimate group of colleagues you want to see succeed. This way, when someone says, "Know any good CPAs?" you can say, "As a matter of fact, I do!"

Look for opportunities to use your network every day! Have a puzzling dilemma? Looking for a new employee? Trying to find a job? Come across something interesting? All of these present you with a chance to reach out to your network.

Best Practice

Print your blog and social-networking site URLs on the back of your business card. If someone is part of the same network as you, this makes connecting a snap. It can also help you establish common ground.

Once you put your mind to networking, you need a reliable contact management system! I highly recommend using a PDA or Smartphone and backing it up regularly. You can even sync with Microsoft Outlook or other contact management software on your computer. It doesn't matter if you use a Rolodex and handwritten note cards, or LinkedIn and micro blogging, just stay in touch!

Over time, as you follow up, people form an opinion of you. They draw conclusions about what type of person you are, what you're good at, and what you're not so good at. The way others perceive you can also be called your brand. What is your personal brand? How can you develop a brand that draws others? These questions are the subject of our next chapter.

The Least You Need to Know

- Building a network is an excellent investment in your future and is a habit of successful people.

- Talk to people everywhere you go and give out as many business cards as possible.

- Strengthening relationships with your existing connections is the easiest place to start networking.

- Networking online isn't about how many connections you have, but rather the quality of those connections.

- The best networkers are generous with their time and freely share information.

- Keep your network alive with regular and frequent contact.

Chapter 13

Build Your Brand

In This Chapter

- ◆ Packaging yourself
- ◆ Shaping how others perceive you
- ◆ Getting recognized
- ◆ Reinforcing and refining your brand

Branding is everywhere! It's on buses, billboards, watches, shoes, hats, pens, and pencils. It's also on cell phones, staplers, bottled water, bread, and butter. It's on the company you work for, the car you drive, and the clothes you wear. Take note of almost any item around, and you'll find that it's brandishing someone's unique name or logo.

Why do businesses spend so much time and money developing their brands? Because branding works!

But how can you brand yourself? How can you develop a unique identity that enhances your value? You aren't a business entity after all. You're a person, made of flesh and blood. You aren't a product to be shamelessly marketed … or are you?

Brand "You"

If I say the name McDonalds, what do you think of? Probably hundreds, if not thousands, of things. If you go to McDonalds for lunch, what do you expect? Ever imagine for a second that fries might not be on the menu? That the arches might not be yellow? That the Big Mac might not come with special sauce and a sesame seed bun? Of course not! You know exactly what to expect because you know the McDonalds brand.

When it comes to personal branding, you are the developer, the manufacturer, the supplier, and the servicer. You are the brand, and you are the product! Your brand isn't your title, and it isn't your job description. It's the sum total of you as a person, and how others perceive that person. Having a desirable personal brand helps you …

- Gain recognition.

- Exert influence.

- Establish your value.

- Become known as an expert.

- Achieve business success.

So what's your brand? What experience do you deliver? When people say your name, what comes to their mind?

Create Your Brand

Whether you're aware of it or not, you already have a personal brand. People perceive you a certain way, good or bad. The questions you need to ask are: Does my brand convey the best image possible? Is my brand contributing toward my success? Am I promoting my brand?

If you can make yourself known as the best, smartest, fastest, funniest (pick an adjective) in a particular area, you have captured the essence of branding.

It shouldn't be hard to identify your brand because you already know yourself. Think for a minute about what makes you unique. What is your greatest strength? Your greatest skill? What have you accomplished that you can really brag about? Let your mind wander, and write everything down.

Now come up with a list of words that describe you. Are you witty, smart, energetic, funny, strong, confident, resilient, resourceful, assertive, or creative? Ask friends and family members for words they think describe you and start another list. Then compare both lists and look for common denominators. You might even find the way you perceive yourself is different from the way others perceive you.

Best Practice

To ensure your personal brand is consistent, condense it to three adjectives or personal attributes, such as creative-confident-reliable, or bold-resourceful-energetic. Once you know what your brand attributes are, you can measure everything you do against them.

Form your brand attributes and accomplishments into a story that reinforces the image you want to project. You can read my personal biography on the inside back cover of this book for an example. Having a personal story/bio comes in handy for introducing yourself to prospective employers and showcasing yourself on blogs and online communities.

Think of your brand like a side business—a concurrent career. Just because you work at ABC, Inc., doesn't mean you can't be president of You, Inc., at the same time. Pick colors for your brand. Pick fonts for your brand. Find a couple nice photos of yourself (your product) or have some taken. Use the same design elements across multiple channels to create an impression.

Heads Up!

It's important to develop your brand thoroughly before you start promoting it. If you promote yourself as one thing and then suddenly change directions, you send the message you are inconsistent.

The elements of a successful brand are B.R.A.N.D.:

- **Behavioral** Attitude, values, goals, and actions
- **Reliable** Consistency; the same thing every time
- **Appealing** Dress, grooming, general appearance, and attractiveness
- **Noteworthy** Achievements, talents, and abilities worthy of recognition
- **Differentiable** Unique value to your intended audience; makes you different from others

Forming a unique identity sets you apart from your competition (other capable young professionals). Instead of competing to sell the most widgets, you're competing to sell yourself. And when you're a little fish in a giant worker sea, getting employers, hiring managers, and recruiters to notice you can be a major challenge. Creating a memorable and unique identity helps you get ahead.

By the time your brand is developed, you should be completely focused on what *you* have to offer. You should be able to communicate what *you* can do that provides measurable value. You should know exactly what *you* want! Your brand should excite you and motivate you! After all, your brand is *you!*

Display Your Brand

Don't let your brand go to waste. Use it to claim your own piece of headspace next to Starbucks, Apple, and Nike! Get out there and sell your brand to the public!

Consider all the media channels at your disposal. Do you have a personal website? A blog? An online resumé? Do you freelance on the side? Do you write a newsletter? Do you contribute articles or opinions to local newspapers or magazines? Do you teach? Volunteer? Are you visible in any way? When you promote yourself through multiple channels, it provides you with a serious competitive edge!

You might be thinking this isn't your cup of tea, that it doesn't interest you. But let me ask you this: Do you want to be included among the best in your field? Because this is what the best are doing. They're out there getting quoted, and interviewed, and offered great opportunities—all because they're visible!

What makes certain actors, actresses, reporters, and sports figures into household names? Their unrelenting conspicuousness! We see their names and faces so many times we can't forget them.

I'm not telling you to be successful in business you have to make yourself famous. I'm just saying you need to be visible to your intended audience. If your goal is to become an independent financial advisor, you could produce a weekly market commentary. If your goal is to become a CPA, you could blog about tax law changes. If your goal is to become a chef, you could share great recipes.

When you consistently showcase your brand and deliver value, your audience will find you. They'll also remember you, which is precisely where personal branding starts to provide a return on investment. Suddenly you find people start coming to you for advice, with business opportunities, and with job offers. Eventually, you'll never have to knock on another door—because everyone is knocking on yours!

Best Practice _____

You don't have to write a syndicated blog for _The Wall Street Journal_ or make an appearance on the _Today Show_ to effectively promote your brand. Start by looking for opportunities in your own community. Not only will such local appearances help you stand out from your local competition, but they will also help you refine and develop your brand for a larger audience.

Reinforce Your Brand

Each avenue you use to promote your brand should reinforce its unique attributes and style. Can you imagine Ben & Jerry's Ice Cream producing a flavor called Vanilla? No way! Their brand is all about "euphoric concoctions." It even says so in their mission statement. So if one of your brand attributes is "energetic," don't choose gray as the primary color for your website!

From your business cards (yes, you should have personal business cards), to your blog, to your resumé—everything should reinforce your brand. Imagine if you could take each remnant of your professional life and lay it on a table. Would everything look like it belongs together? It should. Each individual piece, though separate, should deliver the same substance and the same style. The style of _you!_

Remember, your brand is only as good as people perceive it to be. If you try to send the message you are reliable, but you don't return phone calls, your brand won't resonate. Everything you do either contributes toward, or takes away from, your brand's reputation. Phone calls, e-mails, blog posts, micro-blog posts, meetings, introductions, and attire—everything counts!

Actively reinforce your brand through your network of friends, clients, and colleagues. Their word-of-mouth advertising keeps your brand alive and thriving. Make sure they never forget you are an expert, a leader, and a visionary in your field.

Evolve Your Brand

Personal branding is an ongoing process. Like any successful business, your brand needs to improve with time. Every few months, take a hard look at the management, the product, the distribution, and the presentation of You, Inc. Ask others for feedback to help you evaluate your brand's quality and then listen to them.

As you overcome new challenges, gain experience, and grow emotionally, your brand needs to be refined. Putting forth the effort to do this holds the attention of your audience, keeps your message unique, and forces your professional growth.

The Least You Need to Know

- Your brand should be unique and capture the essence of your personality.

- Come up with three specific brand attributes and measure everything you do against them.

- Think of developing your brand like a side business—a concurrent career.

- Use every media channel at your disposal to promote your brand and establish yourself as an expert.

- Everything you do should reinforce your brand.

- Use life experiences and feedback from others to refine your brand over time.

Part 4

The Leader Inside You

To accomplish great things in business, you need to duplicate your efforts. Instead of relying solely on your own ability, you need capable people supporting you and helping make your dreams a reality. Leading others is no easy task though, especially when you're young!

And while becoming an effective leader should be your goal, becoming an effective manager is also important. That's right, leading and managing are two different things. Both are important to your success, and both are discussed in this part. We also review the unique challenges that first-time managers face, teach you how to leverage the power of teamwork, and how to demand the respect you deserve. Let's get started!

"Hey, let's all spend the rest of the day using our computers only for office business! Who's with me?!"

Chapter 14

Be It Before You've Been It

In This Chapter

- ◆ Committing to personal growth
- ◆ Becoming the expert
- ◆ Running in the right circles
- ◆ Exuding confidence

I was an entry-level worker making $8 an hour and dying to be promoted. When I approached a member of senior management to inquire about my eligibility for a position that had opened up, he responded with something I'll never forget. In his usual authoritative tone, and without hesitation, he said, "Robert, you're a good worker. But if you want to be a manager, you need to start acting like one."

The more I pondered what he said, the more I came to the realization I was totally ill-equipped to fill the position I desired. I lacked leadership skills, I lacked expertise, and I lacked confidence. If I had been ready for the position, I wouldn't have needed to ask for it because it would already have been offered to me.

This chapter keeps you from making the same mistake I did. It teaches you how to think and act like the person you want to become before you become it.

A View from the Other Side

Whether or not to promote someone is a tough decision! The world is full of great salespeople who failed as sales managers, great administrators who failed as office managers, and great designers who failed as creative directors.

Promoting someone to a position of greater responsibility is always a risk. Just because someone is great at their current job doesn't mean he'll be great at their next job.

Let's say you're an administrative assistant who would like to be promoted to office manager. If management is considering you for such a promotion, these are some of the questions they're likely to be asking:

◆ Are you excelling in your current position?

◆ Do you demonstrate an understanding of important company issues and initiatives?

◆ Are you a problem solver, or do you always need help from others?

◆ Do you possess the skills required to do the (next) job?

◆ How well do you interact with other employees and managers?

I can't even count the number of employees who have come to me after I've placed an ad for a position and asked why I didn't consider them. In almost every case, I had considered them, but where they felt they qualified, I knew they didn't. Why the difference in perspective? Because they were only thinking about the first question listed previously.

"But aren't I doing a good job?" they would say.

"Yes" I would tell them. "But there's more to it than that."

And so the cycle would repeat itself. Time and again I've found myself having the same conversation with my employees that my old manager had with me.

The last thing your superiors want is to promote you and then watch you fail. Minimize their perception of risk by showing them you can do your current job, and at the same time, are prepared to move to the next job. This is the fundamental nature of being considered "promotable."

Commit to Growth

Great leaders invest time and energy into helping their subordinates grow professionally. Unfortunately, most people don't work for great leaders. More often than not, management is disinterested in the ambitions of employees in their care. To experience continual professional advancement, you have to take charge of your own internal growth process.

Introspection

After you set your sights on what you want—be it a management position or otherwise—you need to do some serious self-reflection.

Compare yourself with people who are already doing what you aspire to do. What makes them different from you? Are they more committed? More educated? More assertive? More anything? Think hard and be honest with yourself. What is standing between you and your goals? Try to make a list.

When you finish, take a hard look at the list you've just created. How many things are on it that you could already be doing but aren't? Are there things you don't know how to do but could learn on your own? If you can answer "yes" to either of these questions, you aren't doing enough.

Heads Up!

Sometimes, a lack of professional growth can be attributed to surroundings more than actions. If you work for a small company with no advancement options or for a person who insists on keeping you down despite your qualifications, you may need to pursue other employment.

Knowing vs. Doing

Almost every day, I meet smart people with tremendous potential and a wealth of knowledge, but no drive. I recently talked with an old high school buddy who apologetically told me what he did for a living and then said, "I guess I've just been career lazy."

So often, our tendency can be to sit idly by and wait for opportunities to come to us. Then, in what seems like an instant, years have passed and we've gotten nowhere. To help you turn your good intentions into positive actions, remember the following.

- Knowledge alone won't bring success.
- Talking about something won't make it happen.

- Deciding to do something isn't the same as acting on it.
- Planning to do something isn't the same as acting on it.
- The potential for failure is real but shouldn't prevent you from taking action.

Best Practice _____

For help finding your internal motivation and setting the right goals, see Chapter 2.

Successful business people don't procrastinate. They figure out exactly what they need to do, and they do it!

Intrapreneurship

Long before you have your own business or run a piece of someone else's, you should already be displaying the behaviors of an entrepreneur. You should be running your job like it's your own business! This is the essence of _intrapreneurship_.

If you're seeing this word for the first time, you probably think it's misspelled. I assure you, however, it is spelled correctly.

Intrapreneurs possess a number of important qualities:

They try until they succeed. Business owners can't afford to give up when confronted with problems.

In like manner, intrapreneurs are resourceful. They remember their value will be enhanced if they solve problems on their own. Their proactive approach shows management they are capable of operating independently and are worthy of greater responsibility.

They learn constantly. Entrepreneurs realize little mistakes can cause big problems. They also realize if they want to stay ahead of their competition, it will require a program of ongoing business development.

Intrapreneurs likewise face stiff competition. They face it from co-workers on the inside and fresh talent on the outside. They know if they want to keep their job, they must have an edge. They learn from their mistakes and avoid making the same ones twice. They stay up to speed with industry trends. They keep their skills sharp.

They conserve resources. Business owners tend to watch dollars and cents closely because it directly impacts their pocketbook.

Intrapreneurs similarly conserve resources. They avoid unnecessary spending and waste while helping their co-workers do the same. By being good stewards of the assets entrusted to their care, they show they look out for their employers' interests— a quality that procures favor from higher-ups.

They hold themselves accountable. Self-discipline is a vital attribute of most entre-preneurs. If they don't take responsibility for results, their businesses fail.

Intrapreneurs don't need constant supervision to do their job either. In fact, they're better off without it. Gradually, this motivates their boss to give them greater and greater responsibility. After a person has been given a certain degree of latitude, the next logical step is promotion.

They keep their clients happy. Without customers, businesses fail. Entrepreneurs know this and work hard to keep their regulars happy.

Intrapreneurs have customers, too. Their customers are their immediate supervisors or the departments they answer to. They always strive to fulfill any reasonable request that is made of them and provide unflinching support and service. This ensures their boss and co-workers speak highly of them, which makes them likely candidates for better positions.

They improve efficiency. Like a business that brings constant innovation to its cus-tomers, the intrapreneur is always seeking a way to do things better, faster, and more reliably.

They generate a return on investment. Businesses always hope the difference between their income and their expenses will be a profit. Over time, a business that's not profitable fails.

In a similar way, intrapreneurs regularly compare the quantity and quality of their work with what they cost their company. On their figurative balance sheet, they measure whether they are an asset or a liability and ensure they are providing their company with value. This makes their jobs very secure.

 Heads Up!

As an intrapreneur, you still have to operate within set policies and procedures as they relate to scheduling, company protocol, and so on. You also need to adopt the same goals and objectives as your company leadership to ensure you're pro-moting their interests. To do oth-erwise would harm your career rather than help it.

Being an intrapreneur makes you promotable. It also demonstrates that, given extra responsibility, you'll shoulder it superbly.

Are you an intrapreneur?

Management Material

By the time I was promoted to my first management position, I knew more about the inner workings of our company than my immediate supervisor. To this day, each promotion or job offer I have received can be directly attributed to the fact that I was grooming myself for it long before it came along.

Take a look at your co-workers. If your manager was gone tomorrow, which one of them would be the likely replacement? Who seems to be the most qualified? Who knows the most about management's responsibilities? Is there a "number two" person whom people look to for leadership when the manager is away? Who's the guy or girl with all the answers? Is it you?

If senior management is looking to replace someone from within, they generally choose the person who requires the least amount of training.

Just because you don't hold the title of manager or assistant manager, doesn't mean you can't be viewed as one—at least on some level. You can earn expert status by learning everything you can about your job and the jobs of people around you. Take every training class at your disposal. Don't stop until you're the go-to person for everything possible!

Jump at the opportunity to do any task that is normally performed by management. Examples could include passing out paystubs, chairing meetings, writing reports, conveying instructions, or training people. Power and authority are largely products of perception. The more people see you performing management functions, the more they perceive you as management material.

Best Practice

Dressing for success is not out of date. The way you dress is a reflection of your inner person. If you dress slovenly, it tells people your work will be careless and sloppy. If you dress like an executive, people perceive you as an authority figure.

When you emulate the style of your company leadership it becomes easier to join their ranks.

The Company You Keep

The people you associate with influence your thoughts as well as how others view you.

Who do you associate with at work? Are they smart, hard-working, career-minded individuals? Are they highly regarded? Without using any overplayed clichés, let's just say the way people view them is probably the same way they view you. If you want to become a manager, for example, you should socialize with other managers—golf with them, eat lunch with them, be seen with them. (If you're having trouble forming alliances with management, review Chapters 10 through 12.)

The more time you spend with managers, the more you understand about the issues they face, their motivations, and their style of communication. Gradually, human nature causes you to adopt their thinking patterns. If you associate with managers, you begin to think like a manager.

I can personally attest to the power of such influence. When I joined the financial services industry, I thought any salary over six figures was huge. Granted, it's a respectable income, but when you start dealing with people who earn millions of dollars a year, six figures suddenly seems smaller.

When you surround yourself with successful business people, you progressively set your sights on bigger things because you realize how attainable they are. You realize that these people aren't any smarter then you; they just go about things a little differently. You figure out what it takes to walk their walk, you imitate them, and you get the same results. What at one time seemed impossible becomes very possible!

Heads Up!

Just because someone is in management or makes a lot of money doesn't mean they're good company. If you disagree with someone's attitude, habits, or value system, you may still choose to forgo their association.

Confidence Is King

Henry Ford said, "Whether you think you can or think you can't, you're right." If you are confident in your ability to achieve something, you can achieve it! If you doubt your ability, the doubt can lead to complacency and eventually to failure.

Barriers to Confidence

The key to overcoming a lack of confidence is to understand its source. Is it possible your vulnerability has to do with your size, weight, or complexion? Does it stem from your perceived intelligence, your social status, or your family? Do you have irrational fears?

Whatever the case, you must identify the root of the problem! Once self-reflection leads you to its source, your fear decreases. You will also be able to face your problem head on, which is essential to defeating it.

Remember everyone has weaknesses. *Everyone*. What you should do is focus on your strengths! Identify them and then assert yourself in matters where you feel confident first. What so often happens is we allow our weaknesses (or perceived weaknesses) to keep our strengths concealed. Don't let this happen to you!

Become Confident

Studies have shown we can change our feelings by changing our behavior. As we discussed earlier in the book, if we smile a lot, we actually feel happier! And that's just one example.

To help you increase your level of self-confidence, try the following:

- **Plan.** By planning each day in advance you avoid wasting time, forgetting things, and making mistakes that embarrass you and undermine your level of self-confidence.

- **Exercise and get plenty of rest!** Both of these things make you feel better. They also make you look better, which is a confidence booster.

- **Spread positive energy.** If you're nice to people, and compliment them regularly, they do the same for you, thus increasing your confidence.

- **Think in the third person.** Okay, I know this one sounds weird, but it actually works! If you tend to be more forgiving of others than you are of yourself, try looking at yourself from an outsider's point of view. Celebrate your own positive traits and accomplishments just as you would if they were someone else's.

- **Practice self-praise.** Instead of allowing your mind to dwell on negative thoughts, expel them with praise and commendation. Think about things you've recently done well and remind yourself, "I'm really great at …" or "I nailed that meeting yesterday when I …"

◆ **Dream.** Picture yourself speaking up, speaking out, and getting results! The more you can visualize yourself achieving something, whatever it is, the more your confidence that you can achieve it grows!

While not making you confident, here are some tricks to help you appear confident when you may actually be shaking in your boots.

Before interactions, try these tips:

◆ Take a deep breath and let it out.

◆ Clinch your toes inside your shoes.

◆ Shake out all your limbs.

◆ Splash cold water on your face.

◆ Find a quiet, well-insulated place to yell. (I recommend this as a last resort.)

During interactions:

◆ Keep your chin up and shoulders back.

◆ Maintain eye contact, nod, and smile a lot.

◆ Keep your comments brief and to the point.

◆ Refer to people by their first names often. This demonstrates confidence and familiarity.

◆ Hold something like a drink in one hand, and put the other hand in your pocket. This keeps you from fidgeting.

◆ If you have sweaty palms, dry your hands before you shake.

Throughout this book, we've discussed ways to display confidence with body language. Ultimately, though, confidence comes from within. People can sense whether or not you believe in yourself. Those who are truly confident sell the most, earn the most, and achieve the greatest business success!

Heads Up!

Be careful with too much self-praise or it can cause you to have an inflated view of yourself. It's critical to balance positive affirmations with recognition of your limitations and shortcomings. To do otherwise would make you cocky rather than confident.

The Least You Need to Know

◆ Make yourself promotable by showing your superiors you can do your current job, and at the same time, are prepared to move to the next job.

◆ To experience continual professional advancement, you have to take charge of your own internal growth process.

◆ Learn everything you can about your job and the jobs of people around you. Become the go-to person for everything possible.

◆ Jump at the opportunity to do any task that is normally performed by management.

◆ The more people see you performing management functions, the more they perceive you as management material.

◆ The key to overcoming a lack of confidence is to understand its source.

The First-Time Manager

In This Chapter

- ◆ Mastering management basics
- ◆ Avoiding new manager pitfalls
- ◆ Creating a culture of teamwork
- ◆ Gaining the confidence of your team
- ◆ Being a captain and coach—not a boss
- ◆ Cultivating relationships with fellow managers

Being a manager for the first time is at once exciting and daunting. You've worked hard, done your job well, earned the respect of those around you, and suddenly, everything changes. Overnight you go from being responsible for your personal results, to being responsible for the results of others. Your duties change. The dynamics of your work relationships change. People even view you differently.

With so many factors shifting, how can you make a smooth transition to the ranks of management? What pitfalls do you need to avoid? How can you build a collaborative team that drives you to greater heights? Let's see.

The Basics

As a manager, your value will be determined by an entirely new set of rules. Instead of being judged based on your personal achievements, you will be judged based on the achievements of your team. And while the elements of good management are many, your top priority should be to earn their respect and confidence. How can this be done?

Take an Interest

Everyone wants to feel appreciated. We all deserve to be acknowledged for our individual traits, opinions, and strengths. When people work for a manager who treats them more like a number than a person, they usually won't be loyal. If you want your employees to support you, you need to *show* them you value their individuality.

Best Practice

Your first weeks in any management position should be spent learning. Get to know each of your staff members individually. Learn how things operate. Find out who does what, where, when, and how. Don't be in a hurry to make changes. Just soak everything up and try to get a feel for things. Document your observations.

The first thing to do is ask for their feedback. If you're rolling out a new procedure, give your staff a chance to look it over and provide their input. If you're trying to decide where to have the company picnic, throw out a few options and let them choose the location. If something isn't running smoothly, ask a key staff member how they would fix the problem.

Take note of each person's motivational "hot buttons." For some, their motivation might be career growth. For others it might be monetary rewards, a flexible schedule, or recognition (see Chapter 2 for more motivators). Pay attention to what gets your staff fired up and then give it to them whenever possible.

Show personal interest by giving consistent training and feedback. Everyone wants to feel they are doing well and growing in their job, so take note of weaknesses and help your employees overcome these. As their effectiveness grows, they will feel better about themselves and better about you.

While not getting overly personal, give attention to your employee's personal lives through courteous, daily interchanges. Learn what their hobbies are, if they have children, and where they go on vacation. By showing this type of interest, good managers communicate that they value their employees as more than just workers.

When unexpected situations arise in the personal lives of your employees, you should make allowances for them as long as your leniency isn't abused. When a good employee makes a reasonable request that doesn't hurt business, why not make a concession? You can't buy the kind of loyalty you'll receive in return.

Daily Communication

I used to have a manager who set an exceptional example in communicating with his employees. Although he was also one of the most demanding people I've ever known, those who worked for him viewed him as approachable and down to earth. Here's why: every day after lunch, he would spend 30 minutes to an hour visiting each department in the company. With a toothpick still in his mouth, this was no formal meeting. It generally consisted of stepping into each office with an ear-to-ear smile and saying something like, "How is everybody today? Looks like you're all working pretty hard in here. Are we making lots of money?"

His informal meetings were nothing more than a chance for him to be friendly with his employees. Sometimes he would inadvertently step into a crisis situation and would stay a little longer to help work through it. I always respected him for his efforts in this regard, and my fellow teammates did, too. His approach really worked!

While walking to an employee's workstation once a day to check on them is good; it's even better to find specific, measurable things such as a neatly completed report, a performance goal that is exceeded, or a diligently handled customer complaint to commend them for. This type of recognition is more motivating than a generic, "Keep up the good work." Admittedly, it can be easy to go about your business until a problem needs to be addressed, but, if you only address problems, you're likely to become known as a tyrant instead of a supportive leader.

Foster an environment of healthy communication by maintaining an open-door policy. Everyone you supervise should feel comfortable approaching you and have a chance to be heard. This goes a long way in earning their respect. If you're not available to assist your employees when they need you, they're apt to grow frustrated. Can you imagine a football coach spending games shut in the locker room instead of on the field?

 Heads Up!

No one expects you to be gregarious and have a sunny disposition all the time. It's equally important to draw attention to errors and other shortcomings as part of a daily routine of communication.

When I was hired into my first executive level position, one of my chief priorities was to gain the respect of our company's workforce. Looking back, one of the best decisions I made was to choose an office situated on the corner of a major junction in the building. The result was every employee had to walk by my office as they were arriving for work, leaving work, walking to the bathroom, or going on a break. For several months, I made it a point to never shut my door unless I was buried in tasks or working on something confidential. This unique location allowed me to say good morning and goodnight to everyone who worked for me, and enabled them to step in my office whenever they had a question or needed to vent. It soon became apparent the personnel viewed me as approachable and ready to lend a hand.

Of course, for healthy communication to thrive, you have to create the right environment.

Productive Working Climate

A farmer decided to grow an apple tree and set about finding the perfect spot. He eventually decided upon a sandy place in the shade and gently pushed one apple seed about an inch and a half into the ground. He patted the sand back into place and began instructing the seed to grow. "Grow into a giant apple tree," he would say, but it wouldn't grow. Each day he would visit the seed and encourage it to sprout with words that gradually became more forceful. "Grow, grow, grow!" he would demand angrily, but it never grew.

Another farmer also decided to grow an apple tree and set about finding the perfect spot. He eventually decided upon a place with rich, black soil and bright, full sun. He dug a small hole about 15 inches deep, placed the seed inside and gently patted the soil back around it. Each day he would visit the seed and water it just the right amount. In a short time and without a word, it sprouted and grew.

This anecdote illustrates the importance of a productive working environment. Just as an apple seed can't be forced to grow into an apple tree, a person can't be forced to grow into a fruitful worker. The motivation to do so has to come from within. The most a manager can do is provide the proper elements to foster growth and remove obstructions to its progress. Just as an apple seed requires rich soil, full sun, and 12 to 18 inches of depth, employees need a manager who is consistent, lively, cool under pressure, and so on. And just as the farmer decides where to plant the apple seed, it's the manager who decides what the climate will be in the area under his supervision. What contributes to a healthy working climate?

If there's one thing that frustrates people, it's inconsistency. Imagine working for someone who is friendly and easygoing one day but harsh and demanding the next. Doubtless you would find it wearisome adapting to their unpredictable mood swings. Workers need to know they can count on their manager to be the same person from day to day.

If you're known for flying off the handle, it's doubtful you'll foster the kind of work environment where people are comfortable and confident. At best, you'll be motivating with a climate of fear. If this is the case, your employees are likely to spend their breaks browsing the Internet for a new job.

Added pressure is par for the course when you're in management. The way you deal with that pressure is what determines the amount of respect you get from your employees. If you start to feel pressure mounting, you can either redirect it at your staff or absorb it and move on. It took me some time to learn the latter is more effective.

At 23 I was already running the marketing division of a large company and directly supervised 13 people ranging in age between 26 and 55. My department was responsible for generating leads that accounted for more than 30 percent of our gross revenue, and when sales would slacken, the pressure on me would mount! In turn, I would call a department meeting and turn up the pressure on all my employees. I figured if I was going to feel the pinch, they were, too. What I failed to realize is instead of being motivated, they interpreted my demands as the arrogant tirades of an immature manager.

Staying calm, cool, and collected instills confidence in others and causes them to look to you for direction when they face pressures of their own.

Don't make the mistake of thinking you have to be serious all the time. Maintain a lively atmosphere that's spotted with humor. Even an occasional joke at your own expense can make you more approachable. If you start to notice a lifeless attitude among your staff, take some time to walk around and make conversation to liven the mood.

The final key to a productive working climate is keeping everyone busy. Busy workers have a greater sense of accomplishment and job satisfaction. This takes some effort, but with a little planning and forethought, it can be done.

Best Practice

Before they leave work, have your employees write down the 10 most important things they need to accomplish the following day and leave it on their desk. After everyone leaves, walk around the office and read the lists. This allows you to see if more tasks need to be added and enables you to keep your finger on the pulse of individual productivity.

New Manager Pitfalls

Newly found authority has a tendency to puff people up. Mix the pressure to perform with a dash of nervous anxiety and you have a cocktail that can lead to trouble. To help you avoid driving people away with your own sense of self-importance, let's consider some common pitfalls of inexperienced managers.

You think you can do everything yourself. The primary function of a manager is to delegate work and then follow up to ensure it gets done properly. It can be hard to delegate when you know you can do the same job better or faster, but to be effective as a manager, you need to let go!

Focus your time on training instead. Work with your employees until they can perform at the same level as you, or they reach their personal best. Your management ability is determined not by the quantity, quality, or reliability of your work, but rather by the quantity, quality, and reliability of your employees' work.

You think you know it all. Just because you possess the title of Manager, doesn't mean you know everything. Ask for input from the people around you. Try to learn from them. You'll likely be surprised by how many good ideas they have. There's no need to make a show of your authority—everyone already knows you're in charge.

You think you have to change everything. Just because something isn't being done *your* way, doesn't mean it's being done the *wrong* way. Learn to tell the difference. Allow some time to pass before you start making changes. Even then, make them gradually and think them through.

 Heads Up!

If your company leadership is unhappy with results and uses you to replace another manager, they are likely to fill your head with ideas about how you need to be a catalyst for change. They may tell you they expect you to "turn things around."

Don't allow such statements to pressure you into making changes too rapidly. You're much better off easing into things and showing company leadership that you are operating strategically. Make it your goal to have things turned around within 90 days. Even if you use the first month to collect information and plan, you'll still have 60 days to implement changes.

You think nothing is your fault. As a manager, you are responsible for *everything* that happens in your realm. If you didn't know about it, you should have. If it's someone else's mistake, you should have caught it. Just as you are praised for the accomplishments of your team, you are also chastised for their blunders. Excuses only make you appear weak.

You think you don't have to stand up for your people. At one time, you may have only worried about yourself, but now you have other people to worry about. Just as arms can accomplish little without hands, you can accomplish little without your people. Is someone pushing for pay cuts in your department? Fight against them. Is someone trying to dump dirty work on your people? Defend them. In so doing, you'll earn their much-needed loyalty.

You think you can't be wrong. Oh yes you can! And often, you are—especially in the beginning. Always admit your mistakes and don't be afraid to laugh at yourself. You're only human after all.

You forget you have a boss. Just because you're *a* boss, doesn't mean you're *the* boss. Don't forget you still have someone to answer to. Make time for that person. Keep them updated on your progress. Ask them for guidance. Make sure they never get blindsided.

You assume problems resolve themselves. As an entry-level worker, you didn't have to address problems when they arose. As a manager, it's your job to. Senior management put you in your position with the confidence you will keep things running smoothly. When operational or employee issues arise, it's your job to figure out the solution and resolve them.

Go Team!

As a young manager, I quickly learned the combined experience of my employees exceeded that which I personally possessed. And while it takes humility to admit this, you will probably find the same is true in your case. If you choose to operate in "I give instructions and you follow directions" mode, you miss out on valuable help your people can provide.

When you create an environment of teamwork, all your employees collaborate to reach common goals. Instead of doing all the organizing, planning, and directing alone, you have a powerful support structure to help you. By empowering your team to make decisions and encouraging them to hold each other accountable for results, you can achieve superior outcomes.

An easy way to illustrate this is with team sports. Can you imagine if individual players had to wait for signals from their coach before they could pass or try to make goals? In a similar way, players on a business team understand the object of their game and have latitude to act in a way that supports their intended outcome.

FYI
The suggestions in this chapter do not elaborate on every detail of how to build a working team. Nor do they refer to constructing a functional team in the fullest sense. What this chapter portrays could more accurately be described as a modified-team approach.

Rather than going to such extremes as wearing matching T-shirts to the company picnic and equally sharing your authority, I suggest you take a *teamlike* approach with your management style.

Involve your staff members in planning and decision-making processes. Create lively group discussions to help resolve problems. Encourage team members to hold one other accountable for results. All of this can be accomplished without relinquishing your rights as a manager.

While the concept of teamwork is far from new, the majority of companies still operate with a traditional top-down management style. Notice the difference between this and a team approach:

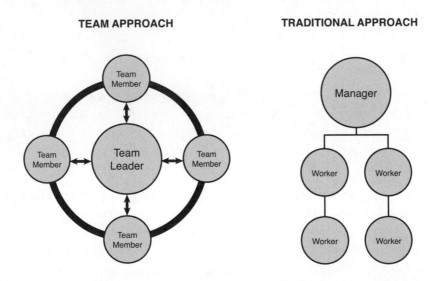

So how can you create a culture of teamwork? There are people who would try to convince you teams result from special retreats where you make Lego buildings, play tug-of-war, and reorganize office furniture. And while team exercises can do some good—like making team members more comfortable with one another—forming a team takes work and strategy.

Group Objectives

Every team needs a common goal. It could be connected with sales, production, service, or anything else. It could be a single thing or made up of many things. Having a shared objective acts like a funnel that keeps everyone moving in the same direction.

Imagine you have two employees who work in purchasing. One thinks the primary goal is to cut costs, while the other thinks the primary goal is to increase quality. Might not the two differ in opinion about what products to buy? This aptly illustrates the need to ensure your whole team understands what is most important.

Individual Expectations

As team leader, it's your job to explain the duties, performance, quality, and time standards that determine each team member's success. Besides the overall team objective, each team member needs his or her unique responsibilities. This is similar to the way a football team shares the goal of making touchdowns, but have different expectations for the quarterback than the wide receiver.

Shared Accountability

There should never be a question among team members about who is responsible for what. Like the wide receiver counts on the quarterback to throw good passes, your employees should count on each other to do their part. In such an environment, you will be required to spend less time counseling employees because they will hold each other accountable.

Best Practice

Peer reviews are a good way for team members to hold one another accountable. At our office, we distribute quarterly, anonymous surveys that require each employee to rate their workmates in six key areas. When the results are compiled, employees with a rating of 90 percent or above receive a bonus.

Shared Consequences and Rewards

Rewards and recognition should be shared right along with reprisals for poor performance. Bonuses and other monetary compensation should be tied to group performance when possible. Team members must be able to see the impact their work is having on the team and the organization as a whole.

Empowerment

For a team to function, its members must be empowered to make decisions about things that affect their work. This requires you to set clear boundaries defining what choices they can and cannot make.

I often tell my employees that as long as they get their work done, they can go about things any way they wish. The boundary I've set is if they make a change affecting other employees or established procedures, they have to discuss it with me first. If you manage a restaurant, for example, you might tell your servers it's acceptable to replace food that is prepared incorrectly, but they need your permission to give away free food or remove charges from someone's bill.

 Heads Up!

Empowerment fails miserably if you second-guess the decisions your employees make or blame them when things go awry. Once you've given your employees a measure of authority, back them up in their decisions. When they make mistakes, use the opportunity to coach them so they'll make better decisions in the future.

Collaboration

Teams are all about sharing information. They are also about giving and getting feedback. The entire team should meet at least weekly. All team members need to be informed about progress, performance, problems, and priorities. They should be encouraged to share any suggestions they have.

Excluding confidential matters, everything should be open for discussion and group problem solving. Such interchanges allow for creative innovations that can improve your business and your results—both of which look good for you as a manager!

Be a Coach, Not a Boss

As a young manager, it's imperative you learn to operate like a coach instead of a boss. Just because you are "the boss" doesn't mean you have to "boss" people around. As we discussed in Chapter 1, there is a good chance it's hard for some of your employees to take direction from you because of your age. Rather than using authority to force them, you should use finesse to motivate them.

Remember, your employees have aspirations of their own. They are not just a means for you to get your job done. The relationship you have with them needs to be mutually beneficial and rewarding.

While not using these words exactly, this is essentially how to align yourself: "I'm here to help this department succeed. I also plan to succeed personally. I would like to help you succeed as well. Here's what you can expect from me. Here's what I expect from you. If you'll help me, I'll help you, and we'll all be successful." Within such a framework, directing and counseling becomes coaching.

Heads Up! _____

As a manager, it's always better to under promise and over deliver. If you make promises but don't fulfill them, you quickly undermine any respect you've earned. Consistency of word and action is paramount to earning the confidence of your team.

All the players on a sports team know their coach wants to win the game. They also know she wants them to become better players. Your employees should essentially view you in the same light—as someone who is going to help them win on a professional level.

Instead of just telling your employees what to do, explain the big picture to them. Enumerate how what you're asking of them relates to their job, your job, their fellow employee's jobs, department goals, and company goals. Show them why doing things a certain way is in their best interests.

Even when things go wrong, your goal should never be to make an employee feel bad. You should show confidence in his or her ability to correct the problem, discuss potential solutions, and create an action plan to prevent further mistakes (see Chapter 17 for more about addressing issues). As individual and team results improve, your employees will begin to sense you are invested in helping them succeed and will be more open to the direction you provide.

FYI

It's easy to think that if you are the only one who knows how to do your job it makes you irreplaceable, but in actuality, it holds you back.

Let's say you head the IT department at your company and the chief technology officer is nearing retirement. You know you're qualified to move into the position when it opens up, but there's nobody in your company that can replace you. Do you think this enhances or hinders your eligibility to assume the position?

If you want to advance professionally, you have to make yourself available by training your replacement. This strategy is in your best interests, and the best interests of your company. It will also come in handy when you call in sick or go on vacation because you'll have someone to look after your responsibilities.

Working With Other Managers

If you're hired as a manager from the outside, people usually acknowledge your qualifications automatically. If you're promoted from within, it can be more difficult to get the respect you deserve.

To understand why this is the case, put yourself in the shoes of those who are now your fellow managers. In all likelihood, they've watched you grow from the ranks of entry-level into the management position you now hold. They had a relationship with the manager you replaced. They know you lack management experience. They may even be jealous of your newly found success.

Overnight, you've gone from their subordinate to their equal and they are being forced to deal with you on a completely different level. Should it be surprising if they show some reluctance to welcome you to their ranks?

Don't expect them to warm up to you overnight. Like all relationships, the ones you have with your fellow managers take time to build. The best thing you can do is show them you are 110 percent dedicated to making a success of your new position. Apply the suggestions in Chapters 9 and 11, and do everything you can to help them when the opportunity arises. You might even try telling them something like this:

> "I wanted to ask a favor of you. As I'm sure you can tell, I'm really excited about this new position and I want to do a great job! I know you have a lot of experience and I admire the things you've accomplished here. What I was wondering is if you would be willing to give me honest feedback whenever you think I need it. Could you do that for me?
>
> I'd also like to know if there is ever a way I can support you—in anything. So please don't hesitate to ask!"

Having such a conversation accomplishes several things. It lets your fellow managers know …

- ◆ You are committed to results.
- ◆ You respect them.
- ◆ You are open to feedback.
- ◆ You are a team player.

It also gets them involved in helping you succeed. Instead of watching you make mistakes from a distance and not saying anything, they know they can approach you with their suggestions. Like quasi mentors, they feel obligated to assist you.

Don't underestimate the power of their experience. Listen attentively as they offer advice. If you disregard them or display an overconfident demeanor, you'll lose their support.

Heads Up! _____

Just because someone has been a manager longer than you doesn't mean they know more than you. So while you should always listen to fellow manager's advice with an open mind, you still need to use good judgment when making decisions. You certainly can't please everyone, and ultimately the responsibility to run your area rests with you.

The Least You Need to Know

◆ Realize as a manager, your value is no longer determined by your personal accomplishments, but rather by what you can accomplish through others.

◆ Take a personal interest in your employees by showing them you value their individual traits, opinions, and strengths.

◆ Look for specific, measurable things to commend your employees for daily.

◆ Don't allow your newly found authority as a manager to puff you up.

◆ Form your employees into a working team by establishing group objectives and shared accountability.

◆ Don't expect your fellow managers to warm up to you immediately, but reach out to them anyway.

Chapter 16

Don't Just Manage—Lead

In This Chapter

 ◆ Managing vs. leading

 ◆ Understanding why leaders go farther, faster

 ◆ Having what it takes to lead

 ◆ Examining 10 traits of effective leaders

To call someone a *manager* refers only to their position; to call someone a *leader* refers to their qualities.

People love to talk about leaders and leadership. People respect leaders. They look up to them. They emulate them. And while many leaders are managers, most managers are not leaders.

Will becoming a leader help you achieve business success? Are people born as leaders, or do they learn to lead? What makes someone a leader? By the time you finish reading this chapter, the answers to these questions will be obvious.

Manager or Leader?

When you hear the word *manager*, what does it call to mind? What about the word *leader*? Do both words evoke the same feelings? They shouldn't. In fact, they have entirely different meanings:

- ◆ **Manager**   A person who is responsible for, or has direction and control over, an activity, an institution, or a group of individuals.

- ◆ **Leader**   One who leads.

So what does it mean to lead? Basically, it means to go first. Dr. Albert Schweitzer said, "example is leadership," and with this statement, he captured the essence of what great leaders do—they set an example. While any decent manager can give directions and hold people accountable, leaders inspire others to follow them with their actions.

Exhibiting the qualities of a leader makes people follow you because they *want* to, not because they feel *obligated* to.

The following table highlights key traits of managers and leaders:

Managers vs. Leaders

Managers	Leaders
Administrate	Create
Obligate people	Inspire people
Focus on procedures	Focus on people
Think short term	Think long term
Accept standards	Raise standards

If you want your employees to be enthusiastic about their work, you have to be enthusiastic about your work. If you expect them to be courteous and helpful to your customers, *you* have to be courteous and helpful to your customers. If you expect them to follow company procedures, you must do the same.

I used to work in an office where the sink was constantly littered with dishes and the microwave was always dirty. Eventually, the office manager got fed up and sent out a memo telling everyone to clean up after themselves. For a while things improved, but instead of picking up after herself like she asked everyone else to do, this particular manager would leave her dirty dishes in the sink for someone else to load in the dishwasher. Her employees quickly caught on to this and reverted back to their old habits. It may be a small example, but the lesson is employees do what they see their manager doing.

As a leader, you must demonstrate a willingness to do whatever you ask your people to do—even if it's dirty work. I hold the position of vice president at an upscale financial planning firm where I wear a suit almost every day. Even so, if I notice the break room trashcan overflowing, I empty it. I'm certainly not required to, but I want to set an example worthy of imitation. I know if our employees see me taking out the trash, they will take out the trash, too.

If there's extra work to be done, help your team out. It shouldn't matter if it's in your job description. They will appreciate your assistance and you will earn their respect.

Working alongside them will also give you an opportunity to train them. Instead of *telling* them to work faster, you will be *showing* them how to work faster. Instead of *telling* them to get organized, you will be *showing* them how to get organized.

Heads Up!

To lead doesn't mean to take over. The last thing you want is to start doing your employees' jobs for them. Your objective should be to set an example and then encourage them to pick up where you leave off. If you bail them out of every situation, they'll never learn to be self-sufficient.

If you are currently in a management position, ask yourself: Do I expect more out of my employees than I expect out of myself? Do I set the best possible example for them to follow? Am I willing to do the things I ask my people to do? Don't be surprised if your honest answers reveal some areas you need to work on.

A Key to Business Success

Henry Ford, Walt Disney, Steve Jobs, Sam Walton—all leaders! What do they have in common? They did something unique, something people had never seen before.

It's only when you stand out that you achieve extraordinary business success. You need to be at the forefront of developing creative ideas, questioning the status quo, and helping others succeed. When you are, you build a tremendous following. It's the power of this following that drives your success.

Think about what happens when someone sees you doing something attention-grabbing and then begins to imitate you. Suddenly you have two people doing something attention-grabbing. Then, someone new sees what the two of you are doing and joins in. Now you have three people doing something attention-grabbing. From there, word spreads fast, and the power of your influence compounds! Such influence allows you to accomplish more than you can on your own because you have a loyal following of people imitating your example. This is how great leaders build great companies!

When you use your leadership ability as a force for positive change, your company and your employees will benefit. They will see you are trying to help them and they will want to help you in turn. They will be drawn to you. They will be loyal to you. They will even want to befriend you.

The ability to lead is a skill you can take anywhere. It prepares you for positions of greater responsibility and it never goes out of style!

FYI

Have you ever heard someone referred to as a "born leader"? If so, you should know this statement is misleading. While it's true certain personality traits—which may or may not be genetically predetermined—can contribute toward your ability to lead, it takes more than that.

Leaders are born from experience! It's the ability to adapt your personality, approach, beliefs, and skills that determine whether or not you become a leader.

Ten Traits of Leaders

If you understand what makes a great leader, you can condition yourself to develop those traits. You can *choose* to become a leader! What qualities are common to most leaders? Let's consider 10 of them. Leaders …

1. **Behave ethically.** Simply put, to behave ethically refers to doing what is right instead of what is wrong—to being morally responsible and honest in your dealings. A reputation for acting honestly convinces others to place their trust in you. Leaders make earning trust a priority! They also expect other people to deal honestly with them (see Chapter 23 for more on ethics).

2. **Are consistent.** Rather than saying one thing and doing another, leaders live the values they promote. If you aren't taking your own advice, people assume it's not worth much.

3. **Are responsible.** Leaders take responsibility for their actions. They admit when they're wrong, and they share blame when necessary. Rather than repeat mistakes, they use them as opportunities to learn and improve. To do this requires humility.

4. **Show compassion.** Compassion manifests itself in a number of ways, but basically it means to be attentive to the needs of others. Leaders treat others the way they want to be treated. They listen to their suggestions and recognize their accomplishments. They strive to help them grow and to make them feel important. They show a personal interest in their welfare. When relationships are strained, they find ways to diffuse tension.

5. **Celebrate success.** Leaders recognize even little accomplishments are worth celebrating. They share their enthusiasm for success with others and they show appreciation for the good things their supporters do.

6. **Take action.** When it comes to decision-making, leaders don't waste time. They immediately get involved in challenging situations and work to find solutions. They aren't afraid to take calculated risks if there is likelihood the outcome will be desirable. They always stay close to the center of the action.

7. **Have vision and passion.** Rather than focusing on the present, leaders look toward the future. They have good imaginations and a questioning mind. Their spirit of adventure motivates them to seek out new and better ways of doing things. They never live in the past. The more they visualize the future, the more their passion for it grows. This passion moves them to be jubilant and convincing, which, in turn, inspires others.

8. **Communicate openly.** Leaders are generally strong communicators. Even when they could potentially hurt someone's feelings, they are open when giving advice and criticism. They actively share their vision with others and try to help people see things their way.

9. **Are determined.** Leaders never quit. Once they fix their sights on what they want, they drive for it tirelessly. Even when things go wrong, they show a thick skin and stay positive in thought and speech. They believe in themselves and their ability to achieve what they set out for. Because of this, they tend to have a competitive nature.

10. **Are willing to be different.** Leaders are true to themselves and their vision even when it's unpopular. Rather than adapt to the whims of others, they are steadfast in their convictions. This makes them visible and is inspiring to onlookers.

Numerous psychological studies have been performed to identify various leadership styles. Among these are authoritarian, participative, delegative, bureaucratic, and charismatic.

Without getting bogged down with a discussion on varying leadership styles (that's another book altogether), it's better to appreciate that each leader develops his or her own unique leadership style. Leaders have even been known to use multiple leadership styles depending on what a situation calls for.

It is worthy of mention, however, that the traits described in this and the preceding chapter are characteristic of a participative leadership style. This style is generally accepted to be the most effective because it encourages group participation, decision-making, and innovation, but leaves final say with the leader.

Take a look at the preceding list and ask yourself: Which of these traits do I possess? Which ones do I lack? Which ones can I cultivate more fully? There's no hard and fast rule saying you can't lead without these specific traits. The main thing to remember is becoming a leader is an ongoing process involving these steps:

1. Identify the traits of other leaders.

2. Seek to develop those traits in yourself.

3. Become a leader over time.

If you don't think you're ready for leadership, understand you don't have to change the world to be considered a leader. You can be a leader on a small scale just by speaking out, making suggestions to improve things, or persisting in your views even when they're unpopular.

Everytime you're the first one to stand up for something you believe in, you're leading. Everytime you change the tone of a negative conversation by saying something positive, you're leading. And everytime you make one of your dreams happen, you're leading! So, can you become a leader? Yes, you can!

The Least You Need to Know

◆ To call someone a manager refers only to their position; to call someone a leader refers to their qualities.

◆ As a leader, you must be willing to do whatever you ask your supporters to do.

- To lead doesn't mean to take over. If you bail your supporters out of every problem they face, they never learn to be self-sufficient.

- Leaders aren't afraid of being different.

- There's no such thing as a "born" leader. Leadership qualities are developed over time.

- You don't have to change the world to be a leader.

Dealing With Disrespect

In This Chapter

- Dealing with difficult subordinates
- Diffusing tense peer relationships
- Commanding respect from your superiors
- How to speak softly and carry a big stick

Everything we've discussed in this book has assumed if you do the right things and exhibit the traits of a leader, people give you the respect and acknowledgement you deserve. Unfortunately this isn't always the case.

There are going to be times when your employees challenge you, your peers disregard you, and your boss railroads you. When such situations arise, your success may depend on your ability to demand the respect you're entitled to.

Among other things, this chapter shows you how to handle confrontation, command respect, and hold others accountable.

Subordinates

Dealing with difficult employees can be a formidable challenge. When tensions are high, it's easy to lash out at inappropriate behavior, or worse yet, ignore it.

As a manager, you have no choice but to calmly and firmly address personnel problems. If you shy away from this responsibility, you won't reach your goals.

FYI

If you apply the suggestions found in Chapters 9, 10, 11, 15, and 16, you are likely to be well respected. In most cases, the respect you receive correlates directly with the respect you deserve. It also is connected with the respect you show others.

The advice in this chapter is designed to help you in situations where you receive treatment that is unwarranted.

Prepare Your Mind

All forms of insubordination and disrespect are totally unacceptable. Once you believe this, you won't be inclined to let incidents slide. Be determined to enforce your disciplinary policy consistently and fairly.

Disregard your desire to be popular. It's more important to be respected than it is to be liked. You can be more objective and firm with your discipline when you aren't worried about damaging friendships or sullying your "nice guy" reputation. Remember, you're the coach, and you have the right to demand the best from your players!

Best Practice

If you notice a regular pattern of insubordination or noncompliance from your employees, take a hard look at yourself to ensure it's not warranted.

Before any problems arise, decide you're going to keep your cool when they do. Emotional outbursts are never productive, and as a manager, you set the standards. If you throw tantrums, your employees will, too. By keeping your composure regardless of what others do, you send a powerful message that you are in control.

Make It Private

If your employees challenge you in public, take them somewhere private to preserve their dignity as well as your own. This prevents them from trying to involve others in the dispute or from arguing just to save face. The last thing you want is a staff vs. management free-for-all.

All you have to do is say something like, "This isn't the right place to discuss this, why don't we talk in the conference room?"

If they still want to make an issue, calmly but firmly say, "Come with me" and start walking in the other direction. Regardless of how they respond, maintain a controlled demeanor. If they become loud or irate, simply restate your request until they comply or until you excuse them for the day.

Once you have the instigator alone, you still need to maintain your composure. Just because you have them behind closed doors, doesn't mean you can fire back. Attacking them only causes the problem to escalate until someone storms off. Remember your job is to solve the problem, not make it worse.

If they won't calm down and discuss the matter in a professional way, send them on a break. Say something like, "I'd really like to discuss this matter with you, but I'm not going to do it while you're worked up. Why don't you go take a break, meet me back here in 15 minutes, and we'll discuss it then."

Isolated Incidents

Before you address specifics, give the difficult employee an opportunity to vent. This can be difficult to do when you know they're out of line, but you get better results by letting them talk first. Otherwise, instead of listening to you, they'll be preoccupied with their own argument. Send the message you are supportive but serious at the same time.

Heads Up!

Before you take the liberty of counseling an employee, make sure you have a thorough understanding of your company's disciplinary policy.

You may be required to document the incident a certain way, or have another person present while counseling them. The employee may even have a history you don't know about.

If you fail to handle the situation properly, you could get yourself in trouble, or even get your company caught up in legal issues.

The manner in which you address a behavioral problem should be determined by a number of factors. First, ask yourself whether it is a first or a repeat offense. Did it stem from a brief lapse in judgment, or was it something more serious? Are you dealing with a generally good employee or a habitual offender?

If you decide it's just a minor issue, you may be able to handle it with a verbal warning. You could say something as simple as, "Overall, I think you're a good employee, but this kind of behavior is totally unacceptable. If you ever lash out like that again, I'll have no choice but to handle it more firmly. Do we understand each other?" You don't need to say this in an aggressive way; you just need to say it with conviction.

Focus on the issue itself and not the person. Refer to "this kind of behavior" or "this incident" rather than "you're *this*," or "you're *that*."

Once you've given someone a verbal warning, let the matter go. Don't rehash it, and don't hold a grudge. Immediately go back to treating them the same as other employees; this helps you maintain a productive working relationship and sends a message to everyone else that you are reasonable.

Anything beyond an isolated incident should be reported to your manager or HR department. Repeat offenders require firmer corrections, such as written warnings, suspensions, or even termination. A verbal warning only carries weight when you follow it up with something stronger the second time.

Repeat Offenders

When it comes to second and third offenses, you need to formalize your meetings. You may even consider having an uninvolved third party sit in as a witness. Even if your company has no written disciplinary policy, take good notes and keep your own file. This is essential in case the incident ever leads to legal action.

When someone acts inappropriately on multiple occasions, you need to consider their motives. Are they acting this way because it usually gets them what they want? Is it because they are unhappy in their job? Is it because you don't have a formal procedure for airing grievances?

Best Practice _____

By maintaining an open-door policy as we discussed in Chapter 15, you can avoid most incidents because minor grumbles are addressed before they become larger issues.

Getting to the root of the matter is important, but you need to be on guard you don't let it cloud the bigger issue—the employee's unsuitable behavior. Don't let someone confuse you with circular reasoning or by rambling about unrelated topics.

When addressing the behavior, you need to do two things:

1. Reiterate to the employee what you expect, and set a time frame for improvement.

2. Schedule a follow-up meeting to review their progress.

If they continue to manifest the same behavior, terminate them. This may seem harsh, but in actuality, you have no use for people who aren't happy in their jobs or aren't performing well. Ultimately they only consume your time and drag down the morale of other employees. When you deal with trouble makers swiftly and firmly, you show you are someone to be taken seriously.

Fellow Managers

Once you become a manager, you are part of a management team. This means your authority, input, and expertise should be valued among your fellow managers. Sometimes though, well-established managers don't treat younger managers with the respect they deserve because they view them as inexperienced. They may say disrespectful things or be unresponsive to your requests. They may give direction to your employees without talking to you first.

If you are dealing with something similar, talk to the perpetrator about it! Have confidence in your own skills and abilities. Don't be afraid to approach them. You can either avoid the problem—in which case they'll continue to walk all over you—or confront it.

The following suggestions will help you earn the respect of your fellow managers:

- Never be afraid to make suggestions.

- Always participate actively in meetings.

- Formulate well-developed arguments that demonstrate good research and thorough understanding.

- Ask questions about things you aren't familiar with.

- Before you speak, consider your audience and how what you are about to say will affect them.

- Express your opinions and listen to the opinions of others.

> **FYI**
>
> The word "confrontation" gets a bad rap, but confrontations aren't always a bad thing. Sometimes, in fact, they're vital. It's a fear of minor confrontation that often leads to fits of repressed rage and other unreasonable acts. The occasional war of words—when handled responsibly—is necessary to progress.

Forethought

When deciding how to address someone, consider their motives. Are they acting a certain way because they feel threatened or jealous? Do they have an agenda? Are they under pressure? By understanding *why* someone is acting a certain way, you are able to make your arguments more persuasive.

Consider your own motives, too. Are you simply reacting because your pride is wounded? Are you concerned about the welfare of your customers? Your company? Your employees? Before you take time out of your day and someone else's, make sure you're not overreacting to a minor incident. Remember everybody has bad days and lapses in judgment. If you take offense over trivial matters, you'll lose respect instead of gaining it.

Before you approach someone, have the goal of your discussion firmly in mind. Do you hope to get their attention? Change their attitude? Reach an agreement? *Note:* Hearing them say you are right is not a valid objective.

Your Approach

When you approach a fellow manager, do it with a cool head and in a confident way. You might try saying, "I've got something important I need to speak with you about. Do you have a second?"

Once you have their attention, if you start by telling them what you think, you may get your point across, but you're likely to damage the relationship in the process. A better approach is to think in terms of "we," "us," and "ours."

You could say, "I think it's important the two of us work well together. How do you think we're doing at that?"

Did you notice the expressions, "we" and "two of us"? You may have also noticed how it ends with an open ended question that lets them express themselves. In confrontational situations, it's usually better to *ask* than it is to *tell*. Avoid expressing your viewpoint or making requests until you've listened first.

While listening, ask questions like, "What do you think we can do to resolve this?" or "How do you think this is affecting our productivity?" Asking questions that start with "what" and "how" show you are interested in their opinions and make you seem open-minded instead of interrogatory.

After you've done your share of listening, all you need to do is make a firm and reasonable request. You might say, "As I mentioned before, I think it's really important we work as a team. The problem is, I find it difficult to work with you when you undermine me in front of my staff. I respect you as a fellow manager, and I would never do that to you, so all I ask is you show me the same consideration. Can you do that for me?" (See Chapter 11 under the heading "Assert Yourself" for more on this subject.)

If this approach works, you'll probably find your relationship starts improving immediately. If it doesn't, keep approaching them until you see results. As a manager you should be able to resolve conflicts on your own. Taking the problem to another manager or to human resources should be your last resort.

Your Superior

Few situations are more uncomfortable than conflicts with your boss. We generally expect our superiors to be helpful, supportive, respectful, and reasonable. When they aren't, it takes courage to confront them. It also takes finesse.

Show Due Respect

If a police officer pulls you over and you immediately start yelling, accusing them of unfair treatment, and calling them names, how do you think it will turn out for you? Doubtless they will use their authority to write you a ticket. On the other hand, if you are calm and respectful, they are more likely to hear you out.

In a similar way, your boss has authority over you. If you become accusatory or boisterous, they'll probably feel forced to use their authority to quiet you. Before you approach your boss, commit to doing so objectively and without anger. Even when wrong, their position entitles them to a measure of respect.

When it comes down to it, your job is to support your boss. Don't be so headstrong or determined to win an argument that you forget this fact. If you win an argument at the expense of your boss's approval, you haven't won anything except problems down the road.

Determine the Approach to Use

After an incident, allow some time to pass so all parties have a chance to calm down. Your boss may even realize his mistake and apologize to you before you have an opportunity to bring it up. When you finally do approach your boss, make sure you do so in private and at an appropriate time.

From the beginning of the meeting, let your boss know you want to support him. Give him the first opportunity to talk by asking a well-chosen question or two. Your introduction could go something like this: "I want you to know my goal is to give you the best support I possibly can. Are you pleased with the job I'm doing?"

This is a powerful opener because it communicates you are eager to please, while at the same time giving him a chance to air any grievances he has with you. If he has a valid complaint, you need to know about it so you can admit your fault in the situation.

Continue by stating your concerns in a calm, matter of fact way, and without pointing fingers. Say something like: "I view this as a professional place to work, and I see myself as a professional. I know I'm not perfect, but I try my best to do a good job for you. When you said _____ to me in front of the entire team, I found it very insulting."

At this point, you'll either get an apology or an excuse. Whichever it is, be willing to compromise. If you take a hard line with your boss, it probably won't benefit you. If he continues to mistreat you, you can bring your concerns to the higher ups, or find a new job.

Is It Legal?

Unlawful harassment is a form of discrimination that violates the Civil Rights Act of 1964. This includes verbal or physical conduct based on race, color, religion, sex, national origin, age, disability, sexual orientation, or retaliation.

For such conduct to constitute harassment, it must be severe enough to create a hostile work environment, or to result in a tangible change in employment status or benefits (i.e., demotion, termination, failure to promote, etc.).

When the unwelcome conduct is based on any of the legally protected characteristics mentioned previously and interferes with an employee's work performance, it is illegal. The victim can be anyone affected by the conduct, not just the person at whom it is directed.

Anti-discrimination laws are not designed to be a code of politeness. Minor teasing, offhand comments, and even foul language do not necessarily constitute harassment. For such conduct to be considered illegal, it must be severe enough to alter the conditions of an individual's employment.

If you are a victim of genuine workplace harassment, you should notify your superiors or human resources department. You can also file a complaint by visiting the Equal Employment Opportunity Commission website at www.eeoc.gov.

You Don't Have to Take It!

"Speak softly and carry a big stick." So said Theodore Roosevelt regarding the way he approached diplomatic relations. When it comes to achieving success in business, such an approach is equally wise. People respect strength. If you never stand up for yourself, you won't be respected.

In the professional world, standing up for yourself doesn't mean fighting or flying off the handle. It means you speak up when people treat you disrespectfully. It means you recognize your worth and aren't afraid to remind people of it. It means you are calm and confident at the same time. Everyone should know you as someone who is friendly and easy to get along with, but at the same time, ready to stand up for yourself when the situation calls for it.

The Least You Need to Know

- Disregard your desire to be popular. It's more important to be respected than it is to be liked.

- By keeping your composure regardless of what others do, you send a powerful message that you are confident and in control.

- Always make confrontations private.

- A verbal warning only carries weight when you follow it up with something stronger the second time.

- Before you approach someone, have the goal of your discussion firmly in mind.

- When confronting your boss, do so in a respectful way and with a calm demeanor.

Part 5

Opportunity Knocks

Do you know someone who seems to be successful at everything they do? Have you ever wondered what makes them that way? In many cases, it's their knack for identifying and creating opportunities.

To achieve business success in your 20s and 30s requires you have a trained eye for spotting profitable opportunities, the courage to take risks, and the determination to create your own opportunities. This part teaches you to do all these things! Related topics include how to know when it's time to change directions in your career, how to succeed at a start-up, and even how to start your own business.

Opportunities are everywhere; you just have to know how to cultivate them!

"Farmer Brown, have you considered wind power?"

Chapter 18

Keep Moving!

In This Chapter

- ◆ Growing your career
- ◆ Understanding growth patterns
- ◆ Keeping your options open
- ◆ Eyeing opportunities
- ◆ Letting go of dead-end jobs

Achieving business success is all about growth. Think of how many words get paired with growth. Personal growth, lateral growth, upward growth, rapid growth. Businesspeople are obsessed with growth—and for good reason! A business that stops growing is quickly overtaken by its ever-growing competition.

Have you heard the expression, "grow or die"? Well, from this day forward you should apply it to your career. Sustaining a measurable growth pattern year after year isn't easy, but it is necessary!

How can you ensure you continue growing professionally? How can you spot worthwhile business opportunities? How can you make a smooth transition from one opportunity to the next? This chapter helps you answer these questions and more.

Grow Up or Grow Out, But Grow

The old days of working 40 years for the same company and retiring with a gold watch and a pension are long gone. This antiquated concept of career growth focused on one thing: moving up. In the new millennium, you have many more options. Up is no longer the only way to grow. You can also grow out, or even down!

Think of your route to business success like a giant web. Instead of climbing a ladder one rung at a time, you have hundreds of little supports running in every possible direction. As you move from one position to another, you broaden your personal and professional skill set. Each move, be it up, down, or across, makes you more valuable to current and future employers.

Lateral

Making a lateral move could be described as accepting a position with a similar level of responsibility and compensation but different duties. Lateral moves give you breadth of experience. They can be made within the same company or between different companies.

Best Practice

To benefit from a lateral move, you don't need to spend an inordinate amount of time in any single position. Your main objective should be to learn needed skills and then move on to other (or bigger) things.

Imagine you work for a company that has three divisions—manufacturing, sales, and service. If you start with an entry level manufacturing position and work your way "up" through that division, you could eventually become the chief manufacturing supervisor. But what if you aspire to lead the entire company? How could you effectively manage a sales or service team if you've never had any sales or service experience?

If, however, you hold entry level or middle management positions with all three divisions, you gain experience that can equip you to run the entire company.

Many people are afraid to accept a new position if it doesn't pay more or have a fancier title. If that new position helps you develop valuable skills though, it could be worth taking. Lateral moves can make you more …

◆ **Marketable.** The more skills you have, the more attractive you will be to potential employers. Even if you are happy with your current job, it pays to keep a well-rounded resumé handy for when the unexpected happens.

♦ **Promotable.** Having more experience and making more contacts within your organization makes you a likely candidate for promotion.

♦ **Secure.** If your company invests time and money on your training and development, you become extremely valuable. Even if your department gets downsized or eliminated, you'll have skills that can be utilized elsewhere.

♦ **Engaged.** When a job gets old, a lateral move can be just the thing to spice it up. If you're tired of the same old tasks or tired of the people you work with, why not move into a different position? You may discover a new passion or, at the very least, realize your company has nothing to offer you and that you need to move on.

Heads Up!

Potential negatives to a lateral move include the perception of others, and the chance of failure.

If your organization has a culture that assumes those who move laterally don't have the ability to get promoted, you may want to avoid this stigma.

Also, when you move laterally, you never know if you'll excel in your new position. You should consider both of these factors before you make a lateral move to ensure it's bringing you closer to your goals rather than farther from them.

Downward

Sometimes, taking a step downward is the only thing that helps you take a step upward. While this strategy is risky, it can also pay off. Although you will likely face the loss of prestige and income, you may be able to bridge an important skill gap.

The rationale behind a downward career move should be one of three things:

1. You have a clear picture of where you want to go in your career and you recognize you can't get there without acquiring the skills that a lower-level position provides.

2. You need special schooling but have so many responsibilities there is no time to pursue it without giving up some of them.

3. You are unhappy and need more time to pursue your passion.

Although you can make such moves at any time during your career, it's better to make them early on. It's much easier to move from the production line to the call center than it is to move from the corner office to the call center because it's not such a big step.

The key to making a downward move successfully lies in planning. You have to know exactly what you want, how to get there, and be single-minded in your career strategy.

Confidence also comes into play when you have to explain your reasons to those who try to discourage you from giving up your highly prized status. To face this psychological challenge successfully, you must be convinced what you are doing is right for your career.

Outward

Next to growing upward, growing outward is the safest way to grow professionally. While you are working to climb the proverbial ladder at one organization, you can be building a second—or even a third—ladder on the side. This way, if one ladder fails, you always have another to grab onto. I call this concept having multiple concurrent careers.

Heads Up!

When pursuing simultaneous careers, be careful not to burn out or lose your balance. If you give so much attention to a side venture that you neglect your primary source of income, you will be doing yourself—and your employer—a disservice.

There are benefits to starting a side business while you are still working for someone else. You have a steady paycheck that keeps you from becoming a starving entrepreneur, and you can use your salary as funding. (For more on how to start your own company and still keep your day job, see Chapter 20.)

Your concurrent career could also consist of pursuing a life-long passion, volunteering, consulting, or even writing a book.

Pursuing multiple career paths helps you broaden your experience, discover your potential, and enhance your credibility.

Keep Growing

Regardless of how you move through the web of business success, your main priority should be to keep growing. How you measure that growth is up to you. Some measure it by the amount of money they make. Others by how much education they acquire. Still others by how much they give back to the community.

To evaluate your level of success, you must have a clear picture of your goals (see Chapter 2). Once you know what your goals are, you will be able gauge how much progress you are making toward reaching them.

Look Past the Trees

When you're laboring every day to make ends meet, it can be easy to lose your vision. Like the old proverb, "He can't see the forest for the trees," our tendency is to get so caught up in our immediate surroundings we forget what we're supposed to be working toward. To combat this snare, there are a couple things you need to do.

Keep Your Options Open

Following the personal branding and networking advice from Chapters 12 and 13 provides you with exposure that can lead to greater and greater opportunities. Studies have shown the majority of six figure positions are filled by word of mouth. If you aren't building a network and creating an online presence, you're missing out on chances to advance your career.

The "keep your options open" mentality is basically a mind-set. Although you may not actively seek new employment, you passively seek it. Being an opportunity seeker motivates you to:

◆ Keep your resumé current and available online at all times.

◆ Maintain a strong social network.

◆ Showcase your skills in the media at every opportunity.

◆ Always be willing to discuss new business opportunities and ventures with others.

◆ Stay focused on the marketplace and look for new areas to capitalize on.

Have an Eye for Opportunity

Whether or not you achieve business success depends much upon how you look at the world. When problems arise, most people do one of two things: they either give up or find a way to overcome. If you have an eye for opportunity though, you'll take things a step farther by developing a universal solution to that problem.

Best Practice _____

Before you decide to pursue a new opportunity or accept a job offer, dedicate time to evaluating it thoroughly. Good questions to ask include:

◆ Have I done everything possible to succeed in my current job? Have I reached my full potential here?

◆ Have I met my prospective boss and co-workers? Do they seem like people I would enjoy working with?

◆ Does the working environment seem like one I will be happy with?

◆ Does the company culture line up with my own values and goals?

◆ Is the pay fair and reasonable? Besides pay, have I evaluated the benefits and perks?

◆ Is the commute manageable?

One example of this can be found in a friend and business associate who spent years in the mortgage industry. When the U.S. housing bubble began to burst in late 2007, his industry suffered and many people lost their jobs. When this happened, he took a look at the resulting problems (rapid rise in foreclosures and empty homes being vandalized) and then developed a unique 24-hour monitoring, detection, and notification system for vacant properties. He started selling his innovative new product to banks, and his business exploded. Instead of being part of a dying industry, he created a dynamic new one!

This is no different than the way Mark Zuckerberg created Facebook to help him stay connected with his friends, or how Ray Croc pioneered the fast food industry with McDonald's in 1954. They both saw an opportunity to fill a need, and they capitalized on it.

Take a look at your industry. Is there a common problem you and your colleagues face? Can you create a solution for it? Can you sell that solution? Even if you aren't currently equipped to start your own business, generating workable solutions makes you valuable to your employer and trains you to think like an opportunist.

Developing an eye for opportunity takes time, and your figurative "eye" has to be trained. Once you start to think this way, though, it's hard to stop. Soon you'll be spotting opportunities everywhere, and your biggest challenge will be deciding which ones to pursue.

Seize the Day!

If you want to keep growing, you must learn to seize opportunities!

Too many people spend too much time waiting for the perfect opportunity to come along—one that is totally safe. When it never does, they assume all the good opportunities must have gone to someone else. They're right! Everytime you pass on an opportunity, know someone else capitalizes on it.

The circumstances surrounding the chance to do something new will never be perfect. There will always be risks involved. So while you should be cautious to a degree, don't let fear and worry hold you back. Each time you grab hold of a new opportunity, you are increasing the likelihood you will achieve something outstanding.

The Politics of Leaving

The ability to spot new opportunities is important, but knowing when to let go of a dead-end job is just as much so! (See Chapter 3 for signs it's time to move on.) How can you move on gracefully and without burning bridges? What do you owe your employer and what do they owe you? It's important to know the answers to these questions.

What You Owe

You may recall from Chapter 1 that we likened your reputation to a painting that develops one brush stroke at a time. If you don't display professional etiquette when quitting a job, it can leave a big, black, blob on your career canvas.

The most important factor in a successful departure is to give adequate notice. In general, two weeks is the standard, but for positions of greater responsibility, as many as four weeks may be expected.

You also need to write a formal resignation letter. This is important because, written properly, it helps you stay on good terms with your old employers. Writing a polished letter can make it easier to get a reference, and also serves as official notice so there is no confusion about your date of departure.

Writing a Resignation Letter

There are a number of ways to write a resignation letter. Some advocate including an explanation. Others suggest expressing regret at leaving. The best way is to be brief, to the point, and express your gratitude along with an offer of support. A good resignation letter looks something like this:

Your Name
Your Address
Your Phone Number

Date

Supervisor Name, Title
Employer Name
Employer Address

Dear Mr. Bossman,

Please accept this letter as formal notification that I am leaving my position as Customer Service Representative on September 20th.

I am grateful for the opportunities I have received at XYZ Corp, and will be pleased to assist you with this transition in any way possible.

Regards,

Robert Sofia

CC Human Resources

After you've given your official notice, it's time for you to really show what you're made of. Do everything in your power to make the transition as smooth as possible for the company you are leaving. Don't give in to the temptation to slack off. Offer to train whoever is going to take over for you, and organize all your work so it's easy for them to pick up where you've left off. Keep an open dialogue with your boss throughout the process and let him know everything you are doing to help.

Heads Up!

Be cautious when using the threat of leaving as a tool to negotiate a higher wage. This strategy can easily backfire because even if they agree to provide better compensation, they may resent you and view you as disloyal. Moreover, if you have no intention of actually leaving, be prepared for the fact they may dismiss you as soon as they receive your resignation.

If you are asked to participate in an exit interview, go ahead, but don't use it to vent, gloat, or apologize for leaving. You are under no obligation to tell them everything they are doing wrong, nor should you badmouth your fellow employees. If you have a legal complaint, talk to a lawyer. If you hate your boss, talk to a friend. On the exit interview, your objective should be to depart peaceably.

Your desire to leave on good terms should be reflected in all your behavior. Don't steal or damage any company property. Don't say negative things to your replacement. Don't try to convince other employees to follow you. By acting professionally and courteously, you will leave a favorable impression of yourself in everyone's mind.

What They Owe

Contrary to how it may seem on television, nobody owes you a cake, a party, or a sappy poem on your last day. If you get a friendly send-off, good for you, but don't expect one. There are a few things, however, you should expect.

Among these is a letter of recommendation. If you've done a good job and fulfilled your obligations, don't be afraid to ask for one. If your boss isn't good at writing letters, offer to write it yourself and then let him or her sign it. I've actually used this technique before and it works quite well. Don't wait until your last day to make this request. You are better off asking early in your notice period so they will have time to write it. You may also need to give them a friendly reminder a few days before your departure. But never wait until after you've already left to request one.

Some unscrupulous companies try to cheat their employees out of wages when they leave. To avoid being wronged in this way, keep good records of your time and the activities you engage in during your notice period. You are entitled to your pay in full, on or before your next scheduled check date.

Under federal laws, your employer may also be required to continue your health insurance coverage until you are able to obtain new coverage. Of course, there are restrictions involved, but it is wise to understand your rights and obtain any necessary paperwork before leaving.

FYI

Most of the guidelines in this chapter assume you will leave your employment voluntarily. If, on the other hand, you are terminated through no fault of your own, you may be entitled to unemployment benefits.

Should you choose to file for benefits, be aware each state administers its own unemployment insurance program and you should contact the Unemployment Insurance Agency in your state as soon as possible after becoming unemployed.

The Least You Need to Know

◆ To attain business success, you must maintain a consistent growth pattern.

◆ Up is no longer the only way to grow. You can also grow out, or even down!

◆ Taking a lateral move can broaden your experience and make you more marketable and promotable.

◆ The circumstances surrounding the chance to do something new will never be perfect.

◆ When leaving a job, always give adequate notice and write a formal resignation letter.

◆ If you have done a good job and fulfilled your obligations, ask for a letter of recommendation.

Chapter 19

It's Alive! Joining a Start-Up

In This Chapter

- ◆ Assessing the risks and rewards
- ◆ Succeeding at a start-up
- ◆ Getting the information you need before jumping in
- ◆ Looking at the financial picture
- ◆ Calibrating your expectations

Start-ups! There's something captivating about the idea of blazing a new trail in the jungle of capitalism. If you're anything like me, the idea of working at a start-up probably calls to mind late night brainstorming sessions, breakthrough innovations, infusions of venture capital, and lucrative stock options.

There's no question start-up culture can be exciting. It can also be tremendously rewarding! But before you go to work at a start-up, there are a number of things you need to consider.

Risk vs. Reward

Working for a start-up can be a valuable learning experience. If you hope to own your own business one day, it's nearly a must. And while the potential rewards are many, the risks are real.

If the start-up fails, you'll be out of a job. If revenues aren't consistent, paychecks can be sketchy. If you're not full of faith and confidence, it's easy to lose steam and get disillusioned when things don't go well—which is bound to happen from time to time. Besides all this, there's the fact that start-ups tend to be disorganized. So if you're looking for formal training and structure in your job, a start-up is not the place to find it.

If you can stomach all of the risks, the potential rewards can make the experience worthwhile. What are those rewards?

Growth. There's nothing like a start-up to help you reach new heights in your career. When you're among the privileged few who orchestrate the launch of a successful company, you benefit from the growth it experiences. When it succeeds, you succeed. As it grows, you grow. As the company opens its doors to more employees, you maintain your seniority. It can be hard to break through the glass ceiling of a well-established company, but when you work at a start-up, you are the ceiling. The value of such positioning can be tremendous when you are young and in the early stages of your career.

Wealth. Cash-poor start-ups usually offer stock options to employees as part of their compensation. When you exercise your options, you become a partial owner in the company you work for. When the company is successful, your shares become valuable and you can sell them for a profit. The more successful the venture, the more valuable the stock options.

Heads Up!

When you purchase stock options, you become an investor in the company you work for. Stock options can be complicated, and like any investor, you are wise to have a thorough understanding of how they work.

Make sure you understand the type of plan being offered, how the stock options work, what vesting opportunities are available, how the stocks are allocated, how they are valued, and any holding periods required.

Education. When you're working with a skeleton crew, everyone has to step out of their comfort zone to tackle jobs they've never done. One day you could be programming a database and the next day pitching it at a conference. Being forced to take on varied responsibilities can teach you valuable skills in a short period of time.

Excitement. Start-up culture is fun! There's nothing like being part of a team that is focused on launching an innovative new product or service. There are fresh challenges to be met every day, and a contagious enthusiasm is fueled by the anticipation of success.

If you are imaginative, creative, and enjoy brainstorming for solutions, you'll feel right at home in a start-up environment. Newly formed companies are hotbeds of bright ideas and thrive on input from everyone working there.

Best Practice

Working at a start-up gives you the chance to build the kind of culture you like—something not usually possible in larger organizations. Want to build an online message board for idea sharing? Want to start a bowling league or softball team? Go for it! These are the kinds of things that make start-up culture fun.

Community. Instead of getting caught up in the turf wars that are so common at larger companies, employees of start-ups share a sense of togetherness and purpose. The traditional hierarchy is quickly thrown out the window when the president and the programmer share a desk every day.

What It Takes to Succeed

Start-up life is only for those with the right mixture of perseverance, initiative, resiliency, and vision. If you have a glamorized view you'll spend a few months building a website and then strike it rich, you'll soon be handed a reality check.

The foremost quality it takes to succeed at a start-up is dedication. Be prepared for the fact the hours are going to be long and your social life is going to be nonexistent for a while. Hard work will be the theme of each day and 60- to 80-hour weeks will be the norm. If you're lazy, you won't last!

The unique demands of start-up culture require you to be flexible as well. Don't expect your tasks, your title, or your schedule to be the same every day. You must be able to juggle several unrelated projects, prioritize them, and see them all to completion. Being eager to learn and quick to pick up new things is critical.

Best Practice _____

If you have a spouse or a significant other, talk to them about your plans to join a start-up. Let them know your free time will be very limited, especially in the beginning. Prepare them for the fact some rough patches are inevitable and you need their support. When you're dealing with the stresses of a new venture, the last thing you want is a troubled relationship adding more pressure.

If you're the type of person who waits for others to tell you what to do, working at a start-up isn't for you. You must be able to look at any given situation, assess what needs to be done, and then work without support. Are you a self-starter who takes initiative? Are you the type who never quits until you achieve what you set out for? Are you somewhat of a perfectionist? All these qualities are valuable when you're trying to create something that will outshine your competition.

The teamwork that is so integral to the success of a start-up will call upon you to work well with others and be quick to offer assistance. Amidst the financial and logistical challenges of start-up life, you want to be the type of teammate who helps others solve problems and keeps your cool under pressure. If you prefer to work alone, you won't fit in.

Do you have what it takes to succeed at a start-up? Are you:

❑ Willing to work long hours?

❑ Able to juggle multiple tasks?

❑ Flexible and adaptable?

❑ A fast learner?

❑ A self-starter?

❑ Good at working without support?

❑ Good at establishing priorities?

❑ Quick to help others?

❑ Passionate?

❑ Creative?

❑ Hard working?

❑ A big-picture thinker?

❑ Self-motivated?

Before You Sign Up

It's easy to be lured into a start-up by the promise of excitement and the prospect of riches. But before you sign on the dotted line, it's good to remind yourself a start-up is essentially a small company, unproven in the marketplace, with little or no revenue. To most people, working at such a place would be laughable. So if you're going to take a leap of faith, there are some critical questions you'll want to ask beyond the basics of compensation and duties.

The Model

Here is the number-one question you need answered: is there a viable need for the product or service being offered by this business? If you aren't sure of the answer, find out.

Research the history of the idea. Is it just the hair-brain musing of a drunken college student, or does it have real business potential? Has the concept already been tried? Has it failed before? What is its competition? Has it been thought through and refined? If you discover the company is only two weeks old, you may want to think twice before you make it your primary source of income. Working for a brand new venture isn't bad; it just requires you do some extra investigating.

Try to get a feel for how the company is structured. Who pulls the strings? Who handles the creative side; the organizational side; the marketing side? Are there plans to hire more people? Are there plans for expansion? Has there been any growth? Attrition? You may not be able to get answers to all these questions, but knowing even a few of them can help you with your decision-making process.

Make sure you comprehend the goals of the venture—what the leadership is really striving for. Do they want to get rich? Get famous? Take the company public? Build something unique? Work with their friends? One answer isn't better than another, but it's important you can stand behind whatever the answer is!

The People

Until there is a tangible product and a track record of results, the most reliable indicator of a business's potential is its people—especially its management!

Ask to meet the founder(s) and anyone else on the management team. This is especially important when the company is small because these are the people who shape the organization. Even if your position is considered entry level, you still have the right to request this, so don't be afraid to ask.

Heads Up!

If you don't know anything about a company's founders or its managers, do a little digging. Try to find out where they've worked before and what they've done. Determine whether they have a history of successes or failures. Ask to see their bios or resumés. Taking such measures may seem extreme, but they can protect you from getting mixed up with the wrong people.

Get to know the entire team you'll be working with. If you're not invited to a social gathering as part of the hiring process, try to create one. This helps you determine whether you like everyone enough to spend 60 to 80 hours a week in their company. If you like them in a social setting, there is a good chance you will like them in a work setting.

See if you share similar values and if everyone gets along. Ask them how they met and whether they've worked together before. Question them about their goals to see if everyone is on the same page. When you work at a start-up, there's no way to hide from people you don't like.

The Money

If you're going to pour your heart and soul into a start-up company, you want to make sure it's going to pay off. Be ready to discuss your compensation and the company's finances in detail. Treat your decision to join like an investment. If you wouldn't be willing to loan the company money, don't offer it your sweat equity.

When it comes to negotiating your stake, there is a good chance you will be making less in cash than you would at a well-established company, and will be offered stock options to make up the difference. While accepting options can be somewhat of a gamble, if you wholeheartedly believe the company will be successful, you should want them. After you are making enough to pay your bills, take the rest in options. If you're afraid this won't pay off, it means you don't have confidence in the venture and probably shouldn't be working there.

When you accept stock options, the most important thing to know is what percentage of ownership your shares equate to. Be careful not to get caught up in the number of shares you receive, as this figure is only important relative to the total number of shares outstanding. (Example: if you receive 1,000 shares out of 100,000 shares issued, your percentage of ownership is only 1 percent.)

FYI

To determine the value of stock options, you must know the total number of fully diluted shares. Fully diluted shares are the total number of shares that would be outstanding if all sources of conversion (i.e., convertible bonds and stock options) were exercised. This is important to know because if a large percentage of option holders exercise their right to claim stock, the share price can plunge.

After you agree on your personal compensation, find out if the entity itself is financially stable. This is where you start to get into some gray areas. Most start-ups aren't financially stable, so you have to make a personal decision how much risk you are willing to take. I have friends who moved back in with their parents until they got their start-ups off the ground. Sometimes, such a move pays off; other times not. Making such a decision is up to you. The safest route is to choose start-ups that are well funded and profitable.

Here are the most important questions to ask:

♦ **How much money is in the bank, and how much is being spent each month?** The answer to this question will give you what is referred to as the burn-rate. In other words, at the current rate of spending, when will the company run out of money?

♦ **If more capital is needed, how will it be raised?** Whether the company is funded by sales, by its founders, or by venture capitalists, make sure money will be available when needed.

♦ **What is the exit strategy and what is its timeframe?** The answer to this question may not be clear in the early stages and could change depending on circumstances, but if there is an exit strategy, you want to know it. Whether the company is being structured for a quick sell or for long-term value can affect its financial standing, the value of your stock options, and your job prospects.

Best Practice

If you want to work at a start-up that's not so risky, offer to join a newly formed office, department, or division of an existing company. Such a scenario can offer you growth potential and the thrill of starting something new without the financial uncertainty.

Along for the Ride

Working at a start-up is a lot like riding a roller coaster. The experience is full of ups and downs, twists and turns, scares and surprises. And just as roller coasters aren't for everyone, start-ups aren't either. For some, the experience is exhilarating; for others, it's nauseating.

Every start-up is different, and the opportunity to join one is rarely perfect. It's critical you understand exactly what you are getting into and are willing to go wherever it takes you.

There's a good chance the business model will change several times, the best ideas will fail, and seemingly bad ideas will pleasantly surprise you. It's just the way things work at a start-up. So if you decide to join one, calibrate your expectations, expect the unexpected, and enjoy the ride!

The Least You Need to Know

- There are many risks and many potential rewards that go along with working at a start-up. Make sure you understand them all before you join one.

- Don't expect to have a formal job description, and don't expect your tasks, your title, or your schedule to be the same every day. Working at a start-up requires hard work and long hours.

- Before you join a start-up, make sure there is a viable need for the product or service it offers.

- Until there is a tangible product and a track record of results, the most reliable indicator of a business's potential can be found in its people.

- Don't be afraid to have a conversation about the start-up's financial stability.

- Start-up life is filled with ups and downs, so if you join one, expect the unexpected.

20

Do Your Own Thing: Starting a Start-Up

In This Chapter

- ◆ Getting started
- ◆ Raising capital
- ◆ Getting help from others
- ◆ Knowing what to expect
- ◆ Reaping the greatest reward

Do you have an unquenchable desire to start your own company? Do you want to be your own boss? Are you tired of laboring to build someone else's empire and ready to build your own? Well if you are, you're in good company! Polls have shown more than half of all young professionals hope to start their own business someday.

As a young entrepreneur, you encounter many obstacles. You have your own inexperience to contend with, people question your credibility, and your connections and circle of influence are limited. Couple this with a lack of financial resources and a negligible credit history, and it can be hard to convince people you should be taken seriously. So what does it take to launch a winning venture?

Groundwork

Before you build a house, you have to lay its foundation. Without doing so, there is nothing to fasten the walls to—nothing to build upon. Starting a business is similar, but instead of metal and concrete, you use materials of a different kind. What are those materials?

◆ An idea

◆ A plan

◆ Experience

Let's take a closer look at each of these start-up building blocks.

An Idea

It takes more than a good idea to build a successful company, but the idea is where it begins. Once you have an idea, take time to mull it over. Consider who will use it, how they'll use it, and why it's needed. Imagine how you will create it, sell it, and service it. Try to visualize every aspect of how your business will operate.

Over time, let your idea evolve. Do as much research as you possibly can, and modify it as you are presented with new information. From your initial idea to its actual development and implementation there should be many changes. This is an important part of the creative process. Such adaptability keeps you on the cutting edge.

A Plan

Until you write your ideas down, they're only fantasies. Once you put them on paper, they become something real. Failure to write a business plan is one of the most common mistakes young entrepreneurs make, and it's one that cheats them out of important problem-solving and planning time.

A properly written business plan articulates your ideas, showcases your credibility, and entices investors. You need one if you plan to do any fundraising, and in some cases, even to lease a location.

A business plan also helps you narrow your focus. Many start-ups fail because they take on too many projects instead of focusing on a niche they can dominate. As you write your plan, you will be forced to acknowledge whether your ideas are reasonable and cost-effective. If you discover they aren't, you can rework them or start over, thus saving yourself time and money.

Your plan doesn't need to be hundreds of pages packed with complex tables and charts. Some of the basics are:

- Summary of the product

- Description of the company and its leadership

- Estimated cost to produce, deliver, and service

- Projected start-up costs

- Sales projections and market data

- Competitive analysis

- Break-even analysis

- Short- and long-term goals

- Potential obstacles

You can structure a business plan in a variety of ways, but the main thing is it suits your unique situation. The idea of writing one can seem daunting, but there are great resources to help you simplify the process (see Appendix A for a list of business planning websites).

> **Best Practice**
>
> Once you've completed your business plan, show it to trusted friends, educators, advisors, and respected professionals. Ask them for suggestions on how to improve it.

Experience

Dreaming about starting your own business is easy. Doing it is another story. If you've never worked at a start-up, never supervised a project, and never taken any classes on business management, you may want to think twice before you quit your day job.

Taking a short-term position in the field you plan to enter is one way to gain needed experience. If you hope to open a restaurant, for example, it would be valuable to log some time as a server or cook in advance. You could also enroll in special courses on how to start your own business. Such classes are generally available at community colleges and technical education centers.

One of the best ways to overcome inexperience is by getting advice from those who have it. Seek out university and alumni networks, your local chamber of commerce, peer groups, and even mentoring organizations (see Appendix A for references). If you have friends or family who are successful in business, run your ideas by them and ask for help. You might be surprised at just how much of it you get!

At one start-up where I worked, the owner put together a panel of his top clients and coined them our "client advisory board." As we launched new products, we would "test" them on this small group of 10 to 12 clients and get their feedback. Who can you test your product on?

Once you have an idea, a plan, and the right experience, your foundation is laid and you're ready to build the walls. Now you only have to figure out how you're going to pay for them.

Funding

Everything costs something. Even if you want to start a lemonade stand, it's going to cost you. The trick is to figure out what your magic number is and then find somebody who will loan that amount to you.

 Heads Up! _____

When writing your business plan, estimate your expenses 15 to 20 percent higher than you expect. It's much easier to raise money up front than it is to go looking for more after you realize you've budgeted incorrectly.

Locating financiers can be a challenge for anyone. When you're young and inexperienced, it's an even bigger challenge because your credibility is called into question. But just because people don't want to loan you money doesn't mean you don't have a good idea. If you're convinced of your venture's viability, don't get discouraged when you hear no a few times.

So where can you find the capital you need?

Your Own Pocket

It was a lot easier to get your hands on venture capital and angel funds in the '90s. (We'll discuss these in a minute.) Nowadays, the popular method of starting businesses is known as bootstrapping. Have you ever heard anyone say, "he pulled himself up by the bootstraps"? Well, that's essentially where the term *bootstrapping*, as used by entrepreneurs, came from. It refers to relying on yourself for funding through savings, conventional bank loans, credit cards, and so on.

The beauty of such self-reliance is you maintain full control of the way your company develops. You also get to hold on to any cash that is generated instead of sharing it with investors. Many successful companies have been founded this way.

There are drawbacks to self-funding. For one, you assume all the risk; and two, getting to market quickly can be difficult unless you have access to a lot of cash.

Best Practice

When bootstrapping, look to places where you can get the lowest interest rate first. This means credit cards should be a last resort.

The Bank

Conventional lending is cheap compared to venture capital and, like self-funding, allows you to maintain full control of your company.

Because banks are typically conservative lenders, they may require you to personally guarantee the funds you borrow, which means you need a good credit score. A score ranging from 680 to 699 is considered good; anything lower and bank lending may not be an option for you.

One negative to conventional lending is if your venture fails and you can't pay off the loan, your credit is damaged. So once you are approved, refinance the balance in your business name as soon as possible to protect your personal credit score.

Family and Friends

If you can't finance your business out of your own pocket, secure funds from investors, or get a second mortgage on your house, asking family and friends may be your best option.

The advantage to asking close associates for loans is they will probably say yes because they care about you. The disadvantage is if your business goes sour, your relationship can sour with it. To protect your financial interests and your relationship, you should take a few precautions.

First, legalize all agreements. Even though you may be the spitting image of your old uncle Elrod, don't settle for a stack of cash and a handshake. Formalize everything with legal documentation (prepared by an attorney) and pay interest on the money you borrow. This prevents anyone from coming back when you strike it rich and insisting you promised them a stake in your venture. If you need help formalizing your agreements, check out www.virginmoneyus.com. This is a great resource that helps manage loans between family and friends.

Second, avoid forming partnerships just because you need money. If you sell stock in your business to family and friends, they have the legal right to stick their nose in. So if they insist on buying shares, make them nonvoting shares.

Lastly, tie all payments to your revenues. When you have a fixed payment schedule and can't honor it, your relationship will be strained. It's better to structure your agreement so the lender receives a percentage of your cash flow until they have been repaid in full with interest.

Angel Investors

Unlike venture capital funds, which are professionally managed, angels manage their own investments. This can make angel funding more accessible to small businesses. Though the typical investment is around half a million, there is no minimum and no limit to what angels can invest. So whether you need $50,000 or $1.5 million, angel investors may be your best option.

> **Heads Up!**
>
> Most investors only care about one thing: generating a return. So if money isn't your primary motivation for going into business, be extra careful who you partner with. If you give away too much control, you can find yourself pushed into situations that don't align with your goals simply because they are profitable.

Angel funds do come at a sizable price. Professional angel investors typically demand at least 10 times (sometimes as much as 30 times) their original investment within five years.

Finding the right angel can be an excellent step for a small business, but it's critical you be satisfied with the amount of control you relinquish and, as with any loan, thoroughly understand the terms. (Resources for finding angel investors are listed in Appendix A.

You may also want to check out Joseph R. Bell's *Finding an Angel Investor in a Day: Get It Done Right, Get It Done Fast!* [The Planning Shop, 2007].)

Venture Capital

Venture capital can come from high net worth individuals, or more commonly from institutional investors such as pension plans and mutual funds. This is often the hardest type of funding to acquire.

Also known as private equity, venture capital (VC) is invested in privately held, early stage companies with large growth potential. Though there is no hard and fast rule, VC is usually provided to those needing $1 million or more.

The niche served by VC includes enterprises that are considered too risky for bank loans, or to be traded on the open market. Because of the risk venture capitalists take, they demand a significant share of ownership and control. Like angel funds, VC also comes with a hefty price tag—usually in excess of 40 percent a year.

As mentioned, venture capitalists are very selective, and getting access to VC isn't easy. Those who receive funding are well under 1 percent of those who seek it. So if you're trying to get your hands on VC, make sure you have a rock solid business plan, a stellar management team, and a foolproof way to deliver returns. Some resources for those seeking venture capital are listed in Appendix A of this book.

Best Practice

When seeking venture capital or angel funding, you may be required to make a pitch directly to potential investors in a face-to-face meeting. These meetings can be very rushed—sometimes under 10 minutes—so it's imperative you prepare well.

The book, *Pitching to Venture Capitalists: Essential Strategies for Approaching VCs, Entering Into Negotiations, and Securing Funding* (West Group, 2004) by Patrick J. Ennis can help you with this.

Grants

While government grants do exist, they are very restrictive and difficult to obtain. Generally they are designed to benefit companies that develop new technologies (utilized by the government), minorities, nonprofits, community improvement programs, and the like. Be wary of claims made on websites or late-night infomercials promising "free money." The only reliable place to seek out government grants is through the official website, www.grants.gov.

Mind Your Money

The number-one reason start-ups fail is because they run out of money. So regardless of where you get your funding, manage it wisely.

Plan on having at least six months' worth of savings so you can survive even if you don't earn anything for a while. Track your expenses in detail to ensure you know exactly what you are making and exactly what you are spending. Use a professional tool like QuickBooks to help you stay organized.

Once you reach profitability, determine the minimum you need to live on, start paying yourself, and reinvest the rest in your company. In the beginning, avoid taking big paychecks or draws. If you make it through your first year and have extra money in the bank, you can always pay yourself a bonus or increase your salary.

Don't let your ego get the best of you by falling into the trap of taking more money out of your business than it can afford. It may be hard to tell your friends you're broke, but by exercising self-control in the beginning, it will pay off in the long run and your company will be more profitable.

Your People

The success of a start-up nearly always results from its people. It's your job as founder to build a team that turns your vision into a reality.

The best place to look for help is among those you've worked with in the past. Once you've labored alongside someone, you understand their strengths, weaknesses, and quirks. You know if they'll complement your skills and provide the expertise you need. Hiring off the street is a much bigger gamble.

If you have friends with special abilities, consider partnering with them. Of course, you wouldn't want to hire someone based on sentimentality, but if they fit the profile, why not offer them a chance to share in your accomplishments?

If you're having a hard time finding the right people to complement your team, talk to your investors. Often they can be helpful because of the experience they bring to the table and the connections they have.

Regardless of whom you choose, make sure they understand what they're getting into, and they have what it takes to succeed at a start-up (see Chapter 19).

What It Takes to Succeed

The nuances to achieving long-term business success could fill volumes. What it takes for a business to succeed one day can dramatically change the next as it is forced to adapt to market conditions. But for the newly formed venture, there are some enduring principles that build the ideal foundation for growth and success. Besides managing your finances and hiring the right people, the following are my top five.

1. Stay Focused and Avoid Distractions

A common start-up killer is taking on side projects that don't support your business model. This can be easy to do when money is tight and you need work, but consulting offers, day jobs, and other diversions steal your focus from where it needs to be—your core business.

I have a friend who started a staffing agency focused on one vertical market. His idea was great and the potential to succeed was there, but when things got slow, he started staffing for other industries, too. Before he knew it, he was no different than any other personnel service and was competing with companies 10 times his size. He lost his niche, and he lost his business.

FYI

In Chapter 18, we talked about having multiple concurrent careers. This may seem to contradict the advice not to let anything distract from your core business. In actuality though, you need to do a lot of legwork before your business is up and running. This can include writing a business plan, building a team, acquiring funding, doing a test market, and more. If you do all these things before you officially "open your doors," you can maintain an income stream by keeping your day job.

If you are starting your company to fill a need within your current industry, you may even be able to turn your employer into your first customer. Better yet, if you can convince them of your idea's value, they might provide you with funding in exchange for your business's services.

---

2. Be Visibly Unique

Don't waste time trying to imitate your competition. Instead, focus on making your business the only one of its kind. Remember your customers are flooded with messages to buy hundreds of products and services every day. It's only the fresh and innovative that will command their attention (see Chapter 13 for a discussion of branding).

3. Deliver More Than Expected

The old adage, "word of mouth is the best advertising" has never been more fitting. In today's information age, people are talking about products and services in a whole new way. Consumers have become the new media. When you deliver what you promise, people are more likely then ever to share it with their network.

Since the advent of online social networking, you never know if Mr. Joe Client has 50,000 "friends" hanging on his every update, post, or video blog entry. While his endorsement could provide just the attention you need, his criticism could shatter any credibility you've worked to build.

Want to ensure people are spreading the good word about you? Don't just offer products and services that are good, offer ones that are surprisingly good. Look for ways to go above and beyond to make your business memorable. A small example: when clients visit our office, instead of offering them bottled water, we offer them a choice of spring water or sparkling mineral water. On top of that, we give them a choice of a dozen soft drinks, six blends of coffee, and an assortment of fresh baked cookies.

4. Think Big

Picture a hotdog stand in your mind … now a hometown café … now a large restaurant chain. They all perform essentially the same function of feeding people, but think how different they are. You could say that, figuratively speaking, every business starts as a hotdog stand. Many would like to be larger but can't seem to get past the opening phase. Why? Because they don't think big enough!

How can you think bigger? Try this: if you'd like to sell your product to 100 people, figure a way to sell it to 500. Want to earn $1 million? Work out a plan to double that figure. Know you can produce 50 widgets a minute? What prevents you from producing 100? Take everything you do and figure out a way to do it better, faster, and more profitably. Don't make the mistake of going after too small a market, charging too little, or settling for less than your best.

5. Don't Give Up

Starting your own business is never as easy as you think it's going to be. Accept this fact in advance and resolve not to get worn down by it. Failure and disappointment are simply part of the growth process. Deals are going to fall through, money is going to be tight, technology is going to fail, and people are going to frustrate you.

No matter how bad things get, be determined not to give up! Not only is this a good principle to run your business by, it's also a good principle to live by. It never ceases to amaze me how far sheer willpower can take you.

Heads Up! _____

Starting your own business takes a tremendous amount of research and planning. This chapter covers some of the basics, but there is much, much more you should know. Just one small mistake—like structuring your company improperly, or failing to obtain the correct insurance coverage—could cost you millions.

At the very least, you should consult an attorney and an accountant, and read a book or take a course on how to start your own business.

The Greatest Reward

There's something miraculous about how a tiny seed can grow into a luxuriant tree. Planting a seed, watching it grow, and then reaping its fruit is one of the most rewarding things a person can do. This is the essence of what starting your own business is all about.

What starts as an idea can blossom into a thriving, fruit-bearing business venture. And just as there are endless types of vegetation, so there are endless types of businesses to build. Whatever you choose to create, it will be uniquely yours—a representation of your creativity, determination, and effort.

So what will you build? Whatever it is, make it something you can be proud of!

The Least You Need to Know

- ◆ It takes more than a good idea to build a successful company.
- ◆ Until you write a business plan, your ideas are only fantasies.

- Make sure you have at least a measure of business experience before you try to start your own company.

- The number-one reason start-ups fail is because they run out of money. So regardless of where you get your funding, manage it wisely.

- The success of a start-up is nearly always dependent on its people, so choose your team carefully.

- Don't waste time trying to imitate your competition. Instead, focus on making your business the only one of its kind.

Part 6

Life Lessons

The success you achieve in business depends much on how you live your life in general. Your view of obstacles, the values you live by, and the balance you maintain either contribute to, or detract from, your success.

This part is designed to positively impact the way you see the world and the opportunities in it. It provides lessons in positive thinking, ethical behavior, and individuality. It teaches you to find satisfaction in your work and profit from it at the same time.

"Dorothy, we understand you're thinking about going into business."

Chapter 21

Overcome Obstacles to Progress

In This Chapter

- ◆ Overcoming mental obstacles to success
- ◆ Escaping the ruts in the road to success
- ◆ Dealing with discouragement
- ◆ Turning mistakes into learning experiences
- ◆ Shattering glass ceilings

Obstacles are everywhere. We face them from the moment we open our eyes until the moment we close them at the end of our day. Some are so small we barely notice them. Others are so large they permanently change us. Obstacles are simply a part of life.

The road to business success is fraught with obstacles. And every person's obstacles are unique to them. Some face obstacles related to their age, race, or sex; others from their upbringing, education, or social status. But by far the most dangerous obstacles are the kind we can't see—the ones that exist only in our mind from imaginary limits we place on ourselves.

To a great degree, the success you achieve in business is determined by how effectively you overcome obstacles. This chapter addresses some of the most common ones, and provides practical advice that helps you surmount them.

Your Biggest Enemy

The Wright brothers are credited with the first controlled, manned, powered flight on December 17th, 1903. Although they failed hundreds of times before they succeeded, they never gave up on their dream. Had they done so, invention of the modern aircraft would have been attributed to someone else.

This example well demonstrates the power that exists in the human mind. At that time, no one had ever seen such a flight. It would have been easy for the brothers to conclude their goal was unachievable. Today, we now know it wasn't. For the Wright brothers, believing was the first step.

All too often though, our minds convince us something is impossible long before we give it our best effort. It's like we create a mental surrender that says, "I can't do this. I'll never make it. It's not possible." Those who let themselves think this way are sure to fail because they stop trying to succeed. How can you conquer such tendencies?

Know your limits. There is a difference between obstacles and limits. Obstacles can be overcome, whereas limits cannot. For example, a blind person cannot drive a car. Real limits are few—obstacles are many.

Knowing your limits keeps you from striving for the unachievable and ending up disappointed. Once you understand your limits, everything outside of them becomes a possibility.

Ignore doubt. At 21, while interviewing for an $8 per hour position, I told the interviewer I expected to be earning six figures within 5 years and be semiretired by 35. "That's a little farfetched," he said with a chuckle.

It may have seemed farfetched to him, but where he saw obstacles I saw opportunity. I knew the obstacles were there. I simply chose to ignore them.

Heads Up!

In saying you should ignore obstacles, I'm referring to imaginary obstacles that haven't materialized. When you face real, tangible obstacles that impede your progress, you can't overcome them by ignoring the facts. To do so would actually hinder your progress instead of advancing it.

Have a plan. A good plan is the secret weapon for combating mental obstacles. When you have a plan and are determined to stick to it, it doesn't matter what you are feeling at a given time because you can simply "proceed as planned."

Conversely, if you are plagued with negative thoughts and a lack direction, it's easy to become complacent and give up.

Visualize your goals. Once you've spent so much time thinking about a goal that you can see, touch, taste, and smell it with your mind's eye, you won't easily give up on it. The desire to achieve it gives you the fortitude to overcome even the most daunting of obstacles. See Chapter 2 for more on visualizing goals.

Embrace positivity. Stay away from people, places, and things that bring you down. Immerse yourself in as many uplifting activities as possible. Choose positive reading material and positive friends. Listen to the prodding of fellow optimists and ignore the criticism of pessimists.

Understand fear. Fear creates imaginary obstacles. Fear can prevent us from introducing ourselves to people (fear of rejection), starting profitable business ventures (fear of failure), and experiencing wonderful things (fear of the unknown). The key to overcoming such fears is to take the following steps:

1. Recognize them in yourself

2. Identify their root

3. Make a plan to deal with them

The next time you have an idea you are hesitant to pursue, ask yourself if fear might be the only thing holding you back.

Get Out!

Like obstacles, ups and downs are a part of life. Sometimes we get stuck in one of the "downs"—more commonly referred to as a rut. If this happens to you, there is really only one question you need to answer: How am I going to get myself out of this situation?

The first step toward answering this is to identify what is keeping you in your rut.

Rut Magnets

Although not directly connected to business, the following items can affect your professional life. As you read about each of them, evaluate yourself to see if one or more of them could be affecting you.

- ◆ **Relationships.** Relationships are extremely complicated. This book is *not* designed to give you relationship advice. But, if you are with someone who destroys your self-esteem, has incompatible goals, or belittles your aspirations, you shouldn't be with them. If you're already married, seek counseling. If you're not, you may want to consider your options.

- ◆ **Depression.** An occasional case of the blues is normal. Frequent bouts of severe depression are not. Left untreated, depression can rob you of your motivation, damage your reputation, and even ruin your life. If you think you could be suffering from clinical depression, seek treatment!

- ◆ **Drugs.** I try not to use too many clichés, but I can't resist using this one: say *no* to drugs! Drug addiction forces you into a rut faster than you can say pot. I wasted a good part of my late teens experimenting with drugs, and I can tell you from experience that they destroy your chances of attaining business success.

- ◆ **Lifestyle.** We're going to talk more about this in Chapter 23, but it's important to note if your lifestyle is one of extremes, you can't give needed attention to your professional goals. Moderation and a balanced life are integral to attaining business success.

- ◆ **Bad habits.** The wrong habits can leave you devoid of time and good health. While some activities may be fine in moderation, their misuse can be a dangerous trap. Wasting time on the Internet, playing video games, watching too much TV, overeating, heavy drinking, and smoking are just a few. Make sure you're not idling away time or money you could be using to improve your lot in life.

- ◆ **Physical appearance.** How do you feel about yourself? Do you like the way you look? It's no secret how we look on the outside affects the way we feel on the inside. If you're not happy with your physical appearance, do something about it. Exercise, go on a diet, see a dermatologist, buy some new clothes, get a new hairstyle—do anything that makes you feel better about yourself. Such a change may provide just the boost you need to pull yourself out of a rut.

- ◆ **Jobs.** If you hate going to work every day, or are working just for a paycheck, why not go job hunting, or start your own business? Not sure if it's time to move on? See Chapters 3 and 18.

◆ **Fear of change.** This particular breed of fear can keep you in a rut longer than anything else. As creatures of habit, our tendency is to fear change, especially when making changes could lead to embarrassment or ridicule from others. Such fear gets in the way of action, and action is what it takes to get out of a rut!

Best Practice _____

If you're feeling stuck in a rut but can't identify a legitimate problem with your life, you may need a vacation. Not the kind of go, go, go vacation that leaves you exhausted, but a kick back, relax, read a book kind of vacation. Sometimes the best way to get out of a rut is to walk away for a little while.

Escape Plan

As you read the preceding points, did you notice how they all included a call to action? When the wheel of a vehicle is "stuck in a rut" it has to roll back and forth or change directions until it gets free. Sometimes the situation may call for more drastic measures, such as towing. The ruts of business and life require no less effort to get out of.

When people tell me they're stuck in a rut, I always ask them the same question: what's your plan to get out of it? Escaping a rut requires a plan! Small ruts call for small changes; large ruts demand drastic ones. Once you have a plan, making changes isn't so overwhelming because you can make them one step at a time.

Make an agreement with yourself and write it down. It could read something like this:

I'm stuck in a rut. My rut exists because I waste too much time on unimportant activities and I hate my job but am afraid to leave. I realize I'm the only person who can get me out of this rut. Starting today, I am going to make the following changes:

◆ Limit my television watching and nonessential Internet browsing to one hour per day

◆ Read a book on self-improvement

◆ Update my resumé and start looking for a job online

◆ Buy a new suit to make me feel good about myself and to wear on interviews

After you write your "plan," post it somewhere you see it every day. Share it with those close to you and ask them for positive reinforcement. Even if nothing dramatic changes right away, you'll already feel better about yourself because you'll have a new sense of purpose!

> **Heads Up!**
>
> If you have a tendency toward laziness or complacency, be careful lazy days don't turn into lazy weeks, and lazy weeks don't turn into lazy months. Left unchecked, you can get used to being nonproductive.
>
> By forcing yourself to be productive every day, you will become a motivated and self-disciplined individual.

The Big D

To be discouraged is to be devoid of courage, hope, or confidence. In a world with so many problems, it's easy to get discouraged. Discouragement can be caused by problems at work, at home, or because of how you perceive your own failings. Many people get discouraged when they feel like their career is going nowhere.

Signs you may be discouraged can include restlessness, sleeplessness, negative thoughts, loss of motivation, and more. The danger of discouragement is it robs you of the desire and will to improve your situation.

All professionals get discouraged on occasion. Layoffs, lost wages, missed opportunities, and many more things can cause discouraging thoughts. What you must learn to do is dismiss them quickly instead of getting enslaved by a cycle of negative thinking.

When faced with discouragement, the first question you should ask yourself is whether you are being rational. Even small problems can seem very large when your judgment is clouded by emotion. Try to take a step back, clear your mind, and examine the source of your discouragement from an outside point of view.

> **Best Practice**
>
> Exercising is a great way to combat discouragement! Not only does it enhance your self-image, but also causes your body to release endorphins that contribute toward mental well-being.

Once you analyze the source of your negative feelings, counter them with something positive. Even if your self-pitying alter ego is telling you to give up, get wasted, or eat a half-gallon of ice cream, none of these things provide long-term relief. What you need is the chance to rejoice in a new success. It doesn't have to be anything monumental, just something that makes you feel positive again. Whenever I start to feel discouraged, I try to complete a small project.

The type of project doesn't matter. What matters is I get to feel the sense of accomplishment that gives me a psychological boost.

If you can't create a new success, at least celebrate your efforts! Even if you failed at something, the fact you tried is worthy of commendation. If you diligently looked for a job all week but couldn't find one, celebrate the fact you exerted yourself. If you took a risk on a new venture that flopped, celebrate the fact you learned something new. When you look hard enough, you can always find something to celebrate!

Not Mistakes—Learning Experiences

"I don't care if you make a mistake. I only care if you make it twice."

I'll never forget those words spoken by one of my first managers. They've resonated with me ever since I made the same dumb mistake twice in a row and got written up for it.

Everyone makes mistakes—lots of mistakes. And while mistakes can be a serious impediment to professional progress, most won't ruin your chances of attaining business success. If you happen to make a major mistake, most people are considerate if it was unintentional. Even the law makes allowances for first time offenders. If, however, you repeatedly make the same mistakes, you destroy your credibility and severely limit your opportunities.

A common trait of successful people is they learn from their mistakes. How can you cultivate the same quality? Follow these steps:

Step 1: Apologize. If your mistake has affected someone else, go to that person and make a sincere apology. It doesn't matter if they are your boss, colleague, or even your employee; they deserve to hear you admit your fault.

Apologizing accomplishes a number of things. It makes you more approachable and likeable, it encourages others to deal leniently with you, and it reinforces in your mind the determination not to make the same mistake again.

> **Heads Up!**
>
> If you refuse to apologize for your mistakes, you gradually become more brazen and arrogant. Arrogance is not a quality that helps you succeed. If anything, it drives others away! It also increases the likelihood you make more mistakes due to overconfidence.

Step 2: Don't justify. Making a mistake always bruises the ego. To avoid humiliation, our tendency can be to shift the blame to another party or justify *why* we did something. Such behavior diminishes the value of an apology and any lessons learned. When you accept your share of the blame unconditionally, it makes you respectable and builds good character.

Step 3: Understand the cause. There is usually a cause for the mistakes we make. Sometimes we are careless, hasty, forgetful, or distracted. Sometimes we need additional training or a new procedure to follow. Whatever the case, make sure you identify what led up to your error. Without identifying the cause, it's impossible to eliminate the risk of repeating the same mistake or a similar one.

Best Practice

Share your plan for improvement with those who were affected by your mistake. They are likely to appreciate hearing you dwelt on what caused it and are determined not to repeat it.

Step 4: Make a plan. Once you identify the cause of your mistake, make a plan to eliminate it. If you need training, take a class. If you were distracted, work on being more focused. If you were forgetful, start writing things down. Whatever the cause, find a way to counter it. This is a step you can't afford to miss!

Step 5: Move on. Unnecessarily dwelling on mistakes can lead to low self-esteem and lack of confidence. Once you've taken all the steps outlined here, let it go. After all, nobody's perfect!

Breaking Glass

Glass ceilings are real. Though unofficial and invisible, they do exist. You'll never see a notice on the top of a job application that says, "This company discriminates against women and minorities," but you may feel the effect of unspoken limitations.

Credentials such as experience and education are required for certain positions—especially prestigious and high-paying ones. Sex and skin color, though, should never be a consideration. Sadly, even in our advanced society, there are still places where such discrimination exists.

On the bright side, women and minorities have more opportunities today than ever before. The 2008 United States presidential election gives evidence of this fact. Even Senator Hillary Clinton acknowledged this when she said (in her speech endorsing Barack Obama), "And although we weren't able to shatter that highest, hardest glass ceiling this time, thanks to you, it's got about 18 million cracks in it." And she's right!

There are 18 million cracks in it—in addition to thousands of other glass ceilings around the world! Thanks to the men and women who have demanded—and even legislated for—equality in the workplace, you face a friendlier business environment than ever before.

Despite the good news, it's worth acknowledging that women, minorities, and other groups face special challenges on the road to business success. Even today, they are highly outnumbered in senior management positions.

If you fall into a group that is commonly discriminated against, what can you do about it?

Be the Best

It may not be fair, but if you want to be treated like an equal, you have to be better than equal. Never take it for granted that you should receive a promotion because you are just as good as someone else. Instead, make the case for why you should be promoted because you are better than someone else.

At the end of the day, it's those who are the most professional, industrious, effective, and assertive who get the coveted jobs. When a person is indisputably the best, their race, sex, disability, or any other distinction rarely holds them back. Recent history has confirmed the truth of these words.

Heads Up!

If you are a woman, be careful not to flaunt your sexuality as a means to get ahead. If you dress in a way that is immodest or revealing, it might get you the wrong kind of attention. You should also be extremely cautious when accepting positions that objectify women or are otherwise demeaning to your sex.

Choose Diversity-Conscious Companies

Before you accept a position, take a hard look at how the organization is structured. What is the company philosophy? Are there any ethnic minorities or women on the senior management team? Does it have a history of dealing with discrimination complaints? Simply put, if you're a woman who's interviewing for a secretarial position and you notice all the entry-level workers are women and all the managers are men, you may want to run for the exit.

Many outstanding companies actively recruit women and other minorities. A quick online search for "women friendly companies" yields over 58,000,000 hits. "Minority friendly" returns 17,000,000. "Disability friendly," just over 11,000,000. The point is opportunities exist for everyone—you just have to find them.

Know Your Rights

None of the advice in this section is meant to encourage you to sacrifice your rights, it's just encouraging you to pick your battles. The fact is, unequal pay and consideration for promotions *is* discrimination. Under the Civil Rights Act, you have a right to equal treatment. If you have time and energy invested with a company and are being held back because of discrimination, you can file a complaint with the EEOC (Equal Employment Opportunity Commission; www.eeoc.gov), or talk to an attorney.

Start Your Own Company or Join a Start-Up

Both of these options can provide terrific upside potential! When you start or join a business enterprise at the ground floor, you have nowhere to go but up. As the company grows, you get to maintain your seniority. Essentially, your floor becomes everyone else's ceiling.

The Choice Is Yours

Most people choose not to exert the energy it requires to escape a rut, overcome discouragement, or shatter a glass ceiling. For them, it's easier to blame obstacles for their lack of personal accomplishment. On the other hand, there are those who forge desire, determination, and hard work into a sledgehammer that demolishes every obstacle in their path.

Which type of person are you?

The Least You Need to Know

- The most dangerous obstacles are found in imaginary limits we place on ourselves.

- The next time you have an idea you are hesitant to pursue, ask yourself if fear might be the only thing holding you back.

♦ To escape a rut, you must identify what is keeping you in it and then remove that thing from your life.

♦ When you face negative feelings, counter them with something positive.

♦ When you make a mistake, try to figure out what caused it, and make a plan that prevents you from repeating it.

♦ Differences aside, it's the most professional, industrious, effective, and assertive people who excel in business.

22

Principles to Work By

In This Chapter

- ◆ Embracing ethical behavior
- ◆ Dealing with gray areas
- ◆ Telling the truth even when it hurts
- ◆ Doing it for your own good

We live in a self-serving society. By and large, people do whatever it takes to get ahead—even at the expense of others. The prevalence of unethical behavior is evident from the inexhaustible media coverage of Ponzi schemes and corporate accounting scandals. Some schools of thought even endorse such behavior by teaching you should maximize personal gain at all cost.

But when you make decisions without regard for how they affect other people—such as your boss, co-workers, customers, and the company you work for—they can actually destroy your chance of achieving and holding on to business success.

Religion and philosophy aside, what do you need to know about ethics? What constitutes right and wrong in a business environment? How can you catch yourself before you venture into questionable territory? And, perhaps most important, why should you do the right thing?

Ethics 101

Ethics and corporate accountability courses are popular at universities around the country. Such courses delve into real-life case studies to show how ethics have been applied (or misapplied). They discuss the application of ethics to accounting, sales, human resources, and other facets of business.

There's no harm in learning about ethics this way, but the problem with focusing on too many specifics is you can never dictate the best response for every situation. There are simply too many sets of unique circumstances to cover.

FYI
Many theologians argue it is impossible to have a discussion about ethics without involving religion and philosophy. They presuppose without a sense of accountability to a higher power, you lack the motivation to behave in an ethical way.

Another way of learning about ethics is to focus on a few, timeless principles that do apply in every situation.

To illustrate: as a child, your mother may have told you not to spoil your dinner. This is a relatively simple standard to follow. On the other hand, she could have told you, "not to eat more than 4 ounces of cookies, candy, chips, ice cream, fast food, or anything else, up to three hours before dinner, on Mondays, Tuesdays, Wednesdays, Thursdays, Fridays, and Saturdays, 365 days a year." Not only is this difficult to remember, but it allows for loopholes and leads to the proliferation of rules.

The following are simplified yet powerful principles that can guide you in business dealings.

Ethical Behavior Involves More Than Obeying the Rules

If you ever examine a written code of ethics, you are likely to find one of its tenets is willing compliance with the law. This is reasonable. After all, engaging in illegal activity is clearly unethical. The majority of ethical decisions, though, will be made separate from law. (In this context, we use the words "law" and "rules" interchangeably to refer to legislative statutes or company policies.)

As an example, assume your company doesn't have a written computer policy. Knowing this, you spend hours every day shopping for personal items on the Internet. Is this illegal? Are you violating any company policies? No. Are you behaving unethically? Yes. Essentially, you are stealing time from your employer.

Just because you technically stay within the bounds of the law, doesn't mean you are behaving ethically. In fact, if you make a habit of exploiting loopholes, there's a good chance you tread into unethical territory.

FYI

Undisclosed conflicts of interests can be unethical even if no improper action takes place. A conflict of interest is basically a situation where your position or authority gives you the opportunity to exploit someone for personal gain. An example would be if you worked as a purchasing agent for a company that acquired supplies from your family business. When such conflicts arise, it's your duty to provide full disclosure to avoid the appearance of impropriety.

Treat Others How You Want to Be Treated

This is the foremost principle that guides you in making right decisions. Though not without critics, the golden rule (or ethic of reciprocity) is the underpinning of ethical codes from cultures around the globe. In its negative form, it states you should not do to others what you would not want done to yourself.

Why does this principle serve as such an indispensable guide? Consider a few examples of how it can be applied:

◆ You are tempted to sell a product to one of your customers to earn a large commission even though you know they don't need it.

   Question: Would you want somebody to do this to you?

◆ Your friend is having a party and asks you to print the flyers on your color printer at work.

   Question: Would you want somebody to use your things without asking, especially if it cost you money?

◆ You are competing with a co-worker for a promotion. To gain an edge, you spread rumors about her and sabotage her work.

   Question: Would you want somebody to do this to you?

This principle never fails. If everyone followed it, no one would steal, lie, cheat, or murder. When you endeavor to live up to this standard as a professional, you will be trusted and admired.

Best Practice _____

Critics have claimed the so-called "golden rule" is flawed because you never know how other people expect to be treated. To a degree this may be true, but if you are genuinely unsure about what they expect, why not ask them?

Do the Right Thing Even When No One Is Watching

So often, the very people who claim to "hold themselves to a higher standard" engage in unethical behavior when they are convinced they won't get caught. It's relatively easy to obey the rules when someone is watching, but ethics demand you be obedient to the unenforceable. Only this shows what kind of a person you really are.

FYI
Aspects of personal and professional ethics:

- Treat others with respect
- Refuse to exploit others
- Treat others impartially and without prejudice
- Be fair and just
- Protect others from harm
- Be honest
- Be thorough and dutiful
- Obey the law
- Maintain confidentiality; respect privacy
- Avoid conflicts of interest

Butterflies and the Evening News

Some situations are extremely complicated. Right and wrong choices may not always be clear. How can you know if something you are tempted to do is unethical?

Even before your conscious mind can process your actions, your subconscious mind may alert you to a wrong course. How? Butterflies. If you are tense, nervous, or unsure of yourself, you may get flutters in your stomach that prompt you to question your actions. When this happens, there is a good chance something is amiss. Don't disregard such feelings. They're a welcome sign that your ethical compass is working properly. Instead of trudging stubbornly ahead, pause and give further consideration to what you are about to do.

If you are still unsure of the best course to follow, try asking yourself this question: would I want my actions broadcast on the evening news for my friends and family to see? If this thought doesn't appeal to you, you're almost certainly in danger of acting improperly.

Must You Always Tell The Truth?

You may have noticed people are quick to condone "little white lies." "They don't hurt anybody" you'll hear them say. Or, "I only lied because I didn't want to hurt their feelings." People lie on resumés, on legal forms, on insurance claims, and to the IRS. Lying is so prevalent that some would argue, "Everybody lies." Considering the popularity of lying, is it really that bad for your career? In a word, *yes*.

Every time you lie, you take a risk—the risk someone will discover your deception. Only one lie is needed to destroy your credibility. Once you have been caught in a lie, supervisors will be less likely to promote you, customers will be less likely to buy from you, and co-workers will be less likely to respect you. Your chances of attaining business success increase when you are trustworthy.

Even when lying makes life easier for the moment, it can make life harder in the long run! Not only do your lies need to be believable, but they also need to be remembered. If you forget the details of a lie, you are likely to say something in the future that contradicts it, which leads to more lies, and lies to cover up the lies. Once you reach this point, you're sure to get tangled in your own web of lies. Lying is a vicious cycle. Once you start, it's hard to stop. If you make a habit of lying, you'll always be enslaved to falsehood. Is that how you want to spend your career—living a lie?

 Heads Up!

Most people have built-in lie detectors. Even if you think you are getting away with a lie, there is a good chance you have "liar" written right across your forehead. Subtle movements of your eyes, hands, and other body language naturally give you away. Even if the recipient of your deception isn't certain you're lying, or doesn't question you, their subconscious mind may remember the fact that you are not someone to be trusted.

Some of the top reasons people lie on the job are to ...

- Cover up mistakes.
- Excuse tardiness and absence.
- Win customers.
- Cover for fellow employees.
- Incriminate fellow employees.

Have you ever lied for one of these reasons? If so, how many times have you done so? Have you noticed an increase in the number of lies you tell? If you don't police yourself, you can fall into a pattern of lying rather easily. When you grow accustomed to lying mistakes away, you gradually become more lenient with yourself. This, in turn, makes you a less productive worker. In one way or another, lying always catches up with you.

Let's think about lying from another angle. If you're a supervisor, you need your employees to trust you. If you lie to them, they won't! Leaders must be able to inspire trust. This calls for being honest with your employees even when it could hurt their feelings.

I have a business partner whom I trust implicitly. Our employees trust him, too. Here's an example of why: Recently, one of our assistants tried to dye her hair strawberry blonde. In the process it turned out melon. She knew it didn't look good, but she was asking everyone for their estimation of it. Not wanting to hurt her feelings, most people told her it looked fine. When she asked my business partner for his opinion, here's what he said: "If you walked out of the bathroom with your fly down, would you want me to tell you?" She got the point, and he didn't have to lie.

When you have a reputation as someone who won't lie under any circumstances, it's amazing what people entrust you with. It may seem trite to say it, but honesty really is the best policy!

Best Practice _____

If your supervisor tells you to lie, does that justify it? Absolutely not! One of my former employers asked me to lie to a customer for him. When I refused, he said, "Fine. Go get Janie. She'll do it." How much do you think he respected Janie?

I've always assured my bosses that, "If I won't lie for you, I won't lie to you!" Over the years, taking this position has served me well and helped me earn trust.

Do It for You

Even if you happen to be a cold, heartless person who doesn't care about anyone but yourself, you should still behave ethically and tell the truth, if for no other reason than it helps you succeed in business! Consider three reasons why:

♦ **People expect it.** Even those who lie and cheat expect others to deal honestly with them (go figure). When you work for someone else, they expect you to act in their best interests. If you break their trust, they'll shun you. Conducting yourself ethically helps keep you off the street.

♦ **You get better results.** When people trust you, they'll do almost anything for you. Your employees will follow you, your clients will refer their friends to you, and your bosses will assign you greater authority.

♦ **You'll enjoy peace of mind.** Worrying you'll get caught for doing something unethical creates anxiety. Trying to keep up with lies you've told clutters your mind. Over time, resulting guilt and anxiety takes a toll on you, your health, and your pocketbook.

There is nothing better than being able to rest your head at night knowing you've made decisions you can be proud of. If you achieve success by cheating, you cheapen everything you accomplish.

Remember, people are watching you—waiting to see what you'll do. Treat them well, and they will treat you well in return. This is the truth about ethics!

The Least You Need to Know

♦ Ethical behavior involves more than obeying the rules.

♦ Treat others how you want to be treated.

♦ Do the right thing even when no one is watching.

♦ If you get butterflies, don't disregard them. They're a welcome sign your ethical compass is working properly.

♦ Only one lie is needed to destroy your credibility.

♦ When people trust you, they'll do almost anything for you.

Chapter 23

Be True to Yourself

In This Chapter

♦ Embracing your individuality

♦ Living your values

♦ Acquiring balance

♦ Taking care of you

♦ Giving back

♦ Finding the true meaning of business success

Many people are convinced money, power, or prestige alone makes them happy. But when a person's life revolves solely around the pursuit of these things, they can never be totally satisfied. Even happiness resulting from great accomplishments fades with time. Those who achieve business success at the expense of their health, family, friendships, or spirituality will inevitably feel empty.

If this is a book about business, why are we discussing such personal matters? Because the way you act and live in general affects the way you perform in business. This chapter addresses key areas—such as lifestyle, health, and money—and shows you how balanced living in these areas can help you achieve and enjoy business success.

Individuality Makes You Strong

Diversity truly is the spice of life! Everything we know in the universe is teeming with variety. And aren't we glad? Imagine how boring things would be if everyone looked and acted the same. Oddly enough, as much as we love variety, we often find it uncomfortable to stand out as different. The social pressures we face can easily cause us to adopt thinking, attitudes, and values that aren't truly our own. This can happen so imperceptibly that, before we realize it, we are living a life we never desired or intended to live.

If fear of rejection, fear of failure, or lack of confidence in your own abilities causes you to throw your individuality out the window, you lose a powerful ally. By understanding your unique strengths, ideals, and motivators, you can live a life that is more fulfilling and more authentic. In turn, you will be more successful at everything you do, including work.

Be Yourself

I have a tendency to be silly. I've never liked that about myself, but it's just the way I am. I tell corny jokes, make childish remarks at my own expense, and invent my own words to songs. For a time, I thought this would keep people from taking me seriously. My solution was to be more serious.

Of course, when I tried to act more seriously I wasn't really being myself and didn't come across naturally. Thankfully, friends and colleagues drew this to my attention, and when I started being myself again, my relationships improved. I became more likeable, more memorable, and most important, more authentic!

Here are three things that help you be yourself:

- ◆ **Know yourself.** You can't be yourself unless you first know yourself. This requires introspection. Take time to think about your likes and dislikes, strengths and weaknesses. Be honest with yourself. Try to grasp what makes you different from others, and make it your goal to understand and accept the person you are.

 Best Practice _____

Want to understand yourself better? Take a personality test. Often, the results reveal things about your makeup that you weren't aware of. At the same time though, be careful you don't let the results totally define you, as they aren't 100 percent reliable.

◆ **Accept that you can't please everyone.** Don't waste your time worrying about what people think of you. When you are true to yourself, you always have critics. If you conform to the liking of one group, there will always be another group that doesn't understand you. It is utterly impossible to make everyone happy, but if you celebrate your individuality, the right people will automatically be attracted to you.

◆ **Stop worrying.** It's okay if you're not perfect. Accepting this is one key to enjoying inner peace.

Heads Up!

Avoid using your "individuality" as an excuse to be discourteous or offensive. Some people have received acclaim by peddling crudeness, but they are certainly not the majority. You get much farther in business by being polite and kind.

Express Yourself

Once you understand who you are, find a way to reveal that person to the world by expressing yourself creatively.

In speaking of creativity, we're not talking about the rare talents of painters, musicians, and designers. Some people aren't creative in artistic ways. To be creative simply refers to having the ability to create something. And in this sense, everyone is creative. You can be creative in math, science, or business. Being creative is about discovering what you find challenging or personally fulfilling and then creating something based on it.

You could create a system, a formula, a new business idea, a book, a website, or a piece of merchandise. By creating something unique to you and then offering it to people, you will ...

◆ Experience personal satisfaction.

◆ Discover new abilities.

◆ Hone existing skills.

◆ Learn about yourself.

◆ Potentially build wealth.

Expressing your creative strengths is one way to find joy in your work and become successful. If you spend your career doing things that aren't your strong suit, you will never reach your true potential.

Live Your Values

Your values are unique to you. They have been shaped by your entire life course. They have been influenced by your parents, family, friends, peers, and education. Your values impact every area of your life. Those who identify their values and then actively live them—at home and at work—are most likely to achieve their dreams. What ideas and beliefs are of chief importance to you? Do you know what you value most?

Let's try a little exercise. Go through the values listed below and circle the 10 that are most important to you. Feel free to add any that aren't listed:

Adventure	Job
Change	Leisure
Competition	Love
Country	Money
Creativity	Music
Economic stability	Our planet
Education	Personal growth
Efficiency	Physical fitness
Ethical behavior	Pleasure
Excitement	Power
Fame	Professional growth
Family	Public service
Freedom	Reputation
Friendships	Sophistication
Helping others	Spirituality
Home	Status
Independence	The arts
Inner peace	Travel
Integrity	Variety
Intelligence	Wisdom

Now that you've selected your top 10 values, eliminate the bottom 5. When you're finished, you should be looking at the five things you value most in life. Write those things in order of priority here and then list the percentage of time you devote to each item in an average week.

My Priorities: **Percent Time:**

1. _____   _____

2. _____   _____

3. _____   _____

4. _____   _____

5. _____   _____

Now take a hard look at the list. Does the way you spend your time really reflect your values? If it doesn't, is there a good reason for it? What can you do to change that?

Countless people have built business empires centered on doing things they love, and widely attribute their success to the fact they pursued their passion. To achieve extraordinary results in any endeavor requires you put your heart into it. How can you put your heart into something that you don't really value?

When you focus your attention on the things you value most, you will inevitably find greater success and contentment!

Best Practice _____

When colleagues, friends, or family members give you advice, check it against your value system before you act on it. In this way, you ensure you are acting based on your own internal motivators and not someone else's.

Analyze Yourself

In Part 1 of this book, we talked extensively about self-analysis as a first step toward choosing a suitable career. Now, yet again, you are being encouraged to analyze yourself. Why? Because self-analysis is an ongoing part of personal and professional development.

As you grow in knowledge and experience, you will find your perception of what is important and the opportunities available to you will change. If you don't think about these dynamics and adjust your priorities and goals accordingly, you can easily find yourself lulled into a routine that isn't making you happy.

Every once in a while, it's critical to take a step back, look at how you are exerting your energy, and then ask yourself: Is this what I really want to do with my life? Am I being true to myself? Am I surviving, or am I living?

Balance Keeps You Sane

If work is the principle thing you value, then compulsively checking your BlackBerry and hauling your laptop to every social engagement may be good for your psyche. But if, like most people, you have competing priorities, finding a work-life balance can help you get more out of your career. The mind is capable of compartmentalizing to a degree, but if it gets overcrowded, things get muddled. The result is your drive, focus, and level of accomplishment diminish.

Balancing Factors

How can you balance the demands of a booming career with a gratifying life outside of work?

- **Adjust your thinking.** It's okay to have a life outside of work. You don't have to feel guilty about it! Just because your boss is a workaholic doesn't mean you have to be. Make up your mind you are going to spend time pursuing activities that are important to you and protect your free time.

- **Create boundaries.** Keep a clear boundary between work and home. If you are connected 100 percent of the time, your mind never gets a chance to rest, which gradually causes work to become burdensome. Technology can be your servant or it can be your master. Don't let it enslave you!

- **Say no.** If you always say yes, people will never stop asking for favors, and you'll always be obligated. Don't agree to do things out of guilt or fear of rejection. If you burnout because you are cramming too much into your schedule, your main livelihood suffers. Learn to say no politely, but firmly.

- **Live by a schedule.** Having specific days or evenings allotted for personal activities can help you manage your time. A morning for laundry; an evening for going out with friends; an afternoon for volunteering. Planning a "life-schedule" gives your personal activities a measure of priority. In this way, they will be less likely to get crowded out.

Heads Up! _____

The term workaholic doesn't always refer to someone who enjoys his or her work. In some cases, it refers to those who overwork themselves due to a compulsion. If you think you could be addicted to work and can't break free, seek professional help. An unhealthy addiction to work can ruin your life and even lead to an early death.

- ◆ **Treat yourself ...** Make time to do something you enjoy every day. It could be reading, taking a walk, listening to music, or whatever rejuvenates you. If you can't spare 30 minutes a day to do something nice for yourself, you have serious time management problems. You should also plan at least one half day per week to engage in recreation. Play golf, go fishing, take a hike, host a barbeque—anything!

- ◆ **... But not too much.** If you place excessive value on recreation and relaxation, it inevitably leaves you feeling empty. On the other hand, when recreation is the complement of hard work, it truly satisfies! So work hard first, and play later—not the other way around.

Why Balance?

By demanding balance from yourself, you create your own freedom. To enjoy a satisfying life, you must take control of your time! If you let your circumstances control you, you become, in essence, a slave.

If this happens, you give less focused attention to your career, and less focused attention to your personal life. Eventually, your existence will be watered down until you are only marginally effective at everything. To attain business success requires you to focus 100 percent on your work while working, and 100 percent on your play while playing. In this way, you refresh yourself to work another day.

Best Practice _____

Discovering your work-life balance is an ongoing process. As your work, family, and interests change, you need to evaluate your situation to ensure you are maintaining harmony in your life.

Invest in Your Body

Your body could be likened to a car. Not just any car, but the only car you'll drive for the rest of your life. How well will you care for your car? Will you drive it recklessly? What quality of gas will you put in it? Will you insure it? Your body is the only vessel that will take you where you want to go in life. If you don't maintain it properly, you'll end up sputtering, broken down, or dead.

The state of our health is never totally within our control. Diseases, genetic disorders, and tragedies threaten us all. But we should care for ourselves to the degree we can! Think how sad it would be if after decades of hard work and accomplishment, you suffered a debilitating sickness—robbed of the chance to enjoy everything you worked for—simply because you lived irresponsibly.

Taking care of your body, like anything worth doing, requires effort. I'm not a nutritionist, and I'm not a fitness instructor, but I do know this: if you take care of your mind and body, you have greater success in everything you do! Here are a few tips:

 ◆ Do aerobic exercise for at least 30 minutes four times per week

 ◆ Lift weights for at least 30 minutes two to three times per week

 ◆ Maintain a healthy percentage of body fat

 ◆ Eat a balanced diet consisting of lean protein, complex carbohydrates, and "good" fats

 ◆ Don't smoke

 ◆ Avoid overdrinking

 ◆ Limit sodium and sugar intake

 ◆ Drink lots of water

 ◆ Wear your seatbelt

 ◆ Get plenty of sleep

If you do these things, you'll have more energy, feel better, and likely live longer! As a young person, it's easy to take good health for granted, but the way you live now determines the quality of life you enjoy later!

Best Practice _____

One of the best ways to get on track with a quality fitness program is to hire a personal trainer. The right trainer can help you develop a diet and exercise plan that is specific to you, provides motivation, and teaches you the proper way to exercise so you don't injure yourself.

Invest in Your Future

Regardless of how much money you make, if you don't manage it wisely, you can still end up penniless. Just ask the host of celebrities who've filed bankruptcy because they assumed their cash would never run out.

With the constant barrage of new technology, changing styles, and inflating prices, there is always something to spend your income on. Uncontrolled spending and lack of savings can exert tremendous pressure on you. Financial pressure can negatively impact your job performance and your overall well-being. It can also limit your job prospects and business opportunities.

As a financial planner, I have seen firsthand there are two ways to become wealthy—make a lot, or save a lot. Here are some good principles of personal finance that help you do the latter:

- **Live below your means.** Saving 10 percent of your annual income isn't that difficult. Before you know it, you'll have a nice cushion that prepares you for the unexpected, helps you fund a future business venture, or creates a nest egg for retirement. (If you only save $25 a week in an account earning 5 percent interest, you'll have over $15,000 in less than 10 years.)

- **Make a budget and stick to it.** Without a budget, you can't see clearly how much money you have or where it's going. You're also likely to overspend on nonessentials. Budgeting is an absolute necessity for the young professional!

Heads Up! _____

Desiring nice things is healthy to a degree because it will motivate you to work hard, but greed is dangerous. If you always feel like you must have the biggest house, the newest car, and the hottest technology, you will never be satisfied, and you will struggle financially.

♦ **Use credit sparingly.** Just because credit is available to you, doesn't mean you should use it. Only use credit cards for emergencies or purchases that can be paid off within two to three months. Always negotiate the lowest possible interest rate when financing purchases.

♦ **Invest in the stock market at regular intervals.** Trying to time the market is unrealistic, but investing regularly over time helps hedge against large market fluctuations. If your employer offers a 401(k), take advantage of it!

Managing your finances properly benefits you in all areas of life. It helps you keep your stress level down, provides you with a measure of security, and prepares you for future business opportunities.

Best Practice _____

The suggestions in this chapter are by no means a comprehensive guide to managing your personal finances. I highly suggest reading *The Complete Idiot's Guide to Personal Finance in your 20s and 30s* by Sarah Young Fisher and Susan Shelly.

Give Back

Business is about more than making money—it's about making a difference! The very root of business involves using your resources to fill a need someone else has. The result is an interchange that impacts lives in a positive way and benefits everyone involved.

Why Give?

As communal creatures, humans are hardwired with a need to give. To deny this need makes life insufferable. Studies have repeatedly shown that even when we give at great personal cost we derive joy from it. Add to the warm and fuzzy feelings the fact that society rewards giving with tax breaks and a good reputation, and you have some pretty compelling reasons to give! Brands like Ethos water and TOMS shoes have built their entire business models around giving and have experienced tremendous success due to this fact. Could you do something similar?

There are opportunities to give to education, the environment, animals, medical research, or your community. You can give of your knowledge, time, or money. If you have a desire to give, the possibilities are endless.

If you're struggling with finding the motivation to give, it's probably because you haven't found the right cause. Joyful giving is about connecting passion with action. Go back and take a look at the values exercise we did earlier. What are your top five values? Among them, there must be at least one you can leverage into an opportunity to give.

> **Heads Up!**
>
> When choosing a charity, exercise extreme caution to avoid scams. Make sure you know what percentage of donated funds actually go toward supporting the cause, and that you are dealing with a legitimate organization. You may want to check a site like www.charitynavigator.org before you donate your hard-earned money.

The Business of Giving

People have a tendency to think business is all about taking—all about personal gain. In actuality though, everything we've discussed in this book is about giving! It's about giving your best to your employer, your co-workers, and your customers. It's about giving your best to every project and every venture you're a part of. It's about giving your best to society and making a contribution of real value. Yes, business and giving are synonymous!

There is more than one way to achieve business success. You can achieve it by greedily exploiting the weaknesses of others and acting without regard for society. Or you can achieve it by taking a genuine interest in your fellowman and acting out of regard for their welfare. The choice is yours, but so are the consequences. The more you cultivate a giving attitude, the happier you will be. And when other people see the good you are doing and the effort you are exerting they will be inspired by your example. They will be motivated to follow you, and they will spur on your success.

Business Success and Life

What you do for a living is only part of who you are; it doesn't define you. Much of society places far too much emphasis on position and title. Should an attorney be considered more successful than a landscaper, or a doctor more successful than a nurse?

Does the manager of a hotel have a greater impact on the quality of your stay than the housekeeper? In other words, isn't every job vital? The answer to that question is a resounding yes! Business success isn't about the title you hold; it's about how well you do whatever it is you choose to do.

Once you earn enough to cover the necessities of life, what motivates you to keep working? Do you want to travel? Pursue a hobby? Leave a legacy? Have more free time? Everyone's motivations are different, and only after you understand what motivates you can you know whether or not you have achieved business success. Remember this: You are successful in business when the work you do allows you to live the life you desire to live.

I'm going to end this book with some simple advice that has served me well. Work hard. Give nothing less than your best. Be trustworthy. Care about people. Take care of yourself. If you do these things, business success will be yours!

The Least You Need to Know

- Money, power, or prestige alone will not make you happy.
- If the fear of rejection causes you to throw your individuality out the window, you lose a powerful ally.
- Make sure the way you spend your time truly reflects your values.
- Take care of your body; you need it.
- Live below your means and save at least 10 percent of your income each year.
- You are successful in business when the work you do allows you to live the life you desire to live.

Business Development Resources

Following are a list of websites related to the subjects of chapters in this book. They will provide you with a wealth of information for success in the business world.

Chapter 1

www.800ceoread.com
Find top business books for sale by category and rating.

Chapter 2

www.myersbriggsreports.com
Provides career personality tests, assessment, and counseling.

www.kolbe.com
Personality test designed to help you identify your strengths and capitalize on them.

www.assessment.com

Motivational Appraisal of Personal Potential (MAPP) is a world-class personal assessment that takes 15 minutes to complete. MAPP identifies your true motivations toward work and allows you to match yourself to job categories to see where you best fit.

Chapter 3

www.princetonreview.com

Complete a brief quiz that analyzes your interests, personality, and work style and then suggests careers that fit.

www.rockportinstitute.com

Provides career change counseling, career coaching, and advanced natural talent and aptitude test services for mid-career change and young adults and students making an original career choice.

www.livecareer.com or **www.rocketcareer.com**

Offers free online career suitability tests.

Chapter 4

www.monster.com

This website allows you to post your resumé online, apply for jobs, research potential employers, get career advice, and participate in online job fairs.

www.flipdog.com

Quickly find information about local jobs. Because Flipdog is powered by Monster, it provides access to one of the largest databases of jobs in the world.

www.jobfox.com

On this website, you can create a profile, find jobs matched to your skills and personality, view potential matches, and request introductions.

www.notchup.com

Free service that allows you to upload your resumé along with a fee. Companies find you and pay you to interview with them.

www.careerbuilder.com

You can search jobs by industry and category on this website. Upload your resumé, apply for jobs, and get career advice.

www.salary.com
Build a personalized salary report tailored to your experience, education, and skills.

www.visualcv.com
Utilize this online resumé tool that allows you to include video, pictures, and a portfolio of your work. Securely share different versions with employers, colleagues, and friends.

www.payscale.com
Access accurate, real-time salary reports based on your job title, location, education, skills, and experience.

www.linkedin.com
Build a professional profile and list your interests. Network with your contacts and request introductions to people in their network. Keep your network informed about changes or openings in your career.

www.jibberjobber.com
Keep track of all of the information involved in a job search. Track the companies that you apply to. Track each job that you apply for, and log the status of each job (date first of interview, thank-you letter sent, etc.).

www.careerperfect.com
A large and experienced resumé writing service established in 1978. Career tools, resources, and professional resumé writing and distribution service.

www.razume.com
Post your resumé and get feedback from other members of the community.

www.emurse.com
Create, store, and share your resumé online. Get a unique URL you can provide to potential employers. Download your resumé in a variety of formats, including PDF.

www.xing.com
Social network for professionals, with more than 7,000,000 users globally. Your resumé can be read in up to 16 languages.

www.resumesocial.com
Post your resumé online and get feedback from other users. Share cover letters and advice.

www.howtowritearesume.net
Assists you in writing a compelling resumé with "phrase builder" technology. Easy-to-use forms and templates you can use to create a resumé easily.

www.pongoresume.com
Resumé builder and publisher that allows you to design, print, fax, and e-mail your resumé quickly and easily.

Chapter 17

www.eeoc.gov
Equal Employment Opportunity Commission website. Provides information and helps enforce federal laws that prohibit discrimination in the workplace.

Chapter 20

www.bpplans.com
Obtain free business plan samples, templates, and instructions on how to create your own.

www.paloalto.com
Maker of heavily endorsed business plan, marketing plan, and legal tool software for small businesses.

www.sba.gov
United States Small Business Administration. Tools and resources to help you with your business from start to finish.

www.entrepreneur.com
Offers help and advice to those starting or running their own business. One section of their website provides insight into the day-to-day aspects of starting and running more than 20 different businesses. They also provide lists of the top venture capital firms and banks for small businesses. Business plan help is available as well.

www.smallbizbooks.com
Business start-up guides from *Entrepreneur* magazine.

www.score.org
Entrepreneurs get free and confidential business advice from working and retired executives and business owners who volunteer as counselors. SCORE was founded in 1964.

www.youngentrepreneur.com
Discussion forum for thousands of young entrepreneurs.

www.nwbc.gov
National Women's Business Council. Offers mentoring and other resources.

www.gobignetwork.com
Community of more than 20,000 start-up investors.

www.virginmoneyus.com
Helps manage and formalize loans between family and friends.

www.garage.com
Early-stage venture capital for entrepreneurs.

www.vfinance.com
A venture capital resource.

www.ovp.com
A venture capital resource from OVP Venture Partners.

www.westlakesecurities.com
Provides a full range of investment banking and financial advisory services to emerging growth and established privately held and publicly traded companies.

www.nvca.org
National Venture Capital Association.

www.angelinvestors.net
www.angelsforum.com
www.commonangels.com
www.newyorkangels.com
Resources for finding angel investors.

www.grants.gov
Government resource that is the central storehouse for information on over 1,000 grant programs.

The 100 Best Business Books of All Time

A great resource for finding what to read next is *The 100 Best Business Books of All Time* by Jack Covert and Todd Sattersten. *The 100 Best* puts the books in context, so readers can quickly find solutions to the problems they face. From *The First 90 Days* in a new job, to how a new business can master *The Art of the Start*, to how to take an existing company from *Good to Great*, I have personally benefited from reading many of these books, and I am confident you will, too!

You

Improving your life, your person, and your strengths.

Flow by Mihaly Csikzentmihalyi

Getting Things Done by David Allen

The Effective Executive by Peter F. Drucker

How to Be a Star at Work by Robert E. Kelley

The 7 Habits of Highly Effective People by Stephen R. Covey

How to Win Friends & Influence People by Dale Carnegie

Swim with the Sharks Without Being Eaten Alive by Harvey B. Mackay

The Power of Intuition by Gary Klein

What Should I Do with My Life? by Po Bronson

Oh, the Places You'll Go by Dr. Seuss/Theodore Geisel

Chasing Daylight by Eugene O'Kelly

Leadership

Inspiration, challenge, courage, and change.

On Becoming a Leader by Warren Bennis

The Leadership Moment by Michael Useem

The Leadership Challenge by James M. Kouzes and Barry Z. Posner

Leadership Is an Art by Max De Pree

The Radical Leap by Steve Farber

Control Your Destiny or Someone Else Will by Tichy and Sherman

Leading Change by John P. Kotter

Questions of Character by Joseph L. Badaracco Jr.

The Story Factor by Annette Simmons

Never Give In! Speeches by Winston Churchill

Strategy

Eight organizational blueprints from which to draft your own.

In Search of Excellence by Thomas J. Peters and Robert H. Waterman Jr.

Good to Great by Jim Collins

The Innovator's Dilemma by Clayton M. Christensen

Only the Paranoid Survive by Andrew S. Grove

Who Says Elephants Can't Dance? by Louis V. Gerstner Jr.

Discovering the Soul of Service by Leonard Berry

Execution by Larry Bossidy and Ram Charan

Competing for the Future by Gary Hamel and C. K. Prahalad

Sales and Marketing

Approaches and pitfalls in the ongoing process of creating customers.

Influence by Robert B. Cialdini, Ph.D.

Positioning by Al Ries and Jack Trout

A New Brand World by Scott Bedbury with Stephen Fenichell

Selling the Invisible by Harry Beckwith

Zag by Marty Neumeier

Crossing the Chasm by Geoffrey A. Moore

Secrets of Closing the Sale by Zig Ziglar

How to Become a Rainmaker by Jeffrey J. Fox

Why We Buy by Paco Underhill

The Experience Economy by B. Joseph Pine II and James H. Gilmore

Purple Cow by Seth Godin

The Tipping Point by Malcolm Gladwell

Rules and Scorekeeping

The all-important numbers behind the game.

Naked Economics by Charles Wheelan

Financial Intelligence by Karen Berman and Joe Knight

The Balanced Scorecard by Robert S. Kaplan and David P. Norton

Management

Guiding and directing the people around you.

The Essential Drucker by Peter Drucker

Out of the Crisis by W. Edwards Deming

Toyota Production System by Taiichi Ohno

Reengineering the Corporation by Michael Hammer and James Champy

The Goal by Eliyahu M. Goldratt and Jeff Cox

The Great Game of Business by Jack Stack with Bo Burlingham

First, Break all the Rules by Marcus Buckingham and Curt Coffman

Now, Discover Your Strengths by Marcus Buckingham and Donald Clifton

The Knowing-Doing Gap by Jeffrey Pfeffer and Robert I. Sutton

The Five Dysfunctions of a Team by Patrick Lencioni

Six Thinking Hats by Edward De Bono

Biographies

Seven lives; unlimited lessons.

Titan by Ron Chernow

My Years with General Motors by Alfred P. Sloan Jr.

The HP Way by David Packard

Personal History by Katharine Graham

Moments of Truth by Jan Carlzon

Sam Walton: Made in America by Sam Walton with John Huey

Losing My Virginity by Richard Branson

Entrepreneurship

Seven guides to the passion and practicality necessary for any new venture.

The Art of the Start by Guy Kawasaki

The E-Myth Revisited by Michael E. Gerber

The Republic of Tea by Mel Ziegler, Patricia Ziegler, and Bill Rosenzweig

The Partnership Charter by David Gage

Growing a Business by Paul Hawken

Guerrilla Marketing by Jay Conrad Levinson

The Monk and the Riddle Randy Komisar with Kent Lineback

Narratives

Six industry tales of both fortune and failure.

McDonald's: Behind the Arches by John F. Love

American Steel by Richard Preston

The Force by David Dorsey

The Smartest Guys in the Room by Bethany McLean and Peter Elkind

When Genius Failed by Roger Lowenstein

Moneyball by Michael Lewis

Innovation and Creativity

Insight into the process of developing new ideas.

Orbiting the Giant Hairball by Gordon MacKenzie

The Art of Innovation by Tom Kelley with Jonathan Littman

Jump Start Your Business Brain by Doug Hall

A Whack on the Side of the Head by Roger Von Oech

The Creative Habit by Twyla Tharp

The Art of Possibility by Rosamund Stone Zander and Benjamin Zander

Big Ideas

The future of business books lies here.

The Age of Unreason by Charles Handy

Out of Control by Kevin Kelly

The Rise of the Creative Class by Richard Florida

Emotional Intelligence by Daniel Goleman

Driven by Paul R. Lawrence and Nitin Nohria

To Engineer Is Human by Henry Petroski

The Wisdom of Crowds by James Surowiecki

Made to Stick by Chip Heath and Dan Heath

Takeaways

What everyone is looking for.

The First 90 Days by Michael Watkins

Up the Organization by Robert Townsend

Beyond the Core by Chris Zook

Little Red Book of Selling by Jeffrey Gitomer

What the CEO Wants You to Know by Ram Charan

The Team Handbook by Peter Scholtes, Brian Joiner, and Barbara Streibel

A Business and Its Belief by Thomas J. Watson Jr.

Lucky or Smart? by Bo Peabody

The Lexus and the Olive Tree by Thomas L. Friedman

Thinkertoys by Michael Michalko

More Than You Know by Michael J. Mauboussin

Sample Resumés and Cover Letters

The following resumé and cover letter samples are courtesy of CareerPerfect.com. They are designed to illustrate a variety of styles, phrasing, and formatting options you can use when crafting a personal resumé or cover letter. When writing your resumé or cover letter, it is important to draw on your own unique experiences, skills, achievements, and abilities. Review Chapter 4 for help with this.

ALLEN ROBERTS

1001 Third Street • New York, New York 10008 • alroberts@myisp.com • (212) 555-8256

February 19, 20XX

Caroll Andersen
Chairman
LCC Corporation
2000 Main Street
New York, NY 10000

Dear Ms. Andersen:

With a stellar track record of increasing market share, profitability, and product offerings, it is a pleasure to submit my resume for President of LCC's North American Division. I believe that, upon review, you will recognize that my innovative strategies are exactly what LCC needs to lead it to the next level.

My greatest strengths match those most necessary to consistent growth and success:

- ◆ Expertise in developing profitable partnerships and forging global strategic alliances.
- ◆ Proficiency in identifying untapped markets and business opportunities both nationally and internationally.
- ◆ Strong track record of bottom-line responsibility for product launch, pricing, marketing and promotional initiatives.
- ◆ A career-long history of consistently increasing productivity and reducing costs.

My keen business insight and in-depth knowledge of improving operations while leading tactical marketing activities will enable me to impact your bottom line. I am confident my combination of drive and experience will provide you with an invaluable resource.

LCC Company intrigues me as an organization that realizes the importance of inspiring teams to reach new heights, which is the very type of vision that has defined and propelled my career. I look forward to discussing your objectives and how we can work together to accomplish them.

Sincerely,

Allen Roberts

Enclosure

ALLEN ROBERTS

1001 Third Street • New York, New York 10008 • alroberts@myisp.com • (212) 555-8256

EXECUTIVE MANAGEMENT

Strategic Planning   •   Product Marketing & Management   •   Global Operations

Accomplished Executive with domestic and international experience in operations, P&L oversight, multichannel product distribution, and marketing involving both start-up and growth organizations. Results-oriented, decisive leader with proven success in new market identification and strategic positioning for multimillion-dollar telecommunications and computer organizations. Track record of increasing sales and growing bottom line while spearheading operational improvements to drive productivity and reduce costs. Excel in dynamic, demanding environments while remaining pragmatic and focused.

CORE COMPETENCIES

• Visionary Leadership	• Key Partnership Development	• Organizational Restructuring
• Global Strategic Alliances	• Tactical Market Planning	• Risk Management
• High-stake Negotiations	• Budget / Sales Forecasting	• Public and Media Relations

PROFESSIONAL EXPERIENCE

INT COMMUNICATIONS CORPORATION, New York, New York   12/2000–Present
President and CEO

Provide executive leadership for $40 million communications infrastructure service provider with eight district offices and net field profit of $3.8 million.

Lead operations and strategic direction with full responsibility for bottom-line factors, including long-range planning, global product management, and software development processes. Provide cross-functional management; direct three Vice Presidents, COO, CFO, and eight District Managers; and general oversight of 500 employees. Direct all operations for installation and service provision for infrastructure systems: LAN, WAN, fiber optics, voice and data networks. Redefine organizational structure; oversee major pricing decisions and perform monthly financial evaluation of company results.

Key Achievements:

➢ Created a more responsive and market-driven organization resulting in increased sales from $22 million to $40 million in five years.

➢ Substantially improved productivity while reducing staffing and operational costs by 28%.

➢ Opened new marketing channels and established strategic alliances in Asia and Europe.

➢ Developed and introduced successful new products for international markets.

➢ Returned company to high profitability through strategic and efficient restructuring.

...continued...

DRIVE TECHNOLOGIES, INC., New York, New York   9/1995–12/2000
Vice President, Marketing

Ensured on-target delivery of all marketing initiatives for $25 million hard drive manufacturer serving global markets.

Directed regional and international marketing organization, including national managers, regional managers, and product managers. Spearheaded vision, strategy, and execution of global business operations. Oversaw staffing, strategic directives, and training of national marketing teams. Developed and implemented strategic marketing plans, established marketing and sales objectives, and prepared company-wide sales forecasts. Directed international project teams through due-diligence, prioritization and development. Participated in research and development of new disk-drive technology. Established Performance Drive Europe and Asia operations. Reported to CEO.

Key Achievements:

➤ Conceived innovative sales strategy that increased annual company revenue by 36%.

➤ Captured extraordinary market share and revenue results leading directly to joint ventures.

➤ Effectively led international project teams to proven results across multiple lines of business, geographic borders, time zones, and cultures.

LOUIS INSTRUMENTS, INC., New York, New York   1/1991–9/1995
Product Manager

Directed product and regional/international marketing operations for $13 million keyboard and peripheral manufacturer.

Participated in development of new keyboard technology. Recruited, trained, mentored, and developed new management team. Negotiated major OEM contracts.

Key Achievements:

➤ Increased revenue from zero to $13 million in five years by expanding market share and establishing alliance initiatives.

➤ Successfully identified and resolved manufacturing issues, resulting in 12% cost reduction.

➤ Earned Top-Performance Achievement Award as result of outstanding contributions.

EDUCATION AND CREDENTIALS

Master of Business Administration (MBA) • BOSTON UNIVERSITY, Boston, Massachusetts

Bachelor of Science, Electrical Engineering (BSEE) • NEW YORK UNIVERSITY, New York, New York

Professional Associations:

INSTITUTE FOR GLOBAL COMMUNICATIONS (1996–Present)

ASIAN AMERICAN MANUFACTURING ASSOCIATION, AAMA (1990–Present)

Patricia Chopin

5540 B Street, Bridgeton, Missouri 63044
(314) 555.1697 • patti@anyisp.com

February 22, 20xx

Cassandra Peri, Manager
Divot Delivery Services
1205 Meridian St., Suite 7
Bridgeton, Missouri 63044

Dear Ms. Peri:

Your posting for an Executive Assistant indicated requirements that closely match my background and expertise. I have enclosed my résumé to provide a summary of my qualifications and background for your review.

Throughout my career, I have maintained the highest performance standards within a diverse range of administrative functions, which is clearly illustrated by my past successes. As Assistant to the Chief Financial Officer of SPTM Systems, Inc., I streamlined operations and reduced costs by consolidating operations and negotiating competitive rates with service providers. Additionally, while serving as an Assistant to a senior partner of Smith, Inc., I facilitated the implementation of a new promotional strategy that significantly increased the company's profile.

Further qualifications I offer include the following:

- Successful track record supporting the efforts of executive-level staff, including CFOs, presidents, and senior partners.
- Strong background in all aspects of office management, from scheduling meetings and coordinating travel to overseeing budget and accounting functions.
- Demonstrated capacity to develop and maintain comprehensive administrative processes that improve the efficiency of day-to-day operations.

With excellent organizational and communication skills, an outstanding work ethic, and the ability to work well in both team-oriented and self-directed environments, I am positioned to exceed your expectations. I would welcome an opportunity to meet with you to discuss my qualifications and candidacy in further detail. Thank you for your time and consideration.

Sincerely,

Patricia Chopin

Enclosure

PATRICIA CHOPIN

5540 B Street, Bridgeton, Missouri 63044
314.555.1697 • patti@anyisp.com

QUALIFICATIONS SUMMARY

Skilled and dedicated **Executive Assistant** with more than 12 years' experience coordinating, planning, and supporting daily operational and administrative functions.

➢ Demonstrated capacity to provide comprehensive support for executive-level staff; excel at scheduling meetings, coordinating travel, and managing all essential tasks.

➢ Proven track record of accurately completing research, reporting, information management, and marketing-support activities within demanding time frames.

➢ Adept at developing and maintaining administrative processes that reduce redundancy, improve accuracy and efficiency, and achieve organizational objectives.

➢ Highly focused and results-oriented in supporting complex, deadline-driven operations; able to identify goals and priorities and resolve issues in initial stages.

➢ Proficient in Microsoft Office Suite (Word, Outlook, Excel, PowerPoint), Visio, QuickBooks; Windows and Mac OS; type 90 wpm with complete accuracy.

PROFESSIONAL EXPERIENCE

SPTM Systems, Inc., St. Louis, Missouri   12/2004 to Present
Executive Assistant

Provide high-level administrative support to Chief Financial Officer of leading manufacturer of solid-imaging products and solutions with more than $75 million in annual revenue.

Perform a variety of key investor-relations functions, addressing inquiries of current and potential shareholders, communicating with marketing department regarding investor-relations initiatives, and maintaining investor database. Collaborate with CFO to oversee distribution of financial releases to NASDAQ. Develop spreadsheets to improve and inform quality and risk-assessment initiatives. Prepare meeting agendas and carefully monitor all action items.

- Reduced company travel expenses by $47,000 within first three months of tenure by identifying cost-effective travel agencies and negotiating vendor contracts.

- Successfully coordinated and hosted numerous client seminars, creating invitations and promotional materials, booking venues, and selecting guest speakers.

SMITH, INC, St. Louis, Missouri   10/2000 to 11/2004
Administrative Assistant

Served as Administrative Assistant for three partners and one principal of financial-services firm with more than 75 locations nationwide.

Directed all administrative and project-support efforts. Conducted in-depth business-development research and compiled results for review by proposal team. Created presentations and scheduled all executive-level meetings and travel. Prepared biweekly time, expense, and travel reports. Managed invoicing and billing processes.

- Proactively developed vital competitive analysis process to facilitate implementation of aggressive company marketing strategy.

- Effectively managed license renewal process for all financial service representatives.

continued…

PATRICIA CHOPIN

– Page Two –

CONSOA, LTD., Bridgeton, Missouri   3/1996 to 10/2000

Regional Assistant

Provide administrative support for five regional medical directors for successful healthcare organization.

Oversaw a wide variety of administrative functions, in support of all director-level projects and information-management processes. Compiled and analyzed data from monthly reports to prepare directors' presentations to executive management. Developed internal correspondence that facilitated effective communication and transfer of information between five regional offices.

- Played key role in design of interoffice intranet, collaborating with Web developers to identify and define essential components of site functionality.
- Significantly reduced time required to prepare and distribute quarterly financial reports by initiating implementation of electronic reporting procedures.

ROBERT & ASSOCIATES, Bridgeton, Missouri   2/1994 to 2/1996

Office Manager

Directed day-to-day office operations, providing fundamental support to company President and team of consultants.

Managed accounts payable, receivable, and payroll. Oversaw administrative budget; prepared expense reports and bank reconciliations. Purchased hardware and software, performed application upgrades, and trained staff.

PROFESSIONAL DEVELOPMENT

The Exceptional Administrative Assistant Seminar ~ *Top Skill Seminars*
Indispensable Executive-level Support ~ *Top Skill Seminars*

CAMILLE REUBENS

2207 Beach Avenue, Los Angeles, California 90045
213.555.1854 • careub@myisp.com

QUALIFICATIONS PROFILE

Highly creative and multitalented **Graphic Designer** with extensive experience in multimedia, marketing and print design. Exceptional collaborative and interpersonal skills; dynamic team player with well-developed written and verbal communication abilities. Highly skilled in client and vendor relations and negotiations; talented at building and maintaining "win-win" partnerships. Passionate and inventive creator of innovative marketing strategies and campaigns; accustomed to performing in deadline-driven environments with an emphasis on working within budget requirements. *Creative experience in the following:*

PRINT	PHOTOGRAPHY	WEB & MULTIMEDIA
• Brochures & Newsletters	• Black & White Photography	• Web Site Design
• Logos & Business Cards	• Lithography	• Video Editing
• Posters & Post Cards	• Retouching	• Video Photomontages
• Stationery	• Photograph Restoration	• CD Cover Design

PROFESSIONAL EXPERIENCE

Cygnet Media Productions, Long Beach, California, 2001–Present

Art Director – Graphic Design

Successfully manage and coordinate graphic design projects from concept through completion. Collaborate with clients to create vision, conceive designs, and consistently meet deadlines and requirements. Effectively build, motivate, and direct design and production teams. Coordinate freelance designers, consultants and vendors to meet all project requirements. Create and conduct highly persuasive sales and marketing presentations. Expertly convert features to benefits to achieve client objectives. Manage all operational, strategic, financial, quote/bid, staffing, and administrative functions.

Key Achievements:

- Successfully completed client projects worth up to $470,000.
- Provided proposal layout and design for million-dollar corporate contracts under extremely tight deadlines.
- Established trusting relationships with designers, vendors, and key clients.

Market Studios, Ltd., Norwalk, California, 1999–2001

Senior Graphic Designer

Successfully translated subject matter into concrete design for newsletters, promotional materials and sales collateral. Created design theme and graphics for marketing and sales presentations, training videos and corporate Web sites. Participated in team effort to produce streamlined production of policy manuals and educational materials for newly hired employees and freelance designers.

Continued…

CAMILLE REUBENS

PAGE 2

Key Achievements:
- Earned several awards for providing graphic design support to both headquarter employees and hundreds of field offices.
- Coordinated staff participation in community-sponsored charitable events.

Dimensions, Huntington Beach, California, 1997–1999
Graphic Designer
Created new design themes for marketing and collateral materials. Collaborated with creative team to design and produce computer-generated artwork for marketing and promotional materials. Participated in production of print and promotional items for key clients under direction of Marketing Department.

Key Achievements:
- Consistently recognized for fresh and innovative ideas and applications.
- Developed new art-proofing system that increased overall quality of production and improved customer satisfaction to 97%.
- Recruited by ABC Corporation to become their Senior Graphic Designer.

EDUCATIONAL BACKGROUND

Bachelor of Arts in Marketing, Minor in Graphic Arts, 1997
UNIVERSITY OF SOUTHERN CALIFORNIA, Los Angeles, California

TECHNICAL PROFICIENCY

Platforms:	Mac OS 9/10, Windows Vista/XP/Me/2000
Applications:	Adobe Photoshop, PageMaker, and Illustrator; Macromedia Flash, Fireworks, and Dreamweaver; QuarkXPress; Aldus Freehand; MS FrontPage, Project, and Office Suite (Word, Excel, Access, PowerPoint, Outlook).

SUSAN FITZGERALD

1010 Conway Ave SE • Minneapolis, MN 55401
s.fitzgerald@myisp.net • 612.555.8000

February 22, 20XX

John Smith
Vice President, Investment Banking
Nova Investment Corporation
137 Kings Way
Minneapolis, Minnesota 55401

Dear Mr. Smith:

With a proven track record of success in the management and marketing of investment services, I believe my experience would contribute greatly towards the continued success of Nova Investment Corporation. I have enclosed my résumé to provide an overview of my career achievements and qualifications.

As you will note, my tenure in investment banking with Visio Lake Bank exhibits continuous advancement in client-base growth and revenue generation. Examples of my key contributions include:

➢ Achieved 127% of the business development goal set at $10 million in assets; maintained 100% or better for all established production goals from 1998 to the present day.

➢ Built client base to more than 600 customer relationships, far exceeding account development and client retention goals and generating solid revenue growth.

➢ Recognized as one of the top 100 advisors worldwide.

In addition, I offer a comprehensive knowledge of numerous investment tools and the ability to deliver products and services seamlessly to customers. My professional experience, combined with my dedication and enthusiasm, will enable me to make an immediate and valuable impact on your organization.

I look forward to meeting with you and learning more about the position, your objectives, and how I can contribute to the success of your department. In the meantime, feel free to contact me if you have any questions.

Sincerely,

Susan Fitzgerald

Enclosure

SUSAN FITZGERALD

1010 Conway Ave SE, Minneapolis, Minnesota 55401
612.555.8002 (c) 612.555.5645 (h) • sfitzgerald@myisp.net

QUALIFICATIONS SUMMARY

Performance-driven, insightful **Investment Banker** with a proven ability to achieve and exceed all revenue and business-development goals in high-pressure environments.

➢ Skilled at consulting with clients to delineate and analyze financial situations while developing strategic solutions that strengthen investment goals.

➢ Relationship-development expertise that complements the ability to aggressively build solid client base and drive revenue growth.

➢ Comprehensive knowledge of, and experience in, leveraging numerous investment instruments in a variety of complex scenarios.

➢ Proven leadership and team-building skills, coupled with the ability to direct strong teams in managing customer relationships and providing investment services.

PROFESSIONAL EXPERIENCE

VISIO LAKE BANK, Minneapolis, Minnesota   1998–Present
Built a solid record of achievement and advancement through increasingly responsible financial investment positions.

Investment Officer, 2003–Present

Manage relationship-banking team with keen focus on maximizing revenue and territory profitability. Lead team in investment product sales and delivery of customer relationship management techniques. Collaborate with clients to assess individual financial situations and develop strategic financial planning solutions. Oversee securities transactions, funds transfers, margin accounts, and option trades.

Selected Accomplishments:

• Consistently maintained 100% or better of established production goals; achieved 127% of 2006 business development goal set at $10 million in assets.

• Recognized for outstanding professional acumen with national awards for annual production of Kicheen Capitol and Persephone mutual funds in 2006 and 2007.

Investment Consultant, Private Banking, 2001–2003

Served as key team member in the brokerage division of fiduciary, investment management, and private banking services to new and existing high-net-worth clientele. Established and maintained strong relationships with fixed-income investment clients to drive revenue growth.

Selected Accomplishments:

• Surpassed customer retention and business development goals by building client base to more than 600 investors.

• Received Alliance Capital Advisory Award for ranking among the top 200 advisors worldwide in new business development.

continued...

SUSAN FITZGERALD

Page 2

Financial Consultant, 1998–2001

Developed client base through network and seminar marketing. Ensured client retention by providing strategic investment recommendations based on evaluation of analyst reports covering fixed-income and equity investing. Employed numerous investment instruments in option hedging strategies and trading scenarios, including fixed-income and equity securities.

Selected Accomplishment:

- Consistently exceeded established account development and revenue-generation goals.

MORRIGAN INSURANCE, Hibbing, Minnesota   1995–1998

Registered Representative

Collaborated with legal counsel and accounting teams to develop marketing strategies for estate and business succession planning insurance. Created proposals exhibiting extensive detail in internal revenue code and estate tax law. Developed solid estate and tax code knowledge base.

Selected Accomplishment:

- Executed strategic sales techniques resulting in a solid account base and consistent performance above quotas.

EDUCATION AND CREDENTIALS

Master of Business Administration (MBA) in Finance, 2002
MINNESOTA STATE UNIVERSITY, Mankato, Minnesota

Bachelor of Science in Business Administration, 1995
SOUTHWEST STATE UNIVERSITY, Marshall, Minnesota

Professional Licenses
NASD SERIES 7, 6, 63, & 65

Professional Training
DALE CARNEGIE SALES TRAINING ▪ ACCOUNT MANAGEMENT SYSTEMS
LEADERSHIP & TEAM BUILDING

DAVID HURSTON

1002 Main Street, Dallas, Texas 75026
cell 972.952.7002 • securitywizard@myisp.net

INFORMATION TECHNOLOGY SECURITY SPECIALIST

Insightful, results-driven IT professional with notable success directing a broad range of corporate IT security initiatives while participating in planning, analysis, and implementation of solutions in support of business objectives. Excel at providing comprehensive secure network design, systems analysis, and full life cycle project management. Hands-on experience leading all stages of system development efforts, including requirements definition, design, architecture, testing, and support. Outstanding project and program leader; able to coordinate and direct all phases of project-based efforts while managing, motivating, and guiding teams.

AREAS OF EXPERTISE:

- Network and Systems Security
- Research and Development
- Regulatory Adherence
- Cost Benefits Analysis
- Policy Planning / Implementation

- Data Integrity / Disaster Recovery
- Risk Assessment / Impact Analysis
- Contingency Planning
- Technical Specifications Development
- Team and Project Leadership

TECHNICAL PROFICIENCIES

Platforms: UNIX (Solaris, HP-UX), Windows 9x/NT/2000/XP/Vista, Linux (Red Hat, Yellow Dog), Sun SPARC, Mac OS, VM/370, OS2 Warp

Networking: TCP/IP, Novell, DECnet, Banyan, ISO/OSI, IPX/SPX, SNA, SMS/SQL, Ethernet, Token Ring, FDDI, VPN, SSH, SecureID, PGP, PKI, HIPAA, CFR-11

Languages: UNIX Shell Scripting, C, HTML, Java, JavaScript, PHP

Tools: LAN Manager, ISS RealSecure, Checkpoint Firewall, Norton Firewall and Ghost, McAfee/Norton Virus Protection Utilities, HP OpenView, Network Flight Recorder, IBM Tivoli, Tripwire, Snort, Lotus Notes, Microsoft Office Suite (Word, Excel, PowerPoint, Access, Project, Outlook), FrontPage

PROFESSIONAL EXPERIENCE

SYSTEMS INTERNATIONAL, Dallas, Texas   2003 – Present
Information Security Analyst

Recruited to establish enterprise-wide information-security program; oversee companywide efforts to identify and evaluate all critical systems. Design and implement security processes and procedures and perform cost benefit analysis on all recommended strategies; manage security budget of $1.1 million. Collaborate with external auditors to conduct in-depth compliance audits and penetration testing, presenting results to senior management. Develop curricula and facilitate awareness training. Supervise daily activities of Computer Security Assistant and Internet Administrator.

Key Achievements:

- Instrumental in developing and implementing Business Continuity and Disaster Recovery (BCP & DRP) Plans for corporate sites throughout Texas, Ohio and Canada.
- Spearheaded creation of four new information-security departments: Risk Assessment, Vulnerability, Penetration Testing, and Security Engineering services.

Continued...

DAVID HURSTON

- Hand selected employees from Information Technology department to build Risk Assessment Team charged with analyzing all critical systems, developing reports to document system vulnerabilities, and recommending appropriate solutions.
- Created company policies and procedures governing corporate security, email and Internet usage, access control, and incident response.

LLCA INFORMATION SYSTEMS, Garland, Texas   1996 – 2003
QA Lead, 1999 – 2003

Promoted to lead system development and new product QA. Ensured accurate release testing for all new applications, providing final approval for bug-free, fully functional commercial solutions. Proactively assigned resources to meet workflow needs. Created development plans, project documentation, and test cases.

Key Achievements:

- Authored numerous ISO 9000 procedures and security policies in support of engineering operations, participating in regular audits to ensure regulatory compliance.
- Managed creation of high-profile HATP (High Availability Transaction Processing) solution, supervising development teams working in multiple locations.
- Developed highly effective software management application to enable disk-free software upgrades deployed through ATMs and desktop systems worldwide.
- Successfully applied for US Patent on new security software design.

Computer System Engineer/Network Developer, 1996 – 1999

Provided remote and on-site support for domestic and international customers, including Tier-III support for LAN/WAN products and sales support for key accounts of all sizes.

Key Achievements:

- Designed and implemented customer call-center support procedures and customer network design strategy for sales and marketing teams.
- Recognized for outstanding quality of customer service with numerous customer-support awards and personal commendation from clients.

EDUCATION & CREDENTIALS

Bachelor of Science in Computer Science
UNIVERSITY OF TEXAS AT DALLAS, Dallas, Texas

Professional Certification

- MCSE – Microsoft Certified Systems Engineer
- CISSP – Certified Information Systems Security Professional

Professional Affiliations

- Information Systems Security Association
- International Information Systems Security Certification Consortium, Inc.

MILES ADAMS

22 Washington Avenue • San Francisco, California 94118
Home 510.555.1297 • Cell 510.555.8439 • miles@myisp.net

LOGISTICS PROFILE

Accomplished in developing effective processes and directing complex logistics functions for multimillion-dollar projects. Excel at coordinating tasks of numerous internal divisions and external agencies to ensure rapid, accurate delivery of equipment, materials, and resources. Advanced expertise in reviewing invoices and shipping manifests to ensure full compliance with local customs and international regulations. Track record of identifying redundancies and maximizing resources to streamline operations. Proficient in a variety of logistics and supply management software, both proprietary and commercial.

AREAS OF EXPERTISE:

- Distribution Management
- Quality Assurance
- Inventory Control Processes
- Standards / Procedures Compliance

- Continuous Process Improvement
- Vendor and Staff Relations
- Transportation / Materials Handling
- Training and Leadership

PROFESSIONAL EXPERIENCE

UNITED STATES ARMY (*various locations*)   1996 – 2006

Logistics/Distribution Supervisor, 2004 – 2006

Directed eight-member team to develop highly efficient routing system for $47 million in supplies and equipment. Monitored all transportation operations, including quality controls, to ensure transportation services met contract obligations as well as local and national government regulatory requirements. Served as transportation liaison between various organizations and countries. Oversaw dispatching, routing, tracking, and shipping activities to ensure safe, prompt, and accurate delivery of transportation equipment. Trained and coached staff on new tracking procedures. Communicated operational needs to senior management.

Key Achievements:

- Achieved 99.5% average delivery rate on all assignments with no loss of materials or assets.
- Identified and corrected efficiency bottlenecks, which saved $1.2 million and resulted in faster, more accurate supply shipments.
- Played an integral role in creating new automated method for property tracking procedures to increase accuracy and accountability.

Logistics Coordinator, 2000 – 2004

Collaborated with and supported Logistics Manager in overseeing up to $25 million in equipment and supplies shipped worldwide to support a wide range of projects. Assured proper authorization for shipments; oversaw tracking and monitored cross-border transportation activities. Held accountability for $11 million in property, equipment, and supplies. Developed and operated automated systems to optimize flow of supplies.

Key Achievements:

...continued...

MILES ADAMS

- Key player on team that consistently exceeded stated objectives on all projects.
- Led smaller teams in developing effective stocking and inventory-management systems to minimize loss and maximize performance.

Logistics Support, 1996 – 2000

Coordinated with staff regarding relocation and transportation arrangements. Prepared documentation and coordinated transport of resources and materials. Marked and labeled freight; documented, verified, and inventoried cargo; and prepared and submitted report documentation. Maintained accurate records and managed office correspondence.

Key Achievement:

- Earned multiple awards for quality and dedication of performance in rapidly changing, fast-paced environment.

EDUCATION & TRAINING

Business Administration Major, 2004 - Present
UNIVERSITY OF MARYLAND

Professional Development:

- Advanced Logistics Management
- Distribution Operations
- Leadership and Supervision
- Advanced Inventory Management
- Standards and Procedures Compliance
- Diversity Training

ADDISON JOYCE, RN

963 E. Main, Helena, MT 59601
406-555-5220 • a.joy@myisp.com

February 22, 20xx

John Smith
Human Resource Manager
Clipper Emergency Center
420 Saddleback Way
Helena, Montana 59601

Dear Mr. Smith:

I was pleased to learn of your need for a dedicated ICU Staff Nurse. With solid experience and education in prevailing ICU practices, acute patient care, family relations, and staff development, I am prepared to become an immediate contributor to your team.

The following are highlights of my qualifications and accomplishments:

- Extensive experience in ICU, CCU, Emergency, and Medical Surgical environments.
- In-depth knowledge of administration that includes admissions, assessment, treatment, referral, and education.
- Frequent commendations by patients and families for providing exceptional care.
- Employee awards for dedication, performance, leadership, and patient advocacy.

My strong initiative and exceptional organizational skills, combined with my ability to work well under pressure, allow me to play a crucial role in fast-paced, patient-centered environments. Furthermore, with a history of success contributing to the healthcare community, patients, and their families, I will immediately impact operations at Clipper Emergency Center.

Enclosed is my resume for your review. I welcome the opportunity to discuss with you personally how my skills and strengths can best serve your hospital.

Sincerely,

Addison Joyce

Enclosure

ADDISON JOYCE, RN

963 E. Main, Helena, MT 59601
406-555-5220 • a.joy@myisp.com

QUALIFICATIONS SUMMARY

Dedicated and patient-focused **Registered Nurse** with proven expertise in acute care, staff development, and family advocacy.

➢ Exceptional capacity to multitask: manage competing priorities with ease while fostering delivery of superior patient care.

➢ Solid administrative and referral experience include admissions, assessment, treatment, referral, and education for a broad range of patients.

➢ Widely recognized as an excellent care provider and patient advocate.

➢ Demonstrated ability to forge, lead, and motivate outstanding healthcare teams that provide top-quality patient care.

➢ Outstanding interpersonal and communication skills; superior accuracy in patient history, charting, and other documentation.

Certifications and Proficiencies

• Ventilator care	• Med/Surg	• Care plan administration
• Telemetry	• ICU and CCU	• NG/Sump and Peg tubes
• Intravenous therapy	• ER Procedures	• Patient/family education
• Phlebotomy	• Triple lumen CVP	• Training and inservices
• Basic life support	• AV fistulas	• Meditech documentation

CAREER EXPERIENCE

ST. ANDREW'S HOSPITAL, Missoula, Montana   2004–Present

Staff Nurse, Intensive Care Unit

Serve as charge nurse caring for patients with life-threatening illnesses, including acute congestive heart failure, acute myocardial infarction, drug overdose, massive trauma, respiratory failure, and disseminated intravascular coagulopathy. Promote health and support patients and families in coping with illness. Skilled in bedside monitoring, 12-lead EKG, and Bennett 7600 ventilator.

• Provide strong contributions as key member of unit quality assurance program designed to identify and evaluate problems, manage patient census, and allocate staff assignments.

• Exhibit motivation and dedication by providing the highest quality of care to each patient.

O'FLANNERY MEDICAL CENTER, Missoula, Montana   2001–2004

Emergency Staff Nurse

Provided care for patients suffering from trauma, acute chest pain, respiratory failure/complaints, drug overdoses, and gastrointestinal bleeds. Acquired and recorded patient information. Prepared patients for surgical and radiological procedures, initiated and maintained intravenous therapy, and operated 12-lead EKG.

• Contributed substantially to successful JCAHO accreditation within the department.

• Implemented and coordinated ongoing staff education program.

Continued...

ADDISON JOYCE, RN

BERKELEY COUNTY HOSPITAL, Helena, Montana   1996–2000
Registered Nurse

Delivered a complete range of RN services and expertise. Accurately obtained and documented patient history and medication lists, assessed individual conditions and needs, as well as selected departmental referrals for acute and chronically ill patients. Prepared equipment; assisted physicians during patient examinations and treatments. Monitored patient reactions to drugs and carefully documented progress of individuals participating in clinical trials.

- Repeatedly commended by patients and supervisors for outstanding quality of care; received consistent mention in care-survey responses.

- Maintained a high degree of accuracy to achieve optimal patient acuity monitoring.

- Significantly improved facility's public image by ensuring exceptional patient satisfaction.

KEILLOR STATE PRISON, Deer Lodge, Montana   1994–1996
Registered Nurse

Provided triage, referrals, direct nursing care, and medication administration to incarcerated population. Organized and managed regular clinics involving external physicians, including ophthalmology, ENT, Med/Surg, orthopedics, and podiatry professionals. Scheduled and managed external medical consultations in concert with security and other necessary personnel. Created, managed, and maintained patient medical and health records.

- Selected to serve as Infection Control Coordinator, maintaining tuberculosis and hepatitis standards and conducted screenings and preventive activities.

- Organized and facilitated meetings with Security Managers to ensure infection-control policy compliance.

EDUCATIONAL BACKGROUND

Bachelor of Science in Nursing, BSN (1994)
MONTANA STATE UNIVERSITY – Bozeman, Montana

Licensure
Registered Nurse (RN), State of Montana

TRACY MORRIS

10 Main Street • Santa Clara, California 95052
tmorris@myisp.com • h 408.555.5011 • c 408.220.0004

SENIOR SALES MANAGER

Strategic Sales Planning • Relationship Management • Market Expansion

Dynamic, results-driven sales strategist with a 15+ year record of achievement and demonstrated success driving multimillion-dollar revenue growth while providing visionary sales leadership in highly competitive markets. Solid track record securing key clients and increasing product distribution to grow market share. Tenacious in building new business, securing customer loyalty, and forging strong relationships with external business partners. Exceptional mentor and coach; combine business acumen with innate leadership abilities to recruit, build, and retain top-performing sales teams.

Key strengths and competencies:

- High-impact Sales Presentations
- Territory Growth Management
- New Product Launch
- Strategic Market Positioning
- Needs Assessment & Product Education

- Multimillion-dollar Negotiations
- Budget Administration / P&L Management
- Recruiting and Staffing Initiatives
- Staff Development Programs
- Team Leadership, Coaching, and Mentoring

PROFESSIONAL EXPERIENCE

SYSTEMS CORPORATION, Santa Clara, California
Director, North American Sales (2004 to Present)

Oversee corporate sales division with eight district offices for leading innovator in data storage and automation with 1500 employees and annual revenues exceeding $100 million.

Direct sales and business development functions, including new product rollouts, key account management, customer relationship development, contract negotiations, and order fulfillment. Manage P&L and budget responsibilities. Conduct cross-functional team training, coaching, and mentoring. Lead district sales managers and marketing associates located throughout the U.S. and Canada. Design, implement, and adjust various sales plans and programs for data storage products, with a focus on building two-tier distribution channel and fostering demand in the Fortune 500 arena.

Selected Achievements:

- Instrumental in complete turnaround of under-performing sales team; set higher expectations and instituted individual accountability resulting in **450% revenue increase** over three years.

- Met or exceeded all quotas throughout tenure; averaged more than **$57 million in annual sales** in North America and earned multiple company awards in recognition of performance.

- Consistently developed strong, sustainable relationships with VAR partners and executive decision makers of Fortune 500 client companies.

DRIVE STORAGE, INC., Chicago, Illinois
Midwest Sales Director (1999 to 2004)

Recruited to build and develop top-producing sales team and manage 12-state territory for computer distributor with $110 million in annual sales.

Managed region comprised of 48 franchisees and independent resellers, with combined total annual sales exceeding $32 million. Developed and implemented strategic plans to market franchises and persuade resellers/VARs to purchase products from company's distribution centers. Accountable for channel and end-

…continued…

TRACY MORRIS • Page 2

user sales development, new market identification and penetration, and large-scale contract negotiations. Monitored operational performance of franchisees to ensure alignment with corporate goals.

Selected Achievements:

- ♦ Team consistently **ranked #1 in company sales** for five consecutive years.
- ♦ Designed and led training and team-building seminars later adopted as company-wide "best practice" standard for franchisees.
- ♦ Impacted business partner revenue, achieving **more than 200% increase** through continual communications and liaison efforts with both franchisees and sales team members.

IMAGE CORPORATION, Rockford, Illinois
Regional Sales Manager (1996 to 1999)
Sales Representative (1994 to 1996)

Promoted to direct product and regional sales operations for one of the world's leading suppliers of office automation equipment including copiers, facsimile machines, and data processors.

Built and developed seven-state dealership network for sale of entry-level reprographic systems. Facilitated sales training for dealer representatives, developed new sales programs, and acted as liaison between dealer channel and direct sales organization.

Selected Achievements:

- ♦ Established company's first-ever Northwest channel sales organization.
- ♦ **Increased territory sales by 127%** or more annually.
- ♦ Rapidly promoted from Sales Representative after earning recognition as Top Sales Producer.

EDUCATION AND CREDENTIALS

Master of Business Administration (MBA) • UNIVERSITY OF MICHIGAN, Ann Arbor, Michigan

Bachelor of Science (BS) • UNIVERSITY OF NOTRE DAME, Notre Dame, Indiana

Professional Development:
Dale Carnegie Sales Training
Leadership through Quality
Account Management-Selling System

Professional Associations:
National Association of Sales Professionals (1995 to Present)
Toastmasters International (1994 to Present)

THAM HUGHES

101 Main Street ◆ New York, New York 10008
thughes@myisp.net ◆ (C) 212.880.8800

QUALIFICATIONS PROFILE

Detail-oriented and thoughtful professional prepared to excel in the field of chemical engineering and contribute to organizational objectives.

☒ **Chemical Engineering:** Prepare water treatment plans for up to 6 million gallons of water per day. Develop water cleanup plan for nuclear reservation. Monitor and test air emissions and evaluate air pollution control processes. Develop physical and chemical methods for controlling air pollution. Utilize gas chromatography and dispersion modeling.

☒ **Process Design:** Analyze plant and equipment needs. Contribute to and develop most economic and effective practices. Establish lab procedures; ensure compliance with EPA guidelines, environmental regulations, and emission standards. Design digital control systems.

☒ **Computers & Administration:** Program in JavaScript and HTML and assist in Web site development. Utilize Windows-based PCs with various software: Matlab, Simulink, Equation Solvers, Lotus; Microsoft Office. Order lab equipment and supplies. Prepare technical reports and documentation.

☒ **Key Strengths:** Finely tuned analytical and research skills with dedication to clear communication and presentations. Adept at maintaining an exceptional rate of productivity, accuracy, and efficiency; well organized and proficient with details.

EDUCATION

Bachelor of Science Degree in Chemical Engineering (2008)
NEW YORK UNIVERSITY, New York, New York
Magna cum Laude Graduate, Academic All-American

Member, Society of Chemical Engineers, 2006 – 2008

EXPERIENCE HIGHLIGHTS

CITY OF NEW YORK, New York, New York

Air Quality Technician (Internship), 2008

Conducted studies in air pollution control and designed spreadsheets in Excel. Measured levels of pollution and made recommendations to improve air quality, including written reports and public speaking presentations.

- Commended by City Manager for contributions to environmental improvement plan.

NEW YORK UNIVERSITY, New York, New York

Teaching Assistant, 2006 – 2007

Assisted professors in chemical and environmental engineering courses. Led small group discussions and answered student questions. Graded tests and assignments. Supervised students in lab. Provided instruction in use of software including Matlab, Simulink, Excel, and Word.

- Selected from 75 students to become a Teaching Assistant.

MANHATTAN COMPUTERS, New York, New York

Sales Associate (concurrent with education), 2004 – 2007

Sold computers, peripherals, and software. Answered technical questions from customers. Demonstrated use of systems and applications. Generated a strong referral business through quality service.

- Built stellar reputation for quickly and effectively resolving issues and ensuring customer satisfaction.

JANICE JOHNSTON

1561 Elm Street · Los Angeles, CA 90406
jan@myisp.com · 323.460.5023

QUALIFICATIONS SUMMARY

- **Film and Television Production:** Wide-ranging knowledge of film and video projects from inception to completion. Effective at organizing and coordinating shoots; experience using production equipment. Conduct script analysis and contribute to script changes. Ability to write and edit scenes, treatments, and scripts; competent in film and sound editing.

- **Administration and Communication:** Provide efficient administrative support for a wide variety of program participants and staff. Prioritize and organize workloads to meet strict deadlines; train and support team members. Establish and maintain strong working relationships with management, staff, and internal and external groups.

- **Technical Proficiencies:** Adobe Premiere, ProTools, Final Cut Pro 4, AVID, Flatbed Editing, Movie Magic Budgeting and Scheduling, MS Office, WordPerfect, Outlook, Internet Browsers, Arriflex 16S and Sony Digital Video Cameras, Studio Floor Camera.

- **Strengths and Accomplishments:** Enthusiastic and creative; demonstrated ability to achieve objectives within strict deadlines. Excellent organizational and communication talents; solid skills in improving productivity and efficiency while reducing costs. Served as Production Sound / Sound Editor for Student Emmy Award-winning film.

EDUCATION

M.F.A. in Film/Video Production (2008) – UNIVERSITY OF SOUTHERN CALIFORNIA, Los Angeles, California

B.A. in Dramatic Art (2006) – UNIVERSITY OF CALIFORNIA, Berkeley, California

SELECTED PROJECTS

Director/ Director of Photography
— "Life" – Digital Video Short Film
— "Locked In" – Digital Video Short Film
— "Unfaithful" – Digital Video Short Film

Director of Photography / Editor
— "Uncomfortable" – 16mm Short Film
— "The Journal" – 16mm Short Film

Writer/Director/Sound Editor
— "Chronicle" – 16mm Short Film

Production Sound / Sound Editor
— "Working the Inner City" – Documentary
— "Blast" – Student Emmy Award-Winning Documentary

Producer
— "Resonance" – 16mm Short Film
— "Swan" – HD Short Film

Assistant Producer
— "No Hope" – 35mm Short Film

EXPERIENCE HIGHLIGHTS

UNIVERSITY OF SOUTHERN CALIFORNIA, SCHOOL OF CINEMA – Los Angeles, CA   2006 – 2008
Film and Production, *Graduate Student*
Cast, directed, and co-produced numerous film and video projects. Planned, organized, and budgeted film shoots utilizing Movie Magic Budgeting and Scheduling. Edited projects

Continued...

JANICE JOHNSTON

Page 2

and assigned scenes using Adobe Premiere and AVID. Performed sound editing in ProTools. Wrote scenes, treatments, and portions of scripts.

- Located and secured approval for land at low cost, assisted in casting, and provided input on final picture and sound edit for Senior Project.
- Commended by Directors for sense of humor that played a key role in diffusing tension and ensuring successful shoots.

LUCERNE PUBLISHING, Los Angeles, California   2006 – 2008

Production Coordinator *(concurrent with education)*

Organized information and edited and composed text for "The Entertainment Guide" (750-page publication). Assisted in determining interview questions in accordance with Production policies.

- Frequently worked numerous additional hours to meet strict deadlines.

UNIVERSITY OF CALIFORNIA, Berkeley, California   2002 – 2006

Academic Advisor

Evaluated petition requests for exceptions to general program requirements, ensuring consistency of policies. Tracked student progress; provided administrative support for more than 100 Ph.D. students and 500 master's degree students. Resolved billing and registration issues. Responded to 50+ e-mail messages daily. Oriented new employees to departmental policies and procedures. Communicated extensively with the Dean, other offices and program coordinators in the U.S., Canada, and Europe.

- Improved efficiency and reduced costs by introducing automated communication processes.
- Successfully organized induction ceremony for Beta Gamma Sigma international society of business school honors graduates.
- Instrumental in major improvement of relations between Student Affairs Office and students.

Index

The *Complete* Business Toolkit

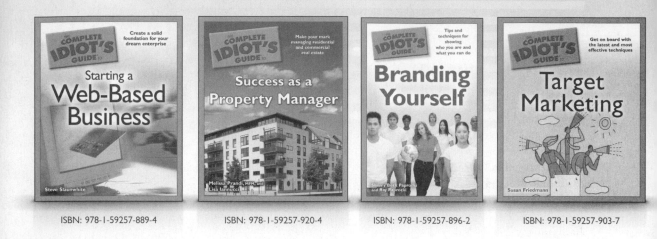